Real Life Stories

By Paul E. Mix

iUniverse, Inc.
Bloomington

Real Life Stories

iUniverse books may be ordered through booksellers or by contacting:

iUniverse
1663 Liberty Drive
Bloomington, IN 47403
www.iuniverse.com
1-800-Authors (1-800-288-4677)

Because of the dynamic nature of the Internet, any Web addresses or links contained in this book may have changed since publication and may no longer be valid. The views expressed in this work are solely those of the author and do not necessarily reflect the views of the publisher, and the publisher hereby disclaims any responsibility for them.

ISBN: 978-1-4502-6591-1 (sc)
ISBN: 978-1-4502-6590-4 (ebook)
ISBN: 978-1-4502-6589-8 (dj)

Printed in the United States of America

iUniverse rev. date: 11/22/2010

Dedication

My book is dedicated to my wife Dixie, our children Donna, John, Linda, and Thomas, our grandchildren, Cheree, Jenifer, Jamie, Matthew, and Miranda, our great granddaughter, Julianne, and all the little children of the world – red and yellow, black and white, all our precious in His sight, Jesus loves the little children of the world.

Acknowledgement

This book was inspired when my daughter Linda gave me a copy of the book below:

A FATHER'S HERITAGE

Your Life Story in Your Own Words

The format of this book was a good start, but too narrow in scope to include many of my real life stories that I wanted to include. For example, my business trip to Saudi Arabia was a little less that 30 days but I unofficially called it *My Thirty Days in Hell*. This true story is officially titled *King Solomon's Mine*. The longest story in the book tells about a young Filipino boy who was severely burned just after a Christmas Holiday. The Ben Hur Shriner's brought Rinor to the United States twice for treatment of his third and fourth degree burns and to add flexibility to his left elbow at the Shriner's Burn's Hospital – Galveston.

Table of Contents

Chapter 1 - The Rooster from Hell

I was born in the small town of Penfield, Pennsylvania on September 26, 1934, with the help of a midwife. My mother, Marion Lucille Curry, was born in the DuBois, Pennsylvania hospital on February 26, 1916. My father, Paul DeVere Mix, was born in his Dad's' house in Penfield, Pennsylvania on September 23, 1909. Grandpa Mix had a two-story framehouse with a nice front porch, and a cold cellar for canned goods.

Back then the family cooked on the top of wood stoves and heated the house with a Pot-bellied wood stove that overheated the house and you, if you stood too close to it. In the Wintertime you were hot in the front and cold in the back and froze your butt off. Mom, Dad, Uncle Leroy Mix, Uncle Bill Thomas, and our family tore the old Mix home down in 1965 and burned the old rotted siding in 1966.

My brother, Keith Mix, was born in the DuBois, Pennsylvania hospital on February 8, 1939. My brother Richard William Mix died as a baby and was buried in an unmarked grave in the DuBois cemetery. I was named Paul Emerson Mix by my mother, who liked the poems and

1

poetry of Ralf Waldo Emerson. I'm glad she didn't name me Waldo.

When my grandmother Rosa Mix died of dropsy, my father comforted me by telling me that she was just sleeping. A short time later our little family moved to my grandfather James C. Curry's farm at Hickory Kingdom, Pennsylvania. I was born on September 26, 1934, so I guess you could call me a Depression baby. I loved the name Hickory Kingdom, and when sitting on the front porch of my grandfather's house, I thought he must have owned all the land as far as the eye could see, but of course that wasn't true.

When I was a small child, our family lived in a converted grain house. It was very cold when the winter winds blew between the old slat sides. One year my pet goldfish froze to death in his bowl. The farm also had a smoke house where meat could be hung in the winter and salted to preserve the cut meat. Grandpa's house was near the top of the hill and it seemed to me it must have been a mile down his long dirt driveway just to get to his mailbox.

As a small boy I had no real friends, only an occasional rabbit that I'd try to catch, the goldfish that froze to death, and the daddy long-legs spiders that walked across the floor. Sometimes when playing with them, I'd accidently pull their legs off. Every Sunday we ate dinner at grandpa's house, and there would always be one piece of meat and plenty of vegetables for everyone. That is when I developed my dislike for cats. One day a house cat jumped up on the table and stole my only piece of chicken. From then on I disliked cats. However, I always loved dogs.

There was an old wooden outhouse about fifty feet from our converted grain-house home. The outhouse had three steps up to the floor level. One day I had to go to the toilet, so I went up a couple of steps so I could reach the old outhouse door latch. When I unlatched the door, there was a rattlesnake looking at me eye to eye. When he sounded his warning rattle, I didn't need to use the toilet anymore. I screamed "Rattlesnake!" and Dad came running with a pitchfork and killed it.

Several older children, cousins I guess, lived in the big farmhouse with Grandpa Curry. One day they thought they would have some fun at my expense, so they shoved me into the chicken coop and latched the door shut. That's where I met the "Rooster from Hell." The rooster pecked me and clawed at me until I was a bloody mess. Finally, I grabbed the rooster around the neck and beat him against the door and shelves. I beat him until he was dead and couldn't hurt me anymore. My mother arrived on the scene, and the other children took off running back to the big house. After Mom tended to my wounds, she headed to the farmhouse to have a talk with grandpa. Needless to say I was never locked in the chicken coop again, and I guess Grandpa had to get a new rooster from somewhere.

Once a year, during the so-called Great Depression, local game wardens allowed farmers to shoot as many deer as they needed to help feed their families. The number of bucks, does, and fawns had to be counted, and the local game warden notified. Since Grandpa's house was near the top of a hill, it had a great view of his cornfields in the valley below on the right. At that time, deer herds in Pennsylvania were very large, and as many as 100 or more could be counted at a time.

On a bright moonlit night in October, Dad and several neighboring farmers, gathered on Grandpa's front porch just before dusk. I asked Dad if I could watch and he told me to "Sit at the front door and don't make any noise!" The men all had ".30-.30" or ".32 Winchester" carbines, and they waited patiently for the deer to arrive. A short time later bucks, does, and fawns slowly came into the corn fields; one of the men whispered "Ready….Aim….Fire" and all Hell broke loose. Fully loaded, each Winchester rifle held seven rounds, and the men had extra ammo in their coat pockets. They reloaded as they hurried down into the cornfields to kill any wounded deer that might try to escape.

To a four-year-old boy it sounded like a war, but only one side was doing all the shooting. Hot brass cases were flying everywhere. After the shooting was over, the dead deer were dragged partway up the hill to the smoke house. There the deer were counted, gutted, skinned, cleaned, quartered, and hung up to be smoked with hickory. Deer that couldn't be hung up were cut into smaller pieces and salted to preserve the meat. Everyone got their fair share of the kill. The next day the local game warden was given the count of bucks, does, and fawns that had been killed.

Later during the Depression Dad also worked for the Works Progress Administration. During that period of time workers built roads, rest stops, and many other things. Several years later Dad found out that work was available in North Tonawanda, New York, the so-called Lumber Capital of the

World. So he went there to find work and earn more money for our family. Later the family moved to an upstairs apartment in Buffalo, New York. One by one Dad's brothers and sisters moved from Pennsylvania to New York State as jobs became more plentiful before the beginning of World War II.

Chapter 2 - The War to End All Wars

I was seven years old when the Japanese bombed Pearl Harbor on December 7, 1941, and our country united and fought back. At that time, Dad worked for the DuPont Company, which made gun powder and other items for the war effort, while Mom worked on an assembly line for Lockheed Aircraft. I did my part by gathering soda-pop bottles in my little red wagon and drying milk weed floss that was hung in burlap bags from the clothesline until the floss dried. The dried milkweed floss was used as the flotation material in Flight Jackets. I often wondered if my dried milkweed floss ever helped save a pilot who was shot down over the ocean. During wartime everyone saved everything that could be saved and used, – from used lard to tin cans, tin foil, old tires, and rubber bands.

I will never forget the day the Japanese bombed Pearl Harbor. It was Sunday afternoon, and I was at a matinee at the local theater watching, *"The Picture of Dorian Gray."* It was a horror film about a man who wished that his painted portrait would grow old but he would stay young forever. However, as he began committing every crime under the sun, his picture grew older and more hideous. Finally he couldn't stand to look at his picture any longer and set it on fire. When he did, his picture returned to its youthful look and his face turned into the hideous face of his portrait. It was truly a great horror film!

When it was announced that "the Japanese had bombed Pearl Harbor and sunk several of our Navy ships," every able-bodied man 18 years old or older in the theater got up out of his seat, went to his local Recruiting Office, and volunteered to join some branch of the U.S. Armed Forces. During the war my dad was also a local air raid warden and would ask people to turn off their lights when there was an air raid warning and the sirens sounded.

I also remember standing on the street in Buffalo as a youngster, when a flight of bombers passed overhead. They were in such tight formation that the sky literally darkened with bombers. I thanked God that they were on our side and felt sorry for the poor people of Japan who would be the targets of our military might. Everywhere you went there were anti- Japanese and anti-Nazi posters. Kids made up jingles like, "Hi Ho Silver, stepping on the gas, Here comes Hitler sliding on his _ _ _!" There were also a lot of pro-American posters like the one with Rosy the Riveter, "Loose Lips Sink Ships," and "Remember Pearl Harbor," to mention a few.

During the war Dad worked for the DuPont Yerkes Plant in Buffalo. One day they asked him to operate a piece of machinery in a new way, hoping it would speed up production.

Instead his left hand caught in the machinery and it wasn't stopped by anyone until it had pushed the flesh and muscle of his left arm up to his elbow.

DuPont paid some of the best surgeons in Buffalo to save his arm if they could, and they were able to pull much of the flesh and muscle back into place and re-attach it so that he had most of the use of his left hand and arm, which was quite an achievement. He could halfway close his left hand and drive a car. There was a lot of scarring and a deep lengthwise gash on the top of his left forearm. After the accident DuPont offered to send Dad to a four-year college with no promise of a future job or two years of college with the promise of a job. Dad took the two years of college and became a Time Studier. They also gave him a substantial number of savings bonds. Later Dad used some of his savings bonds to help pay for my college education.

Shortly after Dad's accident, Mom took my little brother and me to a clothing store owned by two Jewish brothers. She wanted to buy us new clothes for school. The man said he had read about Dad's injuries in the *Buffalo Evening News*. He told Mom to pick out some clothes for both of us boys and a new pair of shoes as well. He told Mom she could pay him later when Dad was feeling better and back at work. Ever since then I have had the deepest respect for Jewish merchants.

**Crew of Enola Gay who dropped
"Little Boy" on Hiroshima.**

**Crew of "Boxcar" who dropped
"Fat Man" on Nagasaki.**

Mushroom cloud from Fat Man atomic bomb over Nagasaki rose 11 miles into the air.

Less impressive cloud resulting over Hiroshima after dropping Little Boy.

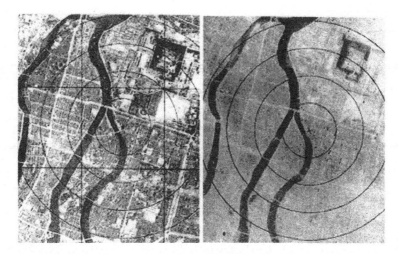

Hiroshima before and after "Little Boy" atomic bomb.

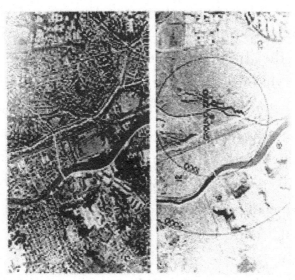

Nagasaki before and after "Fat Man" atomic bomb.00

Chapter 3 - Canadian Border Crossings

World War II essentially ended when the United States Air Force dropped megaton nuclear bombs that totally destroyed the southwest Japanese seaports of Hiroshima and Nagasaki on August 6 and 9, 1945. These were the first nuclear bombs ever used in war. I remember Life Magazine having huge photo spreads of the aftermath. One picture that really impressed me showed the burned surface of a bridge with white shadows on it. The white shadows were of people walking across the bridge when the bomb went off, burning the entire surface of the bridge except for where the pedestrians were cremated as they walked across it. Hiroh Hito, the Emperor of Japan, quickly signed a peace treaty aboard a U.S. aircraft carrier a short time later.

After the Japanese surrender, US troops occupied Japan. My uncle Jack Kehoe said that the Japanese people were some of the nicest people he had ever met. They were very kind and courteous. Uncle Jack brought home a Japanese flag and gave it to me. I kept the flag for several years until the rising-sun emblem and charcoal writing had almost completely faded out. Then it was disposed of by burning. The Japanese people are a very ingenious people. Before the war an American-made Argus C3 35mm camera was the best and most popular U. S. camera made. As a youngster, I saved up a lot of money while working for thirty seven cents an hour at a local department store. Later I made a dollar an hour working for the Great Atlantic & Pacific Tea Company store by stocking shelves after normal operating hours. That was a lot of money for me. After the war, the Japanese exported just about everything, from the little toys in Cracker Jack candy to the finest-made 35 mm cameras like Minolta. It wasn't long before Kodak cameras were made in Japan and exported to the United States.

When I was eleven and my brother Keith was seven, our family moved to North Tonawanda, New York. My sixth-grade teacher was Mrs. Shine. She wasn't my favorite school teacher. She was the oldest gray-haired teacher I had ever seen. She also had some unique ways to punish students. She liked to send me to the coat room or bang the back of my head on the blackboard. Neither made me a better student, but the rest of the class seemed to pay better attention to her. I guess they didn't want their heads banged into the blackboard.

I went to Felton Grammar School and North Tonawanda High School. John Bush became a good friend of mine in grammar school and high school. We were both interested in photography and target shooting. On some weekends, I'd bicycle to John's farm on the outskirts of town and we'd put up some .22 caliber fifty-foot targets for practice.

In our last year of grammar school, John had rheumatic fever and frequent breathing problems. He had to use an inhaler frequently. After that, every time I caught a cold or had a fever, I worried that I might have rheumatic fever. Dad convinced me that rheumatic fever wasn't contagious and assured me that I had nothing to fear.

Shortly after I joined the Boy Scouts, we had a joint campout with some Canadian Boy Scouts. I made friends with one boy in particular named John Hall, who lived in Hamilton, Ontario. We became such good friends that we alternately spent one week of summer vacation at each other's homes for several years. I forgot all about these summer vacations until I applied for work at the Savannah River Plant in South Carolina. The job application asked if I had ever been to a foreign country, and I replied, "No." A short time later two FBI agents dressed in black called me in to a small interrogation room. I told them again that I had not been to a foreign country and they said, "Well, according to our records you spent alternate summers in Canada for several years. "I admitted that I had but I had never thought of Canada as a foreign country. We all had a good laugh, and I did get the job and worked at the SRP for several years.

Another high school friend was Donald Lichtenberger. His family was Danish and everyone in the family had blonde hair and blue eyes. They invited me to go with them to Canada to see Niagara Falls from the Canadian side and do a little shopping. When we crossed the border, Canadian custom agents asked a few questions and waved us through.

Coming home was another story. Canadian custom agents asked Donald's dad to pull off to the side. They took me to a guard shack and began to ask me questions like, "Who is the pitcher of the New York Yankees?"- I didn't know. They asked a couple of other questions I couldn't answer. Finally I said I didn't have any real proof of who I was, but I lived in Buffalo, New York. I told them to call my Dad, that he would be home by now. I gave them my home phone number and said "Please call my father!" They did and my father verified that I was an American student. What I didn't know was that at the time many French Canadian boys were trying to hitch rides into the United States to find better paying jobs for their families. Imagine that!

After the war my dad also tried to cross the Canadian border with our family in a blue 1947 Chevrolet four-door sedan. As soon as we arrived at Canadian customs, they pulled us off to the side. Everyone had to get out of the car and they literally took everything out of it, checking under the seats as well as looking under the frame, in the trunk and under the hood. What we didn't know was that someone in a car with the same description had robbed a bank in Buffalo, and was believed headed for the Canadian border. Dad was very angry when none of the customs agents even offered to help us put things back in the car.

Chapter 4 - High School Friends

Other high school friends were Homer Rieffanaugh, David Elzner, Robert and Dianne Kennedy, Warner "Buddy" Brave, James Oshier, and Howard Menken. Homer and I were good friends during our senior year. We had a chemistry class at the same time. Sometimes I'd borrow paper from him and he'd charge me interest – more paper than I'd borrowed. When he went on vacation with his family, he'd send me a picture postcard, and when I went on vacation with my family, I'd send him a picture postcard. "Wish you were here! Not really."

For chemistry class we had a grumpy old man that reminded me of Scrooge in Dicken's *Christmas Carol*. Toward the end of our senior year he asked, "Who intends to go to college?" I raised my hand, but Homer didn't. Then he told me, "Mr. Mix, you're not smart enough to go to college." I liked chemistry class but I disliked that old geezer. He must have been a real inspiration for me to prove him wrong. Needless to say I earned my share of A's, B's and C's for two and a half years at the University of Buffalo and a year and a half at the University of South Carolina.

Howard Menken and I used to bicycle around town and the neighborhood. He had a bad case of asthma and hard time breathing. He had to stop periodically so he could use his inhaler, and catch his breath. I think his asthma got so bad that his family eventually moved to Arizona where the climate is dry. James Oshier and I lived in the same neighborhood and paled around a lot. On Sundays he had to go to church so we would go to the church, walk in the front door, and come right back out. Then he would tell his mother he had been to church, which of course he had.

Nita Curry was one of my favorite cousins. We were about the same age, and she lived in DuBbois, Pennsylvania. Her father was James Curry, one of my mother's brothers, and we visited them frequently. One of her friends was Linda a very pretty girl. Years later I named our youngest daughter Linda. Later Nita told me that I was lucky I didn't really marry her friend Linda. She turned out to be a fat, slovenly person and an extremely poor housekeeper.

David Elzner built a two-man hydroplane in the North Tonawanda High School woodworking shop. He glued and screwed the wood together so the boat was very sturdy. David insisted that the two of us take the boat out for a test ride on the Erie Canal. His dad had a small 10 HP outboard motor that was barely powerful enough to plane the boat with two teenagers aboard. At this time the Erie Canal was sixty feet deep. In its early days when the canal was much shallower, mules were used to pull barges down the Erie Canal.

On our maiden voyage it took David some time to get the boat planed off, but he finally did. A short time later we noticed we were headed straight toward a steel pier. The boat wouldn't turn in time to miss the steel pier so we dove into the water. When the boat hit the pier, the outboard motor broke off the transom and sank to the bottom of the canal. The boat was badly damaged, but it was repairable.

Later, David's father, who was a Cherokee Indian, dove into the cold canal water a number of times and finally found the motor and brought it to the surface. Unfortunately one of his ear-drums burst on his last dive. The real problem with the hydroplane was that it didn't have a keel to stabilize it. David repaired the damage to the hydroplane and added a keel for stability. Our next test for the hydroplane was in the Niagara River several miles above Niagara Falls. Our plan was to go over to the Grand Island Fairgrounds for a little fun and come back.

When we landed at Grand Island, we spent most of the day having fun until it was time to head for home and supper. We got about halfway back across the Niagara River when the outboard engine ran out of gas. We began drifting fairly fast toward the upper rapids of Niagara Falls. I was wearing a red shirt so I took it off and stood on the deck of the hydroplane trying to flag down a nearby cabin cruiser. A couple of cabin cruisers didn't realize we were in trouble and waved back at us. Finally one cabin cruiser realized what was happening, came to our rescue, and tossed us a line. We attached it to the bow cleat and they towed us safely back to shore. From then on we took an extra can of gas with us when we went out for a ride.

The only thing I built in the high school woodworking shop was a stained plywood box six inches"- wide by five inches" high by eighteen" long for my knick knacks and collectibles. The contents of my plywood box are a pennant, key chain, and neckerchief slide from Scout Expo '67 in Montreal, Canada, August 21-27; souvenirs from the Morristown, Tennessee celebration 1855-1955, preserving the memory of David Crockett by restoring the Crockett Tavern and Davy Crockett Well on the grounds of the proposed David Crockett Memorial Museum plus five wooden tokens featuring Davy Crockett and four important events that happened in 1955; unused 4-cent and 7-cent postcards; ten unused red National Bonus Stamps from the National Stamp System; and a 2 franc note from France with French flag on the reverse side.

The box also contains a United States Treasury Department card dated July 21, 1960, reading, "In appreciation of fine services rendered in behalf of United States Savings Bonds Independence Drive this citation is awarded to Paul Mix (my father) on July 21, 1960 by John W. Lynder, Secretary of the Treasury"; and a North Tonawanda Felton Grammar School 1947-48 bicycle permit which allowed me to ride my bicycle to school, provided I obeyed all the rules and regulations, which I did.

The box also contains a 1952 list of individual averages for the Niagara Frontier Junior Rifle League showing the averages for ninety-eight competitors. The top three shooters were as follows:

1. R. Schultz from the North End Club with an overall average of 269.9.
2. Paul E. Mix from the Twin City Club with an overall average of 269.8.
3. A. Hammill from the North End Club with an overall average of 268.4.

The other ninety-five competitors shot much lower averages. A perfect score would have been 400 for the combined Prone, Sitting, Kneeling, and Standing positions.

Chapter 5 - A 1950 German Pen Pal

In 1950 my German teacher urged us to contact German students to learn more about them and their country. We could write to them in English and they could write back to us in German. The teacher could help translate anything we might not understand.

Herman Prang became a pen pal of mine. He lived at Oberstrassa 83, Saint Goar on the Rhine in the French Zone of Germany. I sent him pictures of my family on February 2, 1950, and he sent me some pictures of his family and his family's store. He thought it was great to have a friend in America. I was fifteen years old at the time and Herman was fourteen. His sister Annemarie was also fifteen. Herman and I both collected stamps, so I sent him some canceled American stamps and he sent me some canceled German and European stamps.

On April 23, 1950, Herman wrote:

"Dear Paul,

This is in reply to your letter of February 2, 1950. I think it is really nice to find a good friend like you in America. Now about myself I am 14 years old and weight about 1.56 gross. I will be out of school for Easter and confirmed by my church on Palm Sunday. I am also working and learning about our recently acquired family business. I have begun to collect some stamps for you and will send you an envelope with some miscellaneous German stamps."

"I have one other request. My sister who is 15-1/2 years old would like to correspond with someone in America. Her name is Annemarie Prang. I am also sending you two photos of myself. Please send me your photo as well. "

"Warmest greetings from your friend, Herman."

On June 13, 1950, Herman wrote,

"I want to thank you for your brief letter of April 30, 1950 and the flag from Washington, D.C. which made me very happy. Please excuse me for not writing sooner but there was a reason. I injured my head while playing soccer as shown in a couple of the pictures I am sending. My head was lacerated but today I am feeling much better and all that remains is a scar."

"You asked about my family. My father and grandfather currently own and operate a food store and delicatessen. We recently rebuilt and remodeled the store as shown in a couple of pictures I have sent to you. You said that someday you would like to visit us in Germany. My parents would like to meet you also."

"It is beautiful here at St. Goar on the Rhine. Someday when I have a little more money I would also like to visit with you in America. Time will tell. Thank you for asking about my Confirmation. Just out of curiosity are you Catholic or Protestant? Today my sister sent a short letter to a girl in America who also wants to be a pen pal."

"Best wishes to you and your family, your friend Herman."

On June 18, 1950, Herman wrote,

"Dear Paul,

Thank you for your letter of April 31, 1950. With regards to your brief letter I will tell you a little bit about our family business. My father and his father, my grandfather, recently bought a food store and delicatessen as shown in the two enclosed pictures."

"I would like to come to America to visit you and your family but unfortunately we don't have enough money right now. Later perhaps when we start making a profit on our business, you could come to Germany to see beautiful St. Goar on the Rhine and meet my family."

"I am sending you some mint stamps today including a 4# Mark stamp from Frauenkirche in Munchen (Hauplstadt von Bayern), a 10# Mark stamp from Kolner Dam and a 20# Mark stamp from Brandenburg near Berlin."

"Thank you for your best wishes concerning my recent confirmation. Are you Protestant or Catholic? As of today my sister still has not received a short letter from the American girl. I will close wishing good health and wealth to you and your family. "

"Your good friend, Herman."

I can't find any further correspondence with my German pen pal and I never made copies of the letters I sent to him. But it really was nice to have a pen pal from Germany. However as one old saying goes, – "All good things must come to an end." Apparently both of our families went their own ways and lived happily ever after.

Herman Prang's Family

Herman near the Rhine River

Herman and Annemarie at garden.

Herman outside his home.

Chapter 6 - Scout Island

Scout Island is in the middle of the Erie Canal and was a great place for weekend Boy Scout campouts. There was a nice log cabin on the island with bunk beds and a potbellied stove. It kept us warm in the winter and provided a safe place to cook. As a boy I loved all outdoor sports such as hunting, fishing, camping, boating, swimming and Scouting.

A local farmer kept a row boat for us on his land across from the island. In the wintertime we could get to the island by taking turns pushing the rowboat across the ice while holding on to the sides. In the summertime we'd row the boat back and forth across the Erie Canal to get to the island. There was a large oak tree on the island with a Tarzan rope on it. We'd swing out over the water, let go, and swim back to the shore. When we'd had enough swimming, we'd dry off and put our clothes back on again.

As teenagers there were three other places we liked to swim, and all of them were very dangerous. These swimming places were the Niagara River, an old abandoned quarry that had filled with water, and the Erie Canal. All of these places were dangerous and our parents didn't really want us to go swimming there, but we did.

We'd go to an upstream pier on the Niagara River and jump into the water feet-first or go down a wooden ladder if there was one. The current was relatively swift, so we'd effortlessly swim and coast to the next abandoned pier, climb out on a ladder, walk to the upstream pier, and go again. One day my brother Keith wanted to dive into the water. We warned him there might be some submerged pilings. He dove off the pier anyhow, hit a submerged piling and tore his thumbnail off. I drove him to a doctor, who patched him up. In time his thumbnail grew back. One spring day we decided to go swimming in the Niagara River when huge ice bergs were floating down from the Great Lakes. We went once, and unfortunately one boy caught pneumonia. That pretty well ended our springtime swimming in the Niagara River.

Our third dangerous swimming place was the Erie Canal, which ran from Albany to Buffalo. There was an abandoned railroad bridge where we had tied another Tarzan rope. A Tarzan rope is a heavy rope with large knots. You can use the knots to shinny down or pull yourself up. You can also use the bottom knot to get the rope swinging and then jump or dive out into the water from there. Swinging and diving from the rope almost cost me my life. I started the rope swinging just before a small cabin cruiser was about to pass beneath us. I dove into the canal, barely missing the side of the cabin cruiser. After I hit the water, I felt the pull of the engine's props trying to pull me into them. All I could do to escape was dive deeper, which I did just in time to avoid the props. None of us ever dove that close to a boat again.

Finally a public swimming pool-complete with lockers, diving boards, and platforms was built about a block from our house in North Tonawanda. Now most of my friends had two safe places to swim, the North Tonawanda High School swimming pool and the North Tonawanda public swimming pool.

Chapter 7 - A High School Bully

Like most high schools North Tonawanda had one bully who was my nemesis. His name was Alfred "Al" Guido, a football player who had the bad habit of hitting me on the left shoulder as hard as he could every time we passed in the high school hallway. I asked him to stop, but he just wouldn't. Al weighed considerably more than I did, and I knew I was caught between a rock and a hard spot. He just didn't like me for some reason.

One day my brother and I were waiting in the car for our parents to get out of church. The back window on the curb side was partly down because it was a hot day. Guido came walking down the street, saw me in the car, and put his fingers on the back window threatening me and I cranked the window up as fast as I could, trapping his fingers on both hands. Al threatened to beat the hell out of me the next time he saw me if I didn't let him go, so I let him go when I was good and ready. I knew Al was going to try to beat the crap out of me at in the high school locker room the next day. We had to pass each other in the locker room as he came to gym class and I tried to leave. In my mind there was only one thing I could do. As Al came down my side of the benches with clenched fists, I hit him in the stomach with my left fist as hard as I could. When he doubled up, I gave him a right uppercut to the jaw that knocked him over the bench. I left as he was picking himself up.

Later Al apologized to me and said he wanted to be my friend. I really didn't trust him until the day he stopped me in the hallway and asked me if I had lost my senior class ring. I told him I had, and he said he found it on the baseball field. He handed me the ring and it was my senior class ring with my initials engraved on the inside. I thanked Al and trusted him from then on.

For my first two and a half years at the University of Buffalo, Dudley Turecki, William Paul Ganley, and I carpooled to school. Dudley and I enrolled in pre-med courses. After my first year of college, I switched over to engineering courses because I thought that if your father wasn't a doctor, you'd probably have a tough time getting into medical school. Dudley stayed in pre-med even though his father was not a doctor; he owned a very successful fish market. Dudley became a doctor but lost his license years later for reasons unknown to me. William Paul Ganley wanted to become a science fiction writer, and apparently he did. Later I heard that some of his early science fiction stories paid his way through college.

I stayed with my uncle Jack Kehoe in Buffalo for one semester while my family residency was established in South Carolina. My father had been transferred from Buffalo's

DuPont plant to the Savannah River Plant near Aiken, South Carolina. I completed my Electric Engineering degree at the University of South Carolina. However, I had to attend one summer session because it took nine more semester hours to graduate from the University of South Carolina than it did to graduate from the University of Buffalo. The three elective courses I chose to take were "Thinking in Practical Logic," "Psychology of Personal Adjustment," and "U. S. History 1865 to Present". I graduated from the University of South Carolina with a B.S. in electrical engineering on August 11, 1956.

Chapter 8 - What Scouting Meant To Me

When I was twelve years old, my father asked what I really wanted to do. Without hesitation I told him I wanted to be a Boy Scout and I wanted to join a Junior Rifle Club. Dad did a little research and found out that Mr. Albert Bulgreen, a World War II army veteran, was a top-notch Scoutmaster for Troop 74 in North Tonawanda. Dad did his part by joining the Troop Committee and helping with transportation and campouts. Dad also introduced me to Mr. Chester Foit, who was in charge of a local NRA Junior Rifle Club in North Tonawanda. I joined both of these clubs and before the age of maturity became an Eagle Scout and Junior Distinguished American Rifleman.

As an Eagle Scout I also had the pleasure of attending the 1950 Boy Scout National Jamboree at Valley Forge, Pennsylvania from June 30th until July 6, 1950. I was sixteen and took a train from Buffalo to Valley Forge, riding with some scout friends. We set up two-man tents in the middle of the night only to learn that someone had placed our campsite in the middle of a poison ivy patch. After setting the tent, we put down a ground cloth. Thanks to the ground cloth we didn't get poison ivy and have to go to the field hospital, but about half the boys in our unit did.

A lot of Boy Scout trading goes on at a National Jamboree. Scout patches of all shapes and sizes are popular items. Some Scouts from Texas brought horned toads to trade. Horned toads are insect eaters, and unfortunately because of fire ants they are now extinct. They would not have lived very long in Pennsylvania or any other cold northern state. After becoming an Eagle Scout I worked as a summer camp counselor at Camp Ti-Wa-Ya-Ee, the Buffalo Area Council's summer camp. I was an assistant rife range instructor the first year and rifle range instructor the second year. For the last two weeks of summer camp I was asked by the camp director if I would act as a Scout leader for a group of Tuscarora Indian Boy Scouts. The adults of the tribe were involved in the annual grape harvest, so I agreed to act as their leader, but I had no idea what I was getting into.

There were about fourteen Indian Boy Scouts, and as a staff member I sat at one of their two tables at meal time. Another staff member sat at the other table, and we swapped tables on a daily basis. The first thing I noticed was that these boys had poor or no table manners at all. They preferred to eat with their fingers. I told them that if they ever wanted to win the "Honor Table Award,"they would have to learn to eat properly with knife, fork, and spoon. In a relatively short time they did. Before the first week was over, the Indian Scouts had earned the "Honor Table Award"- more than once.

At the closing week of summer camp a funny thing happened at the camp store. The store was giving away Vaseline Hair Tonic to scouts who wanted it. The Indian Scouts thought it was mosquito repellent, so they put it in their hair and on their skin. When I saw what they had done, I told them to go take a shower and put a little in their hair only when they wanted to comb it.

When the Indian boys needed to be disciplined for something they had done, I assigned them to work on the wooden steps and handrails leading down to the rifle range. Termites frequently got into the wood, and it had to be replaced. The Indian boys always did what I asked them to do without an argument. They also tried to teach me how to play lacrosse, but they could have killed me with the hard ball, if they had wanted to. There are two sides in a lacrosse game that launch a hard ball at incredible speed using a lacrosse racket. This is a North American Indian game where the ball is caught, carried, or thrown. The object is to take the ball away from the other team and score as many points as you can. I guess you could call it Indian handball instead of football.

I was fascinated by one Indian boy with natural blonde hair, and they were fascinated by my jet black hair. The boys wanted to make me a blood brother in a brief, simple ceremony, which I agreed to. One of the older boys pricked his thumb to get a drop of blood, and I did the same to mine. Then we put our thumbs together so that our blood would mix and we would become blood brothers. They gave me the Indian name of Black Eagle because of my jet black hair and the fact that I was an Eagle Scout, which they held in high esteem. The Indian Scouts presented me with a beaded neckerchief slide with a light blue background and black eagle. They also gave me a beaded belt with a white background that had their tribal symbols on it. I was truly honored. The bead-work was a very beautiful work of art. After all the scouts left camp, the camp staff had numerous chores to do before we could go home. We had to clean up everything and lock up equipment for the following year.

The camp chef was particularly fond of my beaded neckerchief slide and belt. He offered to buy them from me. I told him that they held a lot of meaning for me and that I couldn't sell them to him or anyone else at any price. I should have been smart enough at that time to pack them up and lock them in my footlocker, but I didn't. Unfortunately, the beadwork disappeared, and the only one I ever suspected was the camp chef. I had no proof that he took the items, and none of the camp staff saw anyone near my staff tent. My beautiful beaded belt and neckerchief slide vanished into thin air. Live and learn, die and forget.

Chapter 9 - Artemis Retreat

It was about this time that Dad bought fifty acres of land near Arcade, New York. The land was fifty miles southwest of North Tonawanda. Some of the land had to be cleared. It had a small pond near the back of the property, probably for cattle at one time. My dad and uncles Jack Kehoe and Leroy Mix started building a concrete block hunting cabin there. When it was finished, there was an upstairs loft that was big enough for a couple of beds. You could see the dirt access road from the upstairs window. In the summertime several of my friends David Elzner, Donald Morton, and I hunted groundhogs there. In the wintertime the cabin was used mainly for deer hunting in the general area. My brother Keith named the hunting lodge Artemis Retreat after the goddess of love.

Our land was next door to Fiction Farm, the home of Fran Striker, creator of the Lone Ranger. Tonto was the Lone Ranger's faithful Indian companion. After saving a victim in distress, the Lone Ranger would give him a silver bullet. The last question always asked was, "Who was that masked man?" Fran Striker had half a dozen white stallions on Fiction Farm and they all looked like the Lone Ranger's horse. I asked him if I could hunt groundhogs on his farm with my .22 rifle and he said, "Sure, but make sure you don't shoot in the direction of any of my horses," and I didn't. Mr. Striker was obviously a very wealthy man, but he shared some of his wealth with the people of Arcade every Fourth of July. He had a huge aerial and ground fireworks display set up for the people of Arcade. Residents would bring their folding chairs a little before dark and enjoy the fireworks.

My uncle Russ Curry liked to eat groundhogs, so he put a 50-cent bounty on them. I'd shoot a couple of them with my .22 caliber rifle in a relatively short time. You had to sneak up on them, before they saw you, scampered for their holes, and disappeared. If they saw you first, they wouldn't come out until they thought it was safe again. Rather than wait for a groundhog to come out again, it was easier to sneak up on another one somewhere else on the property.

David Elzner with Groundhog

Dad & Uncle Jack
Laying Artemis Retreat Foundation

Chapter 10 – The Savannah River Plant

I attended the University of Buffalo for two and a half years and the University of South Carolina. Our family moved to South Carolina when my father went to work for the Savannah River Plant, SRP or the Bomb Plant, as it was called by locals. The facility was owned by the Atomic Energy Commission and operated by the E. I. DuPont de Nemours & Co.

After graduating from the University of South Carolina with a B.S. in Electrical Engineering, I also went to work for DuPont at the Savannah River Plant near Aiken. On my first day of employment, I was given a whole-body scan. For the scan you had to remove all metal objects, go inside a huge vertical World War I cannon barrel, and have your body monitored with radiation counting devices.

Everyone has minute amounts of radiation in their body, so the results of a body scan are usually very low but not zero. The reason for using a World War I Canon Barrel was because after World War II all steel was contaminated with nuclear radioactivity. To make a long story short, my whole-body scan radiation count at the end of my employment at SRP was about the same, so my body had not accumulated any additional radiation.

I completed my degree as a B.S. in electrical engineering at the University of South Carolina and met my wife, Dixie. Before long we started our family. In 1965 while living in Aiken I completed Boy Scout leader training in Scout Basic I, II, and III, the Troop Committee, Showando Faculty Training, and Advancement in the Georgia - Carolina Council.

I worked at the Savannah River Plant for several years, first part-time as a metallurgist in the Raw Materials Department, then as an engineer in the Instrument Design and Development Group. Finally I became an engineer in the Nondestructive Testing Group.

Nuclear warheads using enriched uranium 235 and capable of releasing megatons of energy were made at the SRP. When I worked there, tactical tritium warheads, with ten kilotons of energy were also made there. These smaller warheads could be used in cannon shells or small bombs.

During the final stages of World War II in 1945 the United States conducted two atomic bomb attacks against Japan, devastating the cities of Hiroshima and Nagasaki when Emperor Hirohito ignored an ultimatum given by the Potsdam Declaration. President Harry S. Truman issued the executive order for the United States to drop the nuclear weapons "Little Boy" on the city of Hiroshima on Monday, August 6, 1945, followed by the detonation of "Fat Man" over

Nagasaki on August 9, 1945. Thousands of ordinary Japanese people were killed by these bombs. The only justification for this seems to be that millions of innocent American lives were saved.

Within the first two to four months after the bombings the acute effects of the bombing killed an estimated 90,000 to 166,000 people in Hiroshima and 60,000 to 80,000 people in Nagasaki. About 60 to 70 percent of the deaths were believed to have occurred on the first day from flash or flame burns or falling debris.

Almost twenty years later I thought 10 kiloton nuclear warheads might be used in the famous Gulf of Tonkin incident on August 2, 1964, but thank God they weren't. If there is one thing we don't need it's an atomic bomb attack on home shores. At one point it was felt that average homeowners needed underground concrete bomb shelters supplied with food, water, and medical supplies. Posters jokingly said, "In Case of Atomic Attack, Bend Over and Kiss Your Sweet _ _ _ Goodbye!" Think about it. Who wants to crawl out of a hole in the ground only to find out that their neighbors and friends are dead and their food and water supplies are contaminated with radioactivity! Not much to look forward to, is it?

I was unknowing witness to what FBI agents thought was a successful bugging of an atomic energy plant. One day a secretary with access to top secret information saw an unfamiliar shadow under her bookcase. She reached up under the bookcase and found a microphone taped there and a wire running up inside the wall. When the tape got hot, it sagged, making the microphone shadow. The secretary immediately called the FBI.

I was inadvertently involved when one of the technicians who worked in the High Bay Area of the plant asked me if he could borrow an audio amplifier. What I didn't know was that he had also borrowed a microphone and headset from two other people. The fire alarm people had also been in the attic to add sprinkler systems to the building. In a few short hours the FBI had all the answers to their questions.

Earlier a technician had asked the secretary to go to a movie with him, but she refused because she had a boyfriend who worked somewhere else at the plant. When the secretary refused to go out with him, the technician bugged her office. The FBI quickly determined both sides of a telephone conversation could be plainly heard by anyone in the attic with a headset. The technician who bugged the secretary's office was fired immediately, and his security clearance was pulled. He could never work again for any federal government agency.

Later I worked for Jackson Lab Research and Development in New Jersey and finally one of the first pilot plant projects for a new Freon 113/114 plant in Ingleside, Texas.

Chapter 11 – My Son John

Several years later as a married man with three children I was transferred by DuPont to the New Castle, Delaware, Research and Development Laboratory. While living in New Castle, I became the Scoutmaster of Troop 414 from 1970 to 1972. At that time sixth-grade teachers gave students the name, address, and phone number of their local Scoutmaster.

One day I received a call from a foster parent who had a boy named John that wanted to be a Boy Scout. She also had a seven-year-old son and a husband who was seldom home. She said the family had no money for a Boy Scout uniform or scouting equipment. I told her not to worry because we had a Troop Committee that would see to it that any boy who wanted to be a Boy Scout would have a uniform and the equipment he needed. To accomplish this, some scouts who left the troop donated their uniforms back to the troop. Our Troop Committee also provided Scout gear and furnished transportation when needed. John enjoyed being a scout and went on several campouts with the troop.

A few months later, John unexpectedly came to me with tears in his eyes. He wanted me to know that he couldn't be a Boy Scout any longer because his foster mother was asking for him to be moved to another home in the southern part of the state. I didn't know what to say to John, so I just told him I was sorry to hear that he couldn't be a boy scout any longer. Later I called his foster mother and asked her why John had to move. She said, "He started to ask questions about sex" and she thought he would be better off in a foster home with children his own age. It made me wonder what she was going to do with her own son when he started to ask questions about sex.

In Delaware, if a child hasn't seen either parent for one year, they are supposed to be eligible for adoption. John was twelve and had not had contact with his parents since he was eight years old. I called a local adoption agency and told them what I knew about John and asked them why he had never had a chance to be adopted. They asked my wife and me if we would be interested in adopting John, and we said yes we would. We pointed out that John needed to know that his mother and father were no longer living in the state. No one really knew where they were. I found out that his mother was an alcoholic, had left a Delaware rehabilitation center and had disappeared leaving behind only John's birth certificate and a few pictures. Knowing of our interest in John the adoption agency called my wife and I to come in for an interview. They knew that my son Tom and I knew John through Scouting and they wanted our family to spend Saturdays with John so we could get to know him better and vice versa. Any final decision about adoption would be his and his alone. We took

John to the Delaware beach, and went on picnics and fishing trips. John liked both families and felt like he was on the middle of a fence and didn't know what to do.

The social worker said she would talk to John and see if he wanted to come and stay with our family for awhile. We asked if we should go with her, but she wanted to keep the two families separated. So John picked up his belongings and came to live with us for awhile. The next time the social worker came to call on us and interview John privately, he told the her that he liked Mr. Mix and his family just fine and never wanted to be a foster child again. At that time I worked for Jackson Lab Research and Development in New Jersey. A short time later, I was transferred with the DuPont Company and moved our family to Corpus Christi, Texas, for the startup of a new Freon 113/114 plant. We called the social worker to let her know our family would be moving to Corpus Christi. She said she would refer our case to social workers in Corpus Christi. We talked with a Corpus Christi social worker about getting a lawyer to assist us with John's adoption, and she gave us the name of a lawyer she knew who had an adopted child.

Shortly after moving to Corpus Christi John met his new social worker and an adoption hearing was quickly set up. At the hearing the judge spoke only to John and told him the adoption was his decision and his alone. John told the judge that he definitely wanted to become part of the Mix family. To celebrate the occasion we took John's social worker and the family out to dinner. When we got back to social services office, John changed the number of children needing adoption in Texas to one fewer.

While in Corpus Christi I became an adult Sunday School Teacher for a local Christian church. One summer our class planned a picnic at a local park with a small lake. One of the ladies in my Sunday school class found out that we had an adopted child and asked, "How can you love someone else's child the same as your own?" I was flabbergasted and in turn asked her, "How can you not?" When most people found out we had an adopted child, they assumed it was Linda, our youngest daughter who was blonde and the only one with blue eyes. John was always happy when someone told him, "Boy, you sure do look like your dad!"

I was the Scoutmaster of Troop 278 in Corpus Christi, through January 1975. During that period John performed an act of heroism that earned him a Boy Scout Certificate for Life Saving. My father was dead and my mother had moved to Lakewood Village, a small retirement community with a nice in-ground swimming pool. We left the children there and they went swimming. Our daughter Donna started doing back flips from the side of the pool. On one back flip she rotated her body too far, hit the edge of the pool, cut the top of her head, and was knocked out. When John saw the blood, he jumped into the pool and pulled her out. He thought she would be able to stand on the edge of the pool but she fell back into the water again. Without hesitating, John jumped back into the pool and pulled her out again. By this time nearby residents saw what had happened and rushed to help. John was seven months younger than Donna and weighed less than she did. As his Scoutmaster I knew he deserved a BSA Certificate for Life Saving, and it was formally presented to him at the next BSA Court of Honor.

John throwing targets.

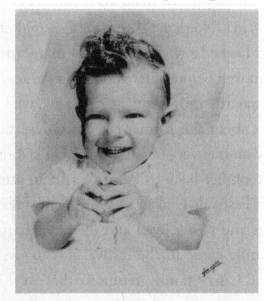

John's baby picture.

Chapter 12 – The Tom Mix Connection

I was born in Penfield, Pennsylvania and Tom Mix, the famous movie cowboy was born in Mix Run, Pennsylvania, a skip and a hop away. My grandfather was a second cousin to Tom Mix, so I thought that made me a third cousin. Another Mix relative said, "No, that makes you a second cousin once removed." So I asked, "Well, then, how many times do you have to be removed before you're not a relative at all?" Be that as it may, I was the only Tom Mix relative who set out to discover more about this former famous movie star.

I loved my mother very much. I think her favorite memory was when I took her back to Pennsylvania to attend one of the Tom Mix Festivals held in DuBois, Pennsylvania, where Tom's mother and father lived and died. Many members of the Curry family came to the festival just to see Mom and talk about the Curry family reunions that were held there for many years. The Tom Mix Festival Committee paid a special tribute to her as well. When we got back home from the trip, that was about all she talked about with her friends at Lakewood Retirement Village. Mom's trip to the DuBois Tom Mix Festival was about the last trip I took with my mother before she ended up with typical smoker's throat cancer even though she never smoked herself. My father, my brother, and I were heavy smokers, so I believe she died of second-hand smoke.

My brother and I never talked about it, but we found out later that we both stopped smoking for good shortly after mom's death. I really believe it is harder to give up a smoking habit than it is a heroin habit. Many of my Shrine friends who were also heavy smokers have died; they just couldn't break the habit. In 2000 my brother Keith and I went on a similar trip to Dubois, Pa. On that trip I had a chance to explain some things that had happened to him when he was younger that he didn't really understand.

When my Aunt Irma, who lived in DuBois PA died, my cousin Nita Curry sent me the 1940 obituary that she had kept about Tom Mix. There were things in it that I knew weren't true about him, especially his birth and boyhood. So I wrote my first book, *"The Life and Legend of Tom Mix"* in 1972, it was an attempt to separate the life from the legend of Tom Mix. I believe it was John Wayne who said you never want to destroy the legend of an American hero. Apparently the legend of Tom Mix was mainly a fabrication by early Hollywood press agents. Chapters in this book are "Boyhood and Family," "Black Powder and Heavy Artillery," "The Years Before Fame," "Sheriff Tom," "The Miller Brothers' 101 Real Wild West Ranch and Real Wild West Ranch Show," "Cowboy

Turns Actor,' "The Big Times," "Publicity and Advertising," "The Sawdust Trail," "The Riderless Pony," "The Legend of Tom Mix," and "A Summary of Thoughts," as well as an Appendix and Index.

My second Tom Mix book was titled just "*Tom Mix*," and it is considered A Heavily Illustrated Biography with a filmography. It was published in September 1994. Chapters in this book include "West Is Where the Heart Is," "I Want to Be a Soldier," "Freelance Lawman and Daredevil," "Early Selig Films," "A 1920s Hollywood Mogul," "The Ralston Phenomenon," "A Tired and Aging Miracle Rider," "The Sawdust Trail: A Trail of Tears," "The Fatal Crash and Its Aftermath," and "Long Live the King of the Cowboys." There are two appendixes and a filmography.

For years Gene Bell of Old Pard Video Productions made videos of the surviving Tom Mix silent and sound films. He had started adding sound effects such as hoof-beats and gun-shots to the silent films to add a little interest. When he died, his brother apparently took his sound editing equipment. To preserve what was left of his business, his wife sent me Gene's video masters and art work so that I could continue to make videos for the Tom Mix Museum in Dewey, Oklahoma. She didn't want me to send her any money, but I insisted on paying her something for Gene's artwork and she accepted it. Later I converted existing Tom Mix videos into DVD's for the Tom Mix Museum and other potential buyers.

Other books I have written are:

1. *The Design and Application of Process Analyzer Systems, Volume 70 in Chemical Analysis: A*

series of Monographs on Analytical Chemistry and its Applications. A John Wiley Inter-Science Application, 1984.

2. *Introduction to Nondestructive Testing: A Training Guide, John Wiley & Sons,* 1987.

3. *Introduction to Nondestructive Testing: A Training Guide, second edition,* John Wiley & Sons 2005. The second edition included a considerable amount of information on computers and real-time processing, which greatly enhanced nondestructive testing.

Chapter 13 – King Solomon's Mine

Author's Note: The Texas Nuclear Corporation in Austin, TX manufactured Inscan systems that were capable of measuring the amounts of gold, silver, and copper in a crushed rock mine slurry stream. We were asked to build three Inscan Probe Systems to measure the amount of gold and silver at King Solomon's Gold Mine in Saudi Arabia. This mine is the world's largest producer of gold and silver. When we received the request for equipment, I had to send Saudi officials a letter stating that no Jews were involved in the manufacture of this equipment or the startup of it.

Memo To: George Luce
From: Ken Blake
Date: February 1, 1988
Subject: Klockner Installation Schedule

George, I received a call today from Graham Midgley with an update on the Klockner installation schedule.

1. Site personnel have applied to local Saudi office for visas in the names of Wallace Daniel and Paul Mix.
2. The local office will apply to Saudi State Department.
3. The Saudi State Department will notify Ramsey/TN and nearest Saudi Embassy to TN with visa reference number. Ramsey/TN will be advised of location of appropriate Saudi Embassy.
4. TN will contact Saudi Embassy to confirm they have the reference number.
5. TN will send Passports for visa stamping.
6. Klockner will provide one airline ticket for one person; TN must pick up expenses for the second person.
7. Graham estimates that TN personnel could leave as early as 6 February, but more likely departure will be mid-week of 8 Feb.

Other Information:

1. Ramsey UK personnel are on the site now and expect to be there another three weeks minimum.

2. The slurry is now flowing through the INSCAN boxes. No problems reported.
3. We are waiting on delivery of coax cable to complete the installation of wiring. Most of the final connections will be left for TN personnel.
4. There is an IBM/AT computer on site available for TN use.

Cc: Wallace Daniel, Paul Mix, and Jim Whitworth

On February 8, 1988 the following fax was sent to Mr. Mahmoud of Klockner in Jeddah. Saudi Arabia. Questions we asked and answers were faxed back. Questions and answers are shown below.
1. Can you advise as to the best air route? Yes, the best route is from Austin, Texas, to Dallas, Texas, to London, Great Brittan., and to Jeddah, Saudi Arabia.
2. Will we need special permits to cover our company tools and test equipment? No.
3. Can we bring prescription medications such as Micronase for diabetics into the country? Yes.
4. Will the company we are working for provide guest quarters on site? Yes.
5. Are there any customs or traditions that we should be aware of? Alcohol and drugs are prohibited.
6. Are cameras and film permitted on site? No.

7. Are TN representatives expected to provide any formal INSCAN training or on the job training only? On the job training only.
8. Is liquid nitrogen on-site yet? Yes, it is on site.
9. Are oscilloscopes and digital voltmeters available for use on the site? Yes.

Wallace and I left the good old USA for London, England then Jeddah, Saudi Arabia on March 3, 1988, and we arrived in Jeddah on March 4, 1988.

On March 3, 1988, our flight to London was 8.5 hours. Wallace was able to get our business class rating upgraded to First Class because of the light load. It was raining lightly when we left Austin, ditto Dallas, ditto London. Food on British Caledonia from Dallas to London was excellent if you like caviar, fish and meat pate's, smoked salmon etc. My main dinner was a crab salad and stuffed crab with potatoes, peas, and carrots. Then we had apple pie and ice cream for dessert, not bad. When we had lunch in Austin, Wallace said to enjoy my last American meal. So far the British meals have been just fine.

We walked all over London today after taking a cab to Buckingham Palace. We could see Big Ben and the spires of Westminster Abby, so we decided to walk over there. Restoration work was going on at the church so we couldn't get any good pictures of the front. The church houses the remains of most (or at least many) of the Kings of England, their families, and other famous English men and women are buried there. It is truly a capsule of the history of the British Empire over the ages.

From there we visited the British Cabinet War Room, where Prime Minister Winston Churchill could conduct the British war efforts in relative safety. The Cabinet War Rooms are about 10' underground beneath the Great George St. government office buildings. From there we walked to Piccadilly Circus, a giant shopping area with licensed soft porno shops and punk rockers galore. It's like an enlarged 6th Street in Austin, Texas. Walking and cabs are about the safest way to get around in this city of ten million or so. It would be suicide for Americans to try to drive here. Big black taxi's make u-turns in the middle of the street during rush hour traffic. They are very skillful but the average American would still consider them reckless, darting in and out of traffic and passing each other and other vehicles by mere inches.

We took the train from Gatwick Station to London. The train is similar to the Amtrack System in northeast U.S.A. Trains travel 60 to 90 mph, pass each other going in opposite directions within a foot, and occasionally stop to let oncoming trains change tracks etc. It takes about 30 minutes to go from Gatwick Station to Victoria Station. The train goes through a couple of tunnels and over the famed Thames River. Large red double-decker buses and black taxi cabs are everywhere in the city. I imagine that the buses and "tube" (underground train) are the most economical way to get around the city.

There is no way that anyone can see London in one or two days. It would be like trying to see all of the interesting sites in New York City in one or two days. London also seems expensive to me. The Church charges 1.6#, about $3, the War Cabinet charged $4.63, and the taxi from the hotel and back cost $14.80 round trip. The train from Gatwick to London cost $9.25 each way, and a good meal costs 8# or $14.80. On the train ride back from London we spotted a little light covering of snow on the ground, so you have some idea what the weather was like. It was cold while we were there and it drizzled all the time. Since we are now leaving England the sun came out and it looks like it is going to be a beautiful day.

March 4, 1988

On our DC10 ride to Saudi Arabia drinking was permitted until we got over Saudi air space. The British Caledonia lunch and dinner stated that "no pork or alcohol" was used in the preparation of the meal for this flight. We saw the movie *"Cry Freedom"* just before we landed in Saudi Arabia-It was an anti-apartheid movie about South America.

When we landed at Jeddah,there was a very long passport visa stamping line. "Re-entries" were processed quite fast but first-timers had to wait a long time. We then expected customs time would take forever with our six suit cases, two of them carrying over 100# of tools. Surprisingly, we got through customs in a short time. After we got through customs two drivers, Lito and Tony, both Filipino, were waiting and holding up a small Wallace Daniel/Paul Mix sign. They had been waiting at the airport for over two hours. On the trip to the mine site we learned that this was the first gold mine in Saudi Arabia. The highway to the mine site was excellent but it was a 3-1/2 hour ride. The trip from London to Jeddah was a six-hour ride and somehow we were ahead of Texas time by nine hours.

The only oddities I noticed about Saudi's at this time were the toilets and the highway patrol. To take a crap,you squat and wash your butt with a small water hose. The highway patrol rides in white vans with yellow emergency lights constantly flashing. According to the tiles on the floor, my room is about 9' x 10'. There is a two door locker, 18" x 4' against one wall, a 6' x 30" single bed against another wall, a cheap desk, two chairs, and a night stand on the wall opposite the door. Each room has a Carrier Air Conditioner along the front wall to one side of the door. Thank God, the AC works fine. There are three wall plugs, European I guess, since they don't look anything like our 110 Volt outlets.

This morning I shaved with the straight razor furnished in the British Caledonia shaving kit. The British Caledonia shaving kit has the essentials we need until we get settled, namely ,a tooth-brush, toothpaste, soap, comb, safety razor, shaving cream, and after-shave cologne. It also contained a foot warmer which I used as wash-cloths and sleeping shades that I wish I had known about last night.

March 5, 1988

My dimensions in the previous paragraph-the floor tiles are more like 16" squares so everything is proportionally bigger. I learned something interesting today. The mine here at Mahd Adh Dahab is actually what was once believed to have been King Solomon's Gold Mine where half of the world's known gold comes from. It is still considered a very rich mine. The back side of the mine shows numerous ditches and caves that were hand-dug by King Solomon's slaves. If a slave brought up good ore he was allowed to come up out of the mine early. If not the slave had to stay in the hole and dig by hand all day. In case of a cave in, nothing was lost-only a slave. Another strange fact I learned today was that there are perhaps 15 times more foreigners in Saudi Arabia than natives-a lot of Pakistani's, and Filipino's. The Saudis do little if any work. They do not believe in getting their hands dirty. They know that they are destined to become boss in this land of theirs. It seems to me that Rome and the Roman Empire was once like that.

As I watched the sun set behind the mountains, I thought of only one thing. If two suns were visible, it would seem like a scene out of *"Star Wars"*. In its own way, the quiet desolation is quite beautiful. Our accomplishments today consisted of checking out all the INSCAN electronics except for the service enclosures and probes. There are lots of flies in Saudi Arabia and hobbled camels somewhere out in the desert. Perhaps I will take my camera if I wake up early enough and walk around the perimeter of the camp looking for camels.

March 6, 1988

Last night after supper we met and talked with our English friends, Alan Dempsey and Gordon Williams about King Solomon's mine and other things. Gordon told us there are vast crevices on the mountain that were dug by hand by slaves suspended with ropes. The crevices vary in width following actual veins of gold ore as they descended into the mountain. These crevices are so deep that they appear bottomless to the casual observer. A rock seems to bounce and ricochet endlessly if thrown into the crevice. One cannot help but wonder how many skeletons may be lying at the bottom of the crevices in King Solomon's Mine.

There is nothing to do here except for work. The Englishmen have accumulated a large number of tapes for their tape recorders. They are very high-quality music by the best American and English recording stars. They are all black market tapes made in countries such as Indonesia that do not recognize or honor American or European copyrights. According to the English , you have to be extremely wealthy to have a single-family residence in London. Too many people and not enough land. Most Englishmen would settle for a two-story, two-family dwelling in the suburbs. Today after familiarizing several technicians with the INSCAN system, we ended up with a little spare time on our hands before supper.

Gordon Williams offered to take Wallace and I around the back side of the mountain to see the ancient diggings. As we left for the mine site we passed the current entrance to the mine, which resembles the entrance to a railroad tunnel through a mountain. The shaft seems to slope downward at about 20 degrees. A mine worker died there yesterday when his earth moving equipment turned over on him. The incident almost went unnoticed by us. However, a Swiss Metallurgist mentioned it to us when we walked past the twisted machine on the way to the Administration Building. Gordon was right, the back side of the mountain looks like Swiss cheese and the huge hand dug crevices seemed bottomless. We dropped a rock down one spot, heard it bounce multiple times, and never could tell when it hit the bottom.

I don't know what good gold ore looks like, but many of the rocks sparkled with fool's gold. There appeared to be copper, amethyst, quartz, and gold in many of the rocks. I was told that other gold mines typically get 37 grams of gold per ton of ore but this gold mine has top quality ore that runs as high as 250 grams of gold per ton of ore. It also has its share of low grade ore. Many of the rocks we looked at glistened and were very pretty. We are still trying to get permission to take pictures on site. Damaron, the Project Manager, gave his informal permission warning us to be discreet and telling us to use his name if we got into any trouble. We are going to be very cautious in this strange but intriguing land.

Liquid nitrogen arrived just before the evening meal so we decided to return to the mine at 7 p.m. and fill all the liquid nitrogen probes. That way we will be able to test them in the morning to verify whether or not we have any probe problems. We are also trying to arrange an afternoon trip into the small town of Mahd to exchange some money and take advantage of the gold prices there. On the way to the mine after lunch, 11:45 to 12:45, we saw the camel herd on the flatlands in front of the mountains. There were a dozen or more camels of various sizes. The larger ones were hobbled to prevent them from wandering too far. Naturally no one had a camera as we were headed back to the work site. The weather seems to be getting hotter every day.

March 7, 1988

There are lots of flies in Saudi Arabia. There are also ants that look like spiders and there are cats all over the work camp. Today started out to be good but ended up in disappointment. At first it appeared that all of our probes were good and as the day progressed one probe appeared to be getting noisy. Wallace is going to check the preamp and fast discriminator tomorrow. If that doesn't fix the problem we may have a major probe failure.

There are Swedes, Germans, English, Americans, Filipino, Pakistanis, Indians from India, and a few Saudi Arabians here. They say there are only two to three million Arabians in the country and they don't believe in doing anything. They contract Germans to engineer the plant, Mountain States Engineering (USA) to start up the plant, Ramsey-England to start up the instruments, the Swedes to run the lab and supervise the Filipino work-force, etc., etc. It's a wonder that anything ever gets done right. They say that English is the language of the plant. As an .American, I can understand the English most of the time, the Germans when they speak English most of the time, the Swiss some of the time, and the Filipinos once in awhile. It's a real international circus. However the plant is supposed to start up tomorrow at 8 a.m. so we shall see. If we are successful in getting slurry into the tanks we should get at least three samples tomorrow. The plant has a maximum throughput of 400 tons of ore per day or 400 ounces of gold per day. $40 American = 150 Riyal, and 1 Riyal = 26 cents or 1 soft drink.

March 8, 1988

Yesterday it rained if you can call it that. I thought a few drops of water were blowing off some of the equipment. The ground never got wet just pockmarked from the rain drops. Today we had a dust storm probably the finest Saudi Arabia has to offer. The top layer of soil is so light and dust-like that the winds whip up great dust clouds, making it difficult to see. We also actually ran the plant today. They started it at 8 a.m. and it was still running at 11:30 a.m.

Yesterday Wallace and I got a Swedish tour of the Gold Refinery. The float material from the mine contains copper, zinc, iron, gold, and silver. Most of the gold is sent out as float concentrate after removing most of the iron, copper, and zinc. The silver and gold from the tailings are leached out of the waste material with a cyanide solution and then it is removed by activated cocoanut charcoal. Finally the material is electrolyzed and the gold and silver is plated out on stainless steel sheets that look like giant Brillo pads. The electrolysis is reversed and gold and silver is replated on steel sheets which have leaf-like silver and gold sheets that are removed by hand scraping. The gold and silver is then melted into ingots, 4" x 6" x 2".

The wind and dust haven't let up at all today. Others tell me a real rain-storm can sometimes follow a dust storm. A real rain-storm is apparently as bad as a Texas down-pour. We had good luck at the mine today. Operations started at 8 a.m. and if all goes well it will end around noon tomorrow. Big wheels will then evaluate the situation and decide when we go to the next phase or extended operation. Today we have taken four samples for each probe. Tomorrow we hope to get two more. That will give us a good calibration for our gold detectors.

I thought the gasket around my door was very tight but I see where the dust storm has found two tiny openings, one on each side of the door and formed two large "C-shaped" sand crescents. Apparently these dust storms are common and the local people cover their noses and mouths with scarves, bandanas, or handkerchiefs. I'm sure they don't use the handkerchiefs for blowing their noses; they just hold one side of their nose and with a hardy blow expel the mucus to the ground or washbasin, if they happen to be near one.

Every day we worked from 6 a.m. in the morning until 6 p.m. except when we want to work later, such as when the liquid nitrogen comes in. Tonight we will work late because we want the lab to take one more set of data. Everyone else here except Wallace and I are making big bucks with special compensation for overseas duty, and time and a half for overtime. We need to put in some extra clauses like that in our T. N. commissioning contracts. To expect an engineer to travel to a place like this and work under these conditions is ridiculous. They expect us to provide on the job training for five instrumentation men and five laboratory technicians, commission the equipment, and doing the bulk of the calibration work.

The Saudi's do nothing and depend on foreigners to act as compartmental groups, going about their work with little concern for the overall "big picture." There is no central organization smart enough to direct the efforts of this multinational effort. Three months from now all the people we have trained will probably be gone and the place will probably fall apart or be in worse shape than it is now. No one who has or is currently working here seems anxious to return when their current work or visitor's permit expires.

Klockner has test run their equipment, proved it worked, got their certificates of completion signed, and left for Germany. When their equipment falls apart which has already started, no one will know how to fix it and if they do they will find out that they don't have any spare-parts. Ramsey employees from England apparently supplied all the electrical glands, elect rical service enclosures, and most of the mercury arc lamps because no one bothered to consider them in the initial design. I could go on and on but this Composition Book is too small.

March 9, 1988

There has been wind and sandstorms for the second day. We are having trouble with the INSCAN calibration program and the plant is having trouble getting started up again. It has been about four days since I sent my laundry to the work camp laundry-I guess I'll try to find it again tonight. Wallace is staying at the mine during lunchtime and trying to figure out what is wrong with the computer program. I will feed data into the IBM program as soon as possible. Wallace wanted a Pepsi for lunch. When I told one of the cooks, he packed Wallace one Pepsi, sliced beef, several chicken parts, plus assorted vegetables. No one can complain about the food around here.

March 10, 1988

Today is the start of the Saudi weekend. Tomorrow will be their Sunday. The plant has run more or less continuously since 8 a.m. this morning. The ball mill shut down once but was restarted almost immediately (within a half hour). Almost everyone here has a camera but the guards have been told to take any camera found and smash it on the ground. The Saudi's check the vehicles entering and leaving the plant and entering and leaving the work camp. However, if the camera is in a soft unmarked zippered case, it is quite safe. The guards have never searched a person's pockets or made them unzip any cased item in a briefcase. Apparently they are only looking for large samples of gold ore. Tomorrow on the Arab Sunday we plan to revisit King Solomon's mine after lunch. Finally the sand storms have subsided without bringing rain.

We have noticed another oddity, the Arabs seem to wash their bottoms first, then their faces, then their arms, and then their feet in that order. This is truly a strange land. Apparently they still have public executions in Jeddah, still stone a woman for adultery and whip a man in public for being misled by a harlot. Stoning an adulterous woman is now high tech. They dump a load of rocks on her with an earth-moving machine. Now that sounds more humane, doesn't it? The former Supervisor of Security is now in jail. He was friendly, educated in America, and always had a kind word for anyone passing in or out of the gates. Rumor has it that he tried to sodomize a young Filipino worker and was turned in by another Filipino worker. After the investigation he was put in jail. He now awaits Islamic Justice. No trial by jury – just a Judge.

Once in jail your friends or relatives must bring you food or you starve to death. Mahd is a very small town. It has a very large jail and way too many police cars. It is as though they are just waiting for someone to make a mistake so they can throw them in jail. It gives me a very uncomfortable feeling.

We took a short trip to Mahd yesterday just one hour before supper. We cashed some American and British Travelers Checks. Gordon Williams went to a salvage shop and bought some glue, then to a drugstore to buy some heart medicine. It cost about one fourth of what it would cost in England, does not require a prescription, and it is even manufactured in England; it was the same medicine exactly.

There are two Gold Shops in Mahd. They have many gold items such as Tiaras, large bracelets, rings, breastplates, and necklaces fit for the Queen of Egypt. Some of these golden items could cover the entire upper portion of a woman's body. The English jokingly call them breastplates, coats of armor, etc. One cannot help but wonder who can afford to buy these things and how often they do. I was told that Arabs come in from the desert, frequent these shops and that the turnover in merchandise is quite amazing. However, once you start inquiring about the cost of these items you soon learn that gold still has a high price here. Small items such as pendants and necklaces sell for about 500 Riyals or $150. Prices however are very reasonable considering American or European costs.

We accomplished quite a bit at the plant today. We had three more sets of standards taken. Probe #3 is still has a little noisy but it is useable. The ROI's were tuned up today and tomorrow we will probably enter more data into the IBM computer. Our three joys in life around here are eating, sleeping, and taking a shower. I will join our English friends in the prison recreation room at 8 p.m. for a Diet 7-Up and some conversation. I hope the walls aren't bugged or surely the Arabs will get an ear full. Later, at 9:30 or 10 p.m., I will take my daily shower. The only interesting thing that I learned tonight was that Gilbert, one of the Filipino technicians we have been training, is actually an employee of Petromin, a first line supervisor and the person that we must satisfy if we ever want to leave this lovely country.

March 11, 1988

The reason it seems so much like a prison here is because the only way we can get about is in company vehicles. There are not very many of them and they are only authorized to go between Mahd, Jeddah, the mine, and the work camp site. No one but the Arabs have a driver's license to drive when and where they want. The Arabs have no auto insurance. If we were to take a company vehicle to Mahd and have a wreck, the driver and passengers would be responsible for the damages. Because of these kinds of restrictions there are few sight-seeing opportunities at this desolate location. I saw a few beetles or scarabs to add to my list of insects. I think they're harmless.

Since today is the Arabian Sunday, it is like a ghost-town around the mine. Almost everyone from Petromin is gone and there are only a handful of foreigners at the mine site. Wallace upped the high voltage on Probe #3 and lowered the heater voltage in hopes of lowering the background noise level. It seems to have worked but we still have to leave it run on the copper standard for an hour or so to see if there is any permanent improvement.

I have been gathering analysis data from the DEC Computer to put back into the IBM Computer when Petromin personnel return. Tomorrow there should be more lab data available to enter. It appears to take a long time to get lab data back. We get solids data about 24 hours ahead of other lab results. I think the Iron analysis is the big delay. I'm not sure their method of analysis has been perfected.

I learned two things about the Islamic Holy Day (Thursday 4 p.m. to Friday 4 p.m.). Nobody works except for us infidels and nobody makes up your bunk in the work camp. Today Wallace transferred several spectrums, deleted those with improper ROI's, and resaved them with current ROI's. I checked some more analysis data before going around the mountain to visit the ancient site of King Solomon's mine. Since today was an Arab Holy Day and very few people were at the mine, it was an excellent day for taking pictures although we are still waiting for official approval to take pictures of our own installed equipment. Three of us went around the mountain and took a couple dozen "unofficial" pictures of King Solomon's Gold Mine. We probably could have been put in jail for that.

Apparently Gold Field Mining of South Africa had the first official contract to build a new, or should I say modern day, mine at Mahd. The story goes that they could not fulfill the terms of their contract,so the Saudi's (Petromin) kicked them out. The South Africans took the ouster pretty hard, put tons of explosives in the mine shafts, and blew up everything in sight. They apparently did a lot of damage before they left. I don't know if the present entrance to the mine is anywhere near the Gold Field entrance or not,but I doubt it.

I don't know why a lot of people talk about the mine like it was a new mine. There appears to be abandoned equipment from the 1890's, 1930's, and 1950's until the present time. The mine has obviously been mined for centuries. The mine in its present form is new perhaps in regards to plant location and in the fact that it employs the latest mining technology. It is not a fully- automated mine in any sense of the word, and it appears to have been designed more for batch handling of ore than fully automated operation.

I think there are plans to start the mine tomorrow, and if so we have a standing order with the lab to get samples every three hours when running. Getting multiple samples or splitting samples and holding them back is out of the question under current operating conditions. We are lucky to get one sample of ore every three hours and have it analyzed. As we left the mine tonight, some of the longer-term residents of the work camp joked with a guard that some gold was in the back of their 4-wheel-drive vehicle. The guard asked one of the guys to open his briefcase and the owner said, "Sure, the gold rocks are in here." "No, replied the guard jokingly, "the pure gold Kilos are in there!"

They say the King of Saudi Arabia came to the "Grand Opening" of the new mine a short time back and the highways to and from the mine were lined with armed guards standing every 100 yards. The guards are also Arabian. They say mine security will really be beefed up when the mine is fully operational. Apparently,a new electrical barbed-wire fence will be installed along with a host of guards carrying machine guns. Maybe yes maybe no. In any case, the taking of "unofficial" pictures of the Mahd site will probably come to an end very soon.

Seeing the mine and actually being there has inspired me to do a little more research on King Solomon's Gold Mine when I return home. The novelty of this visit has began to wear off. From now on it will probably seem like eternity before we go home. One of my English friends assures me the guards are Arabian. He says a book titled, "The Kingdom" is excellent on Saudi history and background. Maybe I will buy one when I get home.

March 12, 1988

No one in this country knows what a teaspoon is. We eat every meal with a tablespoon. Ice cream and some form of pastry are served as dessert with almost every meal. This time for lunch we had a special treat-banana pudding, white cake, and yellow cake. Before lunch was over, they were back to serving yellow cake and ice cream. Today I added the data for five more sample points to the Petromin Computer. This afternoon Alan Dempsey and I will run multiple regressions using the best data points. We will then compare results with the five-point linear regressions taken earlier.

Wallace was told today that he would get his official camera pass tomorrow. Therefore, I brought my contraband camera back to camp at supper-time. I had what I wanted, mostly pictures of King Solomon's mountain. If a guard is assigned to stay with Wallace he will only be able to take pictures of the Texas Nuclear equipment. If a guard is not assigned to him he will be able to take pictures of whatever he wants. I expect the young Arab instrument technician will have his camera at work tomorrow also because the first line Filipino supervisor wants to have his picture taken with me. People here are very class conscious – managers are better than supervisors and supervisors are better than workers etc. Tonight Wallace went back to the plant to enter Chemistry Lab data on disk. He had to do it over because he added wire as an analyte and the solids information I entered and analytes were stored improperly.

Gordon Williams will be going back to England next Thursday. Apparently he handles all the paperwork for Ramsey while Alan Dempsey checks out the Ramsey equipment. Alan is the curious, eager type who sticks his nose into everything and occasionally does more harm than good. Gordon is in his early 60's and Alan is in his mid 20's. Gordon has offered to get our equipment list that we hope to return with to the

U.S., typed up in English and Arabic. That should help us get our equipment out of Saudi Arabia.

No laundry came back again today so I will get another bag full ready to return to the camp laundry. Lots of people are moving in. Some of the original Klockner people are returning and there has been a big turnover in the Filipino work-force. Joel Tiel tells me the plant plans to start up tomorrow morning at 7a.m. and run at a little less than half capacity and stay running at that rate as long as they can. It should be a very interesting day.

All the food is brought into camp by the Arabian Food Company. The milk is whole milk, not skim milk, not chocolate milk, not low-fat milk. There is only one kind of milk in Saudi Arabia, whole milk.

March 13, 1988

Wallace finally got permission in Arabic to take pictures with no restrictions as to when or where, time or date. So he skipped lunch today to go around the site taking pictures. I packed him a lunch of fruit, cheese, and crackers along with a little piece of meat. He won't get fat on what I've packed him. At the present time I don't see why we shouldn't go back home to the good old U.S.A. next weekend. We plan to go to Jeddah on Thursday, spend Thursday night in the Klockner approved hotel, spend Friday in Jeddah, and leave at 2a.m. Saturday morning. We also have to get Klockner's permission to leave.

It costs Petromin 50 Riyals a day or $15 a day for food and lodging for each American and European. It probably costs considerably less for each Filipino. The Filipino's don't eat as well and three of them bunk in the same room. We are housed in blocks here; cell blocks might be a more appropriate term. Each block has 12 rooms, six to a side, with a double-wide bathroom at the end. The bathroom area has 3 showers, 4 toilets, 6 sinks, and a janitor's closet. Most of the time the toilet seats are wet from the Arabs using little water hoses to wash their bottoms. We think this is a disgusting way to clean your bottom but they think the use of toilet paper is equally disgusting. They don't know how we can sit on a toilet seat that everybody else and his brother sits on. They also don't know why anyone would want to blow their nose on a little white cloth, then stick it in their pocket and walk around with it all day. I guess they have a point there.

March 14, 1988

Arabs brush their teeth with their index finger. They only brush sideways, never up and down. I wonder how long their teeth last compared to Americans. Yesterday morning a young Arab came into the control room and extended his hand in friendship to me. Then he shook hands with Wallace. Some Arabs seem to want to be friends yet they are somewhat hesitant in lieu of their religious training about Infidels and hearing other Muslim countries calling Americans "White Satan's." However they seem to enjoy having their pictures taken with us so I suspect we are somewhat of an oddity to them.

Today I went on a tour of the mine with the Swedish Mine Safety Engineer. We entered the main decline and observed some of the work going on at the 1,050 meters above sea level. Small scoop trucks load 3 tons of ore at a time onto 10-ton ore trucks. The mine produces about 120,000 tons of ore a year or 1.2 million tons over a 10-year period with Swedes running it. They say they have a half-year supply already, but claim that mining operations are very expensive due to logistics. The Swedes are hopping this one will average 100 grams of gold per ton. They have seen limited amounts assaying at 600 grams per ton and even 1,000 grams per ton. However, the mine at Mahd is not designed to handle high-grade ore, so it is mixed with lower-grade ore for processing.

I finally found out what a vein of gold looks like in the Mahd mine. All the rocks are gray in color. Gold ore veins are marbleized with white quartz that has blue/green copper chloride stains. Generally as the amount of copper chloride increases so does the amount of gold. Based on our INSCAN results the ore here also appears rich in zinc, iron and copper. Obviously all copper mines do not produce gold. The plant logo is half silver and half gold in color.

The mine mill ran all night but shut-down early this morning. We didn't get any samples today. We tried to put data into the Petromin computers but they were doing budget work and the computers were not available. We took advantage of the time to let the technicians input data into the DEC computer and run regressions under varying conditions. Two of the men are getting quite proficient with the INSCAN equipment. Tomorrow we hope to get the use of the Petromin computer to run various regressions and "fine tune" our system.

March 15, 1988

Well Gordon Williams and Alan Dempsey are headed back for England today. They say the final search before leaving the work camp was quite thorough because the guards are looking for little rocks. It's not worth the effort to me because the gold is microscopic and can't be seen with the naked eye. Anything that looks like gold is "fools gold". I have the pictures I want from King Solomon's Mine and that's good enough for me. Gilbert is required to sign our last release. I am giving him intensive training on the IBM since that is the material he feels most familiar with. The mine is having major problems – filters, dryers, pumps, and fans. It will probably be a long time before they can get a 15-day continuous run. If we are successful in getting out of here this Thursday I think we will be getting out at the right time.

Hostilities are bound to increase between Petromin, Mountain States, and Klockner once Petromin realizes the plant probably won't run at design rates for a long time to come. We didn't have a dust storm today but dust-laden clouds hung low to the ground, producing a somewhat eerie setting. Mr. Damarow had no objection to our leaving. As long as the plant isn't really running we are just wasting our time here.

March 16, 1988

It is colder now than when we first arrived and I don't have a long-sleeve shirt or sweater. I'm glad we'll be leaving soon. We had trouble with static electricity. We have thrown two disks away, a system master, and a copy. I have lost their automatic boot feature. And I am almost certain that the automatic boot worked several times when we first arrived. I will try to get technicians back on the IBM computer program today if possible.

At lunch time I wanted to take a picture of the Arab Mosque right across the street from the entrance to the work camp but the Arab guard on duty wouldn't let me so I walked back to camp taking a few pictures of Arabic – English signs. I got as close to the Mosque as I could and took a picture of it. It will probably look very amateurish. These people have a real fetish against cameras. No tourists, no visitors, and no need for cameras. I think I'll make it my unwritten policy only to travel to countries where cameras may freely be used.

It's strange how people so different can have English as their second language. Tonight I will throw away my pretty little piece of pyrite. No use spending three months in a Saudi Arabian jail for a worthless piece of rock. The pyrite looks like gold,but the real gold bearing rock looks nothing like pyrite.

I had a lengthy discussion with the mill manager this afternoon. In general he seems pleased with our INSCAN SYSTEM. In the morning I am scheduled to give a brief review of the system to some of the Arab dignitaries. I have been told to keep my talk simple because these are a simple people in some ways.

Wallace will get one of the drivers to help him load up all of our tools and test gear by mid-morning. Once the guards are convinced we are not hiding anything in our tool cases we will have only our personal luggage to worry about. It is times like this that I wish Coca-Cola didn't have a bottling plant in Israel. Nothing that Israel has or consumes can be used or purchased in Saudi Arabia. Diet Pepsi's, canned by the Saudi Fruit Juice and Beverage Industry, taste terrible and are flat. Saudi Arabia also has some really big spiders. I just killed one in my room tonight. Apparently, the startup of the Gold Mine has been postponed today. An expert from Allis Chalmers arrived and spent most of the day with Joel Teal, the head Mountain States man.

March 17, 1988

The plant was running well when we left it at about 10 a.m. this morning. Earlier we met with Julius O. Rojo, the Mineral Processing Advisor for Petromin. He gave us blue lines of an enlarged flow sheet for the mine and process area. It is quite informative and may be suitable for framing. Wallace got our tools and spare parts past the camp guards with proper written permission of course. We will eat lunch here and then go through the camp gate for one last time with proper written authority. We still have Customs to look forward to. Some final thoughts as we prepare to leave the work camp. Two pair of shoes is enough. One pair of loafers would make a good choice and a comfortable pair of sneakers would make a good second choice. You should also bring a wash-cloth, towel, laundry bag, emergency roll of toilet paper, and a package of tissues.

In addition to a Sports Jacket, a couple of long sleeve shirts would come in handy. A cheap, small portable radio would also be nice to have. A spy camera would be nice, the smaller the better with the ability to turn the flash off. Since the humidity is so low here most of the time Chap-stick or some sort of lip balm is helpful. It's good to have both reading and writing material. Soon we will see what the seaport of Jeddah, S.A. has to offer the weary traveler. Our four hour car ride from the work camp to Jeddah was very interesting. The first third of the trip was through a sand desert. We saw many camels in this area and tried to take pictures of them through the car windows. The second third of the trip was through the desert covered with rocks. First we saw small gray and black rocks increasing in size to huge boulders. Then we were back to a sand desert with gullies and plains just before arriving at Jeddah, S.A.

In Jeddah young men frequently hold hands and kiss in public but they are not gay. It is an accepted custom here. Finally we found what might be called a shopping mart, and picked up a few souvenirs for our families. The people here are very dedicated to their religion. They close up shop for about 20 minutes at 6:30, 8:30, and 10:30 p.m. Apparently they pray for 15 to 20 minutes every two hours all day long. The Mullah (Priest) sings passages from the Quran. English translation of the Quran passages reminds me of the Old Testament.

March 18, 1988

As we left the work camp yesterday, it was obvious that many local Arabs live in even poorer surroundings than our work camp environment. We saw what appeared to be Nomad tents in the desert. Some of the nomads appear to have camels and goats. I thought I also saw some sheep but they were too far away to positively indentify.

There were numerous wrecked cars about 100 yards off the highway. It appears that wrecked cars are abandoned at the scene of the accident. As we approached Jeddah, the traffic grew heavier and the six-lane highway didn't seem deserted like it was on the way in. The majority of Arabs appear to own Datsun or Toyota pickup trucks. You also see a lot of Japanese cars, and a few Mercedes. There were also a few metal- bodied trucks and buses on the road in Jeddah. Some of the trucks were gaily painted, with more conservative and geometric designs than the gaudy murals on Mexican and Panamanian buses.

We took a quick tour of Jeddah by cab on Friday the Holy Day. We took pictures from the cab windows, but the cab driver got very nervous when he saw any Police. We were very careful not to take pictures of Arabs, the Police, and Government buildings. After we took several "safe" pictures, we returned to Hotel Harithy, the official Klockner hotel.

March 19, 1988

Our return reservations were all screwed up by Lito and Mr. Mahmound in Mahd and Jeddah. We were both booked from Jeddah to London O. K. But only I was booked from London to Dallas. No one was booked from Dallas to Austin, TX. It would seem to me that the best thing we could do is handle our own booking arrangements in cases like this.

We tried to sleep on the 6.5 hour flight from Jeddah to London but we didn't sleep long. It was cold, about 40 degrees or less, damp, and quite unpleasant in London. About the only thing that we did there was have dinner at the Hard Rock Café and buy a few T-shirt souvenirs. The London Hard Rock Café is a very popular spot for lunch. Many guitar's from original rock stars, their pictures, etc. adorn the café. They play loud hard rock music while you eat. The food is reasonable and good by London standards. Tomorrow we leave for Dallas. Wallace is trying to unscramble our reservations and book us both from Dallas to Austin, TX.

March 20, 1988

London's Gatwick Airport was a mob scene when we tried to leave this morning. School children of every age filled the station. Most of the children appeared to be with their teachers. I don't know whether they were coming, going, or both. Our flight to Dallas went without a hitch. When we got to Dallas it was obvious that this weekend was either the beginning or end of the Spring Break. I have never seen so many young people at any airport in my life.

We could not get a confirmed booking on American or Delta. After traveling ten and a half hours by air from London it looked like we were going to be stranded in Dallas for one night. We missed our 3:45 p.m. Delta flight. They took several standbys but not us. We were standby on the next Delta flight at 4:49 p.m. also. Wallace and I were two of the last three selected standbys for this flight. We finally arrived back home in Austin, TX, at about 6 p.m. Due to time changes we had been without sleep since midnight. We were dead tired but relieved to be home in Austin, Texas, and the good old U.S.A.

My Workcamp Desk

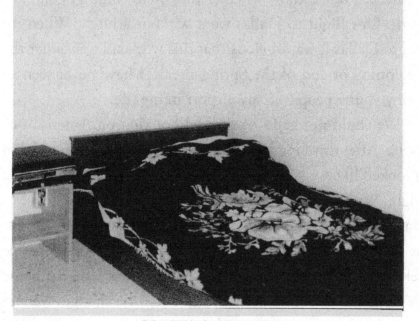

My Workcamp Bed

Entrance to King Solomon's Mine.

Modern Day Saudi Gold Mine.

Looking back at the modern gold mine from the top of King Solomons mountain of gold.

The small cement building under the big roof is the silver and gold refinery with armed guards.

Abandoned 1930's Control Shack.

Abandoned Miniature Railroad Cars from the 1930's.

Abandoned Playground Jedda, S.A.

Other Abandoned Facilities, Jedda, S.A.

Hard Rock Cafe' in London.

Picadilly Circus in London.

Chapter 14 – Movies, Politicians and God

<u>Movies</u>

Some of the best movies I have seen are:

1. The *Yearling*
2. *Old Yeller*
3. *The Grapes of Wrath*
4. *Gone with the Wind*
5. John Wayne and Kevin Costner movies
6. *The Greatest Story Ever Told*
7. *The Ten Commandments*
8. *Oliver*
9. *Matilda*
10. *The Passion of the Christ*
11. *The Picture of Dorian Gray*

If I could play a role in a movie, I thought I might like to play an utterly evil character such as Jack Elan, Malcomb McDowell, and Hannibal Lecter are perfect examples of evil characters. These characters are utterly evil. Everyone loves to hate an utterly evil character. If nothing else, many of these movies make you laugh, cry, or think about important issues. One thing my father always said was," "Don't steal anything, unless you have a chance to steal a million dollars." Dad thought the penalty for stealing a million dollars was about the same as stealing anything of value, and the chances of getting away with robbery were better if you didn't spend the money too fast. Of course neither Dad nor I ever had the chance to steal a million dollars, and anything less just isn't worth the effort.

Politicians

Politically I guess I would consider myself a moderate, not an ultra conservative or extreme liberal. I don't like the extreme left or right. I believe that all crimes are sins and our laws are basically founded on Christian principles.

When it comes to America, I think you should love it or leave it. If you don't believe in our country's principles, then don't come here. As far as I am concerned, illegal aliens deserve nothing more than a trip back across the border. If you are illegally here, you are already breaking our laws. Go back to where you came from and apply for legal U.S.A. citizenship.

I think Dwight D. Eisenhower and Ronald Reagan were very note-worthy presidents. The first several presidents who served this country did so without pay. That's what I consider read l dedication. Today, congressmen vote themselves pay raises whenever they want one.

God

At twelve years of age I prayed that God would come into my heart today, come in to stay, come into my heart, Lord Jesus. I was baptized and accepted Jesus Christ as my savior, and I felt great. As a Boy Scout, I went out of my way to "do a good turn daily" and I felt great doing good turns and helping other people. I believed in the twelve points of the Scout Law, namely that a Scout is: trustworthy, loyal, helpful, friendly, courteous, kind, obedient, cheerful, thrifty, brave, clean, and reverent. I may have turned my back on God, but he never turned his back on me. God has come to my rescue several times.

Once when I was shot and thought I might be dying, God's Holy Spirit descended on me from above and energized every living cell in my body. Instantly I knew that I would be all right. Before the Holy Spirit's intervention, I had selfishly prayed for myself and my family. When I realized what I had done, I said the Lord's Prayer several times and completely surrendered myself to God by saying, "Thy will be done." It was then that the Holy Spirit came as pure energy from above and energized every cell in my body. At that point, I knew I knew that I had no feeling on the right side of my right leg. But I also knew without a doubt that God saved me, I would live, and someday I would walk again.

I was taken to the Laredo Hospital on a bench in the back of my covered pickup truck by one of my hunting buddies who lived in Laredo. When we arrived at the Laredo Hospital, a young priest gave me the last rights, just in case I didn't make it. I thanked him for praying for me because I knew I needed all the help I could get. Later, a doctor removed the bullet that had passed through my leather belt, and between the large and small intestine, and lodged just beneath the skin at the front of my body. Where the bullet stopped felt like a ball of fire.

The doctor told me it was a real miracle that the bullet passed between the large and small intestine without burning either or doing any other damage, except for severing an outside nerve in my right leg. It took several months for the nerve to grow back so I had to learn to walk on a right leg with little or no feeling. I told the doctor I definitely believed in miracles and I always will.

Chapter 15 – Paradise Lost

This is the inspiring story of Rinor Marcial, who at age eight was badly burned by gasoline. It happened while he and his brother Norman, nine, were watching a thirteen year-old friend trying to ignite a traditional bamboo bazooka shortly after the 1988 Christmas holiday in the Philippines. I would especially like to thank Gordon Irwin for his help and cooperation in telling Rinor's story.

Rinor's third - and fourth - degree burns on his left side of covered 25 percent of his total body area. His family became destitute while seeking medical help for their son, the youngest of seven children. His mother and father sold all their worldly possessions, down to their last spoon, to pay for Rinor's hospitalization, clinic care, whole blood transfusions, and medicine.

After selling their home the Marcial family moved their seven children to a one-room bamboo bungalow built by their father. Rinor's father and older brothers worked the rice fields for a generous land owner in exchange for the use of the land.

However, Rinor still additional hospitalization, making the family destitute a second time.

A year and a half after the accident missionary Jocy Johnson found Rinor lying on a pad on the floor of his family's bamboo bungalow. He was naked and covered only with mosquito netting. The lower part of his left arm was tied in the bamboo ceiling to prevent it from touching his body. Rinor was a pitiful sight, and he was unable to walk or use his left arm. He was dying from his original burn injuries and third-degree malnutrition.

This is the story of Rinor's accident, his slow and painful recovery, and the long-overdue surgery that would eventually allow him to use his left arm and leg again. This is also the story of many Christian people and charitable organizations that helped Rinor along the way in turn, were inspired by him.

A brief history of the Philippines will prove useful to the reader in understanding Rinor, his family, and their way of life. We are all influenced by the historical, geographical, social, and economic factors affecting our homelands.

Many years ago the Philippine Islands were a tropical paradise. Some of the islands were lush tropical rain forests that provided homes for native wildlife such as water buffalo, monkeys, reptiles, and a large variety of fish, and tropical birds. Most of the tropical rain forests have been depleted by large, powerful Malaysian and Indonesian logging companies. Renewed government efforts in re-planting them have helped but not enough, and they continue to be harvested for their timber at an alarming rate. Asian loggers now have their sights set on the rain forests of the Amazon, and European loggers are eyeing the rich African forests.

The Republic of the Philippines consists of thousands of tropical, volcanic islands, lying just north of the equator and northeast of Malaysia. The twelve largest islands are Luzon, Mindanao, Negros, Samar, Palawan, Panay, Mindoro, Leyte, Bohol, Catanduanes, Cebu, and Masbate. Most cities and residential areas lie on the perimeter of the islands and are connected by roads to a main perimeter highway. The terrain is primarily mountainous with population centers in the flat coastal plains and river deltas.

The climate throughout the Philippines is monsoonal in nature with well-defined wet and dry seasons. Average monthly temperatures range from 68 to 93 degrees Fahrenheit with the hottest months March through June. Monthly rainfall varies from a few inches in January through April and typically peaks to more than sixteen inches a month during July and August. The islands average six typhoons a year that are similar to Atlantic hurricanes. Winds are commonly more than 100 miles per hour and accompanied by very heavy rains. The strong winds and heavy rains are capable of uprooting trees and knocking down homes. Storm surges and floods can cause heavy loss of life and property.

Pigs, buffalo, goats, cattle, chickens, and corn are raised on the islands, but rice and fish are the main food of the masses. Most of the Filipino people have low-paying jobs either in agriculture or in the garment and shoe manufacturing industries in the major cities.

Coconuts, sugar-cane, timber, bananas, mangos, pine-apples, manila, hemp, tobacco, coffee, and cotton are the main crops exported. The islands also export mining products such as copper, nickel, gold, silver, chromium, manganese, lead, and iron ore. The Philippine government continues to try to exert a strong influence over management of the nation's natural resources.

For years the Filipino people have been influenced by the Malaysian, Spanish and American cultures. As a result the public school system is very similar to that of the United States and English is spoken as a second language. Tagalog is the primary language of the Philippines. The major religions are also diverse, being Roman Catholic, Aglipayan (Philippine Independent Church), and Islam. Despite the diverse Malaysian, Spanish, and American heritage the Filipino people share a strong sense of national unity and identity.

The Filipino people travel from island to island by airplane, ship, and ferry-boat. Buses, commuter trains, Jeepneys (small, colorful, open Jeep buses), and taxis are used for public transportation. Motorbikes and motorcycles with seats or sidecars for one to three passengers are also used for local transportation.

Despite the tropical beauty of these islands poverty continues to abound. Reasons for poverty include the low wages paid in the agricultural and manufacturing industries, the trade deficit, exploitation of the native people by logging giants ,and other long-time exploitation by foreign countries. Add to these the political upheavals involving students, communists, peasants and Muslims, and natural disasters such as typhoons, floods, earthquakes, and volcanic eruptions. Finally, consider the high birth rate and overpopulation problem, and then you can begin to understand the reasons for this nation's poverty. This is the world into which young Rinor was born.

Rinor's story begins in 1971, when Ricardo Marcial met and married a small, attractive Filipino girl named Norma Labiga. Norma is fairly well educated, attending the Far Eastern University for her first and second years and Adamson University for her third and fourth years. Both of these universities are in Manila. Norma studied Chemistry in five years of college, and English from the first grade through her college years. The English language was taught in all her classes.

Nine years later the Marcials were the proud parents of seven children, five boys and two girls. Ricardito hired on as a driver with the Arrow Freight Company on January 10, 1983, to help support his large family. He went to work in Saudi Arabia and Jordan. One of Norma's relatives was married to one of the owners of the company. This family connection probably helped Ricardito land his first good-paying job. While working in Saudi Arabia and Jordan, Ricardito drove an eighteen-wheeler, hauling rice one way and potassium sulfate the other way during one of the Middle East conflicts. The project was known as the JOSYCO project. During this time Ricardito faithfully sent money home to his family every month. When Ricardito returned home to the Philippines in October 1984, the Arrow Freight Corporation gave him a letter of certification that read as follows:

"To Whom It May Concern:

"This is to certify that Mr. Ricardito Marcial has worked with Arrow Freight Corporation in the overseas project with the Jordan-Syrian Land Transport Company in Jordan. He was a trailer driver from January 10, 1983 to October 7, 1984. He drove a Mercedes Benz truck Model 2624 and hauled cargo from the Port of Aqaba. He delivered cargo to different points in Jordan and Iraq. Mr. Marcial has completed his contract with our company and is observed to be a good driver during his employment with us. Issued October 7, 1984, as an employment reference for Mr. Marcial."

The letter was signed by E. C. Bolus, project officer-in-charge.

For the most part the Marcial family spent a quiet time at home. Norma remembers taking the family to the beach once shortly after her husband returned from Jordan. The beach trip was to celebrate Sidney's seventh birthday in 1985. It would be the last family outing for a long time to come.

Thanks to Ricardito's former employment he and his family were able to buy an old two-story house made of bamboo with floors and a bamboo leaf roof. The Marchials had to repair the floor of their home with bamboo that was about a foot in diameter. Eventually they changed the roof to galvanized steel. The family lived downstairs and slept upstairs. The upstairs rooms were much cooler at night. The galvanized roof made the upstairs rooms too hot in the heat of the day.

Negros is divided into two provinces, Negros Oriental and Negros Occidental. The Marcials settled in a residential area in the Don Salvador District of Negros Occidental in the town of Pontrevedra. Ricardito worked at home for a couple of years and then was off again this time to the island of Palawan, which is about 250 miles away as the crow flies.

Palawan is noted for its tropical rain forests, caves, deserted beaches, coves, coral gardens, wild orchids, butterflies, birds, and, primitive tribes. While in Palawan Ricardito drove a pay-loader hauling cut logs from the rain forests to nearby lumber mills. At the lumber mills the logs were converted into lumber for the building industry. Again Ricardito was working a long way from home and sending his monthly paycheck back to his family.

The Marcial family's seven children ranged in age from eight to seventeen. They were considered a middle-class family in 1988 by Filipino standards. The children's names are Marcial, Angelo, Kurt, Sidney, Cindy, Norman, and Rinor, with Marcial being the oldest and Rinor the youngest. As a young boy Rinor liked to run and play. He liked to play basketball with the older boys. His favorite game was hide-and-seek. Rinor loved to play hide-and-seek after dark because he was small and hard to find.

The family's four-room, two-story home in the residential area of Barangay, Don Salvador, had a concrete floor and concrete-block first floor. The second floor was wood frame and bamboo construction. The two youngest boys slept with their parents in one bedroom upstairs, and the rest of the children slept in the other upstairs bedroom. Downstairs were the kitchen and family area.

Cooking was done on the floor. A wood fire was built on top of a dirt cooking area. Then an iron stove-top with three round openings, and short iron legs was positioned over the fire. Pots and pans of food were placed over the stove-top opening. City water was supplied by the National Water and Sewage Association, which charged a monthly fee for the service. A typical meal for the family consisted of fish, rice, beans, and vegetables such as egg-plant or spinach. Pork, beef, and chicken cost too much and were eaten only on special occasions such as birthdays and major holidays like Christmas.

The house had an indoor toilet connected by a large pipe to an outdoor block-lined pit. Sewage was flushed to the pit with a bucket of water. The pit was covered with a wooden shelter consisting of walls, roof, and a door to keep out rain and people. When the pit was almost full, it was covered with dirt and a new outdoor pit was dug, lined, and covered with the same wooden shelter.

Household furnishings included a TV set, refrigerator, and a tape cassette recorder and player. Other furniture included an iron-frame couch and two matching iron-frame chairs with padded cushions, a china hutch, a wardrobe with glass doors, an electric fan, a wall clock, and beds with mattresses. This modest amount of wealth did not go unnoticed. One night a thief broke into the Marcial home through the kitchen drain area and stole the electric clock and tape recorder. When Norma came downstairs in the morning, she looked up at the clock only to discover it was missing. Then she discovered that the tape recorder was also missing along with several bananas as evidenced by the peels left behind on the table.

On another occasion Ricardito brought a company car home along with a guard dog to guard it. The next morning, when he awoke, the car was still there but the guard dog was missing; it was assumed that someone had eaten it. According to Norma little could be done when property was stolen in a residential area. The police were too far away and not concerned with petty thievery. About the only thing that could be done was to give the neighbors a description of the missing property in case the thief tried to sell it quickly in a nearby neighborhood.

Usually, the Marcial's celebrated Christmas quietly at home. Norma would cook plenty of food, have lots of fruit, and perhaps serve chicken or beef for a special Christmas dinner. The Christmas decorations were very simple, and the family did not give or receive gifts. Sometimes they would decorate the hallway with a homemade Star of Bethlehem or a small white Christmas tree made from a painted bamboo broom. However, the younger children always hung their stockings in the kitchen in anticipation of Santa's arrival, and the kindly old elf always found the stockings and filled them with candy. Just having the family together and celebrating the birth of their savior was more than enough Christmas for the Marcial family.

Chapter 16 – Bamboo Bazookas

Often the men and youth of the village celebrated Christmas with a loud display of homemade fireworks. First they would make bamboo bazookas by cleaning out the center of a large piece of bamboo about five inches in diameter by three feet long. They would leave one end open and plug the other end. Then they would cut a small hole in the middle of the bazooka's length. Next they would build a shallow ground fire and prop the bamboo rod across the fire on rocks or concrete blocks. Finally, they would position the small hole at the top and carefully pour about a cup of gasoline into the hole. The hot bamboo quickly vaporized the gasoline. Finally they would strike a match and throw it or a small burning twig into the hole. The gasoline in the bamboo bazooka would explode with a loud noise. The explosion would also damage the bamboo bazooka so it could be used only once. Many bamboo bazookas were made before the Christmas celebration since bamboo is plentiful.

No one could have guessed the tragic turn of events during the 1988 Christmas season that would forever change the lives of the Marcial family. Shortly before Christmas Norma's cousin Roque Espiritu, Jr. died from liver cancer. Roque was the son of Norma's aunt and close to Norma in age. To comfort the family and help in their time of sorrow Norma decided she should go to Roque's funeral and visit with the Espiritu family. She gathered up a few belongings and her two youngest sons, Norman and Rinor. They walked for about an hour to get to the Espiritu home in the Antipolo District of Pontreverdra about three kilometers away.

While staying at the Espiritu home nine-year-old Norman and eight-year-old Rinor became friends with thirteen-year-old Juan, who lived next door. On the morning of December 28, 1988 the boys were playing in Juan's back yard. Jaun showed the younger boys a bamboo bazooka he had made and asked Rinor if he could get some money from his mother for candy. Norma gave Rinor 50 centavos for candy. Then Rinor ran back to the other boys and gave the money to his brother Norman. Norman took the money and an empty pint bottle down to the corner store, where he bought gasoline instead of candy.

Now that Juan had the gasoline he needed, he built a small ground fire and stacked a few rocks on each side of the fire. He told the two smaller boys to stand back out of the way. Then Juan laid the bamboo bazooka across the rocks and began pouring gas in the small hole at the top. Some of the gas ran down the side of the bamboo and caught the bottle of gas on fire. Juan panicked and threw the flaming gasoline up in the air behind him. Unfortunately the flaming bottle of gasoline hit Rinor squarely on the left shoulder. As the burning gas ran down the left side of his body, it turned Rinor into a human torch.

The small boy took off running screaming in agony. He could not run across the backyard because a wire fence and drainage ditch ran between the two homes. Rinor ran to the front of Juan's house and headed down the gravel street toward the front of the Espiritu house where he was staying. Then from out of nowhere, a man who apparently had heard the boys' screams and saw what had happening, knocked Rinor to the ground. He rolled the boy over and over until the fire was extinguished. Then he left as suddenly as he had appeared.

By that time Norma had heard the commotion and arrived on the scene. The fire was out, and both Juan and the heroic man who had put out the fire had disappeared. It all happened so fast that Rinor wonders if it was an angel who saved him. Perhaps it was or maybe it was just a poor man who did a good deed and burned his hands as well. Norma immediately removed Rinor's clothes. After being burned so badly, Rinor wanted to go back to the house and flush his burns with cold water. Rinor was in such pain that he thought he was still on fire!

When his mother saw the blackened flesh starting to fall off the little boy's body she instinctively hailed the driver of a motorcycle with sidecar. She hired the driver to take her and her son to the Don Salvador Memorial Hospital in La Carlota City. On the trip to the hospital Norma cradled her son in her lap keeping the burned side of his body up to prevent further injury. The small hospital was more like a U.S. medical clinic.

After Norma and Rinor arrived at the hospital, a doctor began to clean his wounds while Norma went to a local pharmacy to buy Flammazine ointment for Rinor's burns. When she returned, the doctor applied the ointment and dressed the boy's wounds. Most importantly a medical attendant gave Rinor an I.V. to help replace his lost body fluids. After administering the I.V. the doctor suggested that Norma take Rinor to the hospital in Bacolod for further treatment because there was nothing more the local hospital could do for him. Norma then hired a Jeepney driver to take her and Rinor to the hospital in Bacolod, which was more than an hour away. They arrived at the Bacolod emergency room about 3 p.m.

Norma and Rinor waited and waited for what seemed like an eternity. Finally Norma could wait no longer, Rinor was badly burned and in a great deal of pain. He needed someone to look at him and evaluate his condition. She asked to talk to Dr. Garcia her family doctor who had delivered her children. Finally she was able to talk to Dr. Garcia. Initially Dr. Garcia wanted 5,000 pesos to admit Rinor but Norma had only 300 pesos. After looking at the boy the doctor saw that Rinor was bleeding, and he admitted the boy and placed him in a second-floor room.

Dr. Garcia saw Rinor daily while he was at the Bacolod hospital. Rinor's daily treatment consisted of being bathed in warm soapy water and having his wounds medicated and dressed with Flammazine ointment. This routine was very painful for Rinor but not as painful as the wound-scraping procedure. Twice during Rinor's stay his wounds were scraped. This is a very painful treatment where dead skin cells and scabs are removed from burned areas. Rinor cried a lot during these treatments. Rinor was also given oral antibiotics and penicillin shots. If the doctor had Flammazine ointment on hand, he would apply it to Rinor. If he did not have any ointment, Norma would buy it at a local pharmacy. While at the hospital in Bacolod, Norma's nephew Pacifico Labiga Jr. donated 500 ml of Type A blood for Rinor.

Norma stayed with Rinor everyday he was in the hospital, held his hand, and prayed for him. She encouraged her son to "be strong, be brave." In Norma's mind there was never any doubt that Rinor would live and make a full recovery.

The day after the accident Norma sent a telegram to her husband, Ricardito, who was driving a logging truck on the island of Palawan. Ricardito traveled by company plane from Palawan to Manila. Then he traveled by ship from Manila to the island of Negros. From the time he received the telegram, it took a week for Ricardito to make the necessary arrangements and return home.

After he arrived home, Ricardito brought food to Norma and Rinor at the hospital and took food to the other children who were home. Rinor's hospital room had electricity but no air conditioning. Norma would hold Rinor's hand and fan him in the daytime. At night Ricardito would comfort the boy and fan him while Norma slept. Norma slept whenever she could by propping herself up between two chairs. Sometimes she would sleep on the floor.

After two months the family's money was gone. They owed the hospital 8,000 pesos and the doctor 600 pesos. They sold their block-and-frame home in Don Salvador and all its furnishings for 13,000 pesos. They paid the hospital, and the doctor forgave them his bill. The doctor offered to let Rinor stay in his clinic but told the family there wasn't anything else he or the hospital could do for Rinor. The doctor encouraged the family to care for Rinor at home. It was near the end of February 1989 when the family was forced to take Rinor out of the overcrowded hospital. The extra 5,000 pesos they received from the sale of their block home was needed to build a new home and pay for food, clothing, and transportation.

Chapter 17 – A One-Room Bungalow

Almost immediately Ricardito and his older sons built a small one-room bamboo bungalow on the island of Panay not far from Iloilo City. It was two weeks before the building was far enough along for the family to move into it. The bamboo bungalow was built on land owned by a wealthy and generous man named Carlos Brazas. He was a friend of the family and had been Ricardo's sponsor when he was baptized.

The bungalow was built on bamboo stilts and had a bamboo floor and walls. The roof was covered with palm tree branches and the bungalow was nestled among the palm trees in the middle of some rice fields. The doorway and windows were just openings in the bamboo walls. The bamboo floor was three steps above the ground, and there was always a cool comfortable breeze blowing.

Rinor was laid on a woven mat and the mat covered with a blanket. His mat was positioned where he could look out the doorway and watch his brothers and sisters as they played.

Sometimes Marcial would carry Rinor outside in a chair so he could be closer to the fun. Most of the time Rinor lay on his right side with his left hand and mosquito netting tied to the roof of the bamboo bungalow by a small rope. Rinor was naked and cold, but he could not stand the pain of having a cover put on him. His left hand was tied in the air to keep the open sores on the inside of his left arm from touching the open sores on his left side.

The mosquito netting helped keep the bugs and flies from biting the boy, and infecting his wounds. Every day Ricardito prepared warm water by boiling cold water over an open fire and mixing the hot and cold water to get the right temperature for bathing Rinor. Ricardito would clean and dress Rinor's wounds. For drinking, cooking, and bathing Rinor, Ricardito got sterile water from a Jetmatic pump a half mile away. Water for bathing the rest of the family and for the laundry was obtained from a Jetmatic pump closer to the bamboo bungalow.

In May 1989 Rinor was taken to the Western Visayas Medical Center in Iloilo because his wounds were not healing properly and he was bleeding. His family had not scraped the wounds while he was home. While at Western Visayas a charitable group known as the "Band of Mercy" set up an account of 5,000 pesos at the local pharmacy for Rinor's medications. Flammazine ointment and other medications could be obtained from this account. Rinor was in the Western Visayas hospital in Iloilo for about nine months. His wounds were cleaned and dressed daily, but he was also bandaged tightly from time to time. To remove the bandages

Rinor was placed in a whirlpool bath so that the bandages and scabs would soften and be easier to remove. Despite this presoak, the removal of the bandages was very painful for Rinor, and he cried a lot.

Again Rinor's mother stayed by his side and prayed for his recovery every day. Sometimes to break up the monotony she would hold her son up to the window so he could look outside. Rinor depended on his mother's prayers because he did not pray for himself while he was in the Iloilo hospital. The boy seemed to sense that he was not getting any better. It was also at Western Visayas that Rinor's left arm began to grow to his left side. His left calf also began to grow to the backside of his upper leg. Rinor slept in the fetal position all the time, which contributed to these problems. Recently Rinor was asked if there was ever a time when he thought he might die. He said, "Yes, I thought I was going to die once when I was in the hospital at Iloilo." When asked why he replied, "Because I knew I wasn't getting any better and I could not walk!"

Rinor needed blood three times while he was at the Western Visayas hospital. To get the blood she needed, Norma went to the Red Cross. Volunteers frequently waited at the Red Cross hoping to be paid for their blood donations. Rinor needed Type A positive blood. Norma would ask for Type A positive blood donors and the Red Cross would cross-type the potential donor's blood and make sure it was disease free. The Red Cross would collect 500 ml of blood in a plastic bag, tie it off, and give it to Norma. Norma would pay the donor 200 pesos and hire a Jeepney to take her back to the

Iloilo hospital. Norma said it was a strange feeling, "holding the warm blood in her lap on the trip back to the hospital." Back at the hospital the whole blood was given to Rinor. The frequent blood infusions helped strengthen the young boy.

By August the family ran out of money again, although both Ricardito and Marcial were working in the fields harvesting rice and fruit. By the end of January 1990 the family was again destitute and forced to make room for other people in the crowded hospital. The family moved Rinor back to the bamboo bungalow and retied his left hand and mosquito netting to the roof. This time they could not raise his arm as high. Rinor's mother was by his side most of the time, and he became overly dependent on her.

Norma still cooked fish and rice for the family, but this time without the luxury of her iron stove-top. The cooking area had dirt spread over the bamboo floor. A small wood fire was built on the dirt, and the cooking pot was set on three rocks. The only vent for the smoke was a hole in the roof; there was no vent pipe to direct the smoke. Sometimes Rinor's mother would spoon-feed him as he lay on his mat. Sometimes Rinor would feed himself since he had the use of his right hand and arm. Many times Rinor would not eat all the food his mother had prepared for him. She would encourage him to eat, but he would tell her that he wasn't hungry and refused to eat more.

The family toilet was an unlined pit outside. They would just squat and use it - no one was around, and no one was looking. If Rinor had to go to the bathroom, his mother would slip a piece of paper under his bottom. When he was through, she would fold it up and wipe his bottom with clean tissue. If he had to urinate, she would hand him a plastic bottle and some tissue.

Rinor's daily care never ceased. His mother or father bathed him daily. They applied Flammazine ointment to his burns. They saw that he took his oral antibiotics, but they failed to scrape his wounds, and they could not give him penicillin shots because they didn't have any.

As the boy continued to lie in the bamboo bungalow, a large, heavy scab began to form over his wounds. When the family tried to move him, the scab would crack and bleed. If Marcial carried him outside in a chair, his scab would crack and bleed. On one occasion Norma hired a Jeepney to take Rinor to the school grounds so that he could watch his school friends at play. Although Rinor's family loved and cared for him, his health and physical condition continued to deteriorate.

Rinor's physical condition continued to decline even though several hospitals and clinics "had done all they could" for him. Apparently part of the problem was that although Rinor was eating fairly regularly, he should have been eating twice as much. As the hours turned into days and the days melted into weeks and months, time lost all meaning, and Rinor lost all interest even in eating. By the time missionary Jocy Johnson saw the boy on June 9, 1990, he was still suffering from his third-and-fourth degree burns and by now was also suffering from third-degree malnutrition. It had been eighteen months since Rinor had been burned by gasoline in that tragic Christmas season accident, and he was slowly dying from his injuries.

Chapter 18 – The Healing Begins

Jocy Johnson was truly the stranger from America with one mission in mind:-to save Rinor's Life! The boy was slowly dying, and the changes were probably so gradually that his parents did not even notice his decline. Hospital after hospital had treated his surface wounds and released him. He received blood about every month to boost his energy. He continued to eat, take oral antibiotics, and have his wounds cleaned and treated with Flammazine ointment.

Despite all the care given to Rinor and the fact that his family was destitute as the result of paying for all his medical treatments, the boy was not making any progress. It is truly a miracle that he did not get a bad infection and die during those first eighteen months. To this poor Filipino family missionary Jocy Johnson must have seemed like an angel of mercy.

Jocy Johnson was a divorcee with four children and eight grandchildren and had been active in church work since she was a teenager. Before going to the Philippines Jocy lived in Copperas Cove, Texas, for a number of years. She attended the Eastside Baptist Church and was known for her good works in distributing food baskets and Christmas presents to the needy during the holidays. For thirteen years she also owned and operated a gift shop known as Dove International in Copperas Cove.

Through her missionary friends Jocy learned there was a great need for missionaries and a children's mission in the Iloilo area of Panay island. She visited the island in 1988 and saw for herself that the need was real. Jocy returned home. Although she hoped to return to Iloilo early in 1989, she was unexpectedly delayed. She returned to Manila in the fall of 1989 where she stayed with a friend who was a Filipino minister. From Manila she went to Iloilo City, where with the help of friends she founded God's Precious Promises, Inc. Children's Mission. The mission was funded by the sale of her business and donations from friends. Then she returned to the United States toward the end of the year to register the mission as a non-profit corporation for tax purposes. Jocy was prevented from immediately returning to Iloilo because of a coup in Manila restricted air traffic. By mid-January 1990 air traffic had returned to normal in Manila and Jocy returned to Iloilo City where she began work on her mission.

Jocy Johnson came to Zarraga near Iloilo looking for land where she could expand her mission facilities. Former governor Cornelio Villarreal of Capiz was on Jocy's board of directors and wanted her to look at some land in Zarraga. He thought the land would make a good location for a feeding center, work shop, out-patient clinic, and training center for mothers. So Jocy and Dr. Tidon, who worked at the mission hospital arranged with Carlos Brazas to take a look at the land.

As Jocy was riding around in a Jeep with Carlos Brazas and Dr. Tidon on June 9, Carlos told them about a little boy who was badly burned and living in a bamboo bungalow among the rice fields. Suddenly it started raining, and because Marcial's bamboo bungalow was only a short distance away, they drove there looking for shelter. Carlos told Jocy about Rinor's burns and mentioned that Rinor had previously been hospitalized in Iloilo.

When Jocy saw the small, weakened boy lying on his pad on the floor, her heart was moved with compassion and she began to cry. She could not help noticing that the burns covering his left arm, his thigh, part of his back, and his shoulder were still quite raw. She also noted that his left calf muscle was fusing to his thigh and his left arm was growing to his chest. She promised the boy she would try to come back to him on June 12, but she was unable to return for a few days.

Jocy describes Rinor as suffering from third degree burns, and malnutrition, a nine-year-old boy who was the size of a five-or six-year-old child. Jocy was unable to return to the Marcial home until Saturday the 14th. Then she hired a car and driver and returned to Zarraga with Angie Arragon, her assistant director, Dwight Palmquest, a visiting missionary, and Eva Villegas, a medical technician. Jocy's only thought at the time was to save Rinor. The four rescuers drove as far as they could, then they walked on a levee around the rice field to get to the Marcial's bamboo bungalow in the back.

Rinor was very happy to see Jocy and told her he had wondered what had taken her so long. Jocy told Norma she was going to put her son in the hospital where he could get the medical attention and treatment he needed. She also told Norma it would not cost her a single cent. However, instead of taking Rinor to the hospital, Jocy had the driver take Rinor, Norma, Ricardito, and Eva back to her converted warehouse apartment in Jaro, Iloilo. The driver was instructed to drive very slowly with the injured boy.

Meanwhile Angie, Dwight, and Jocy walked to the main road and took public transportation back to the apartment. Since they did not have to drive slowly, they arrived first. When Rinor arrived, they placed him on a hospital bed donated to Jocy by the Scandinavian Children's Mission Hospital. Rinor and his mother stayed in Jocy's apartment overnight. Jocy wanted Dr. Tidon to do what he could for Rinor before admitting him to the hospital. On Sunday, the following day, Norma began to get anxious about Rinor going to the hospital. Jocy told Norma that Dr. Tidon would be arriving soon, but he did not arrive until 3 p.m. After he arrived, Dr. Tidon removed Rinor's bandages as Dwight watched. Some of Rinor's skin and scabs stuck to the gauze, and Dwight became so upset by the sight the raw wounds, that he nearly fainted.

Dr. Tidon planned to return the next morning to change Rinor's bandages, but Rinor started bleeding from one spot under his left arm. Jocy was unable to contact Dr. Tidon so she called the director of the Iloilo Mission Hospital. Jocy was afraid Rinor might bleed to death, but she had no transportation and desperately wanted to get Rinor to the Iloilo Mission Hospital. She went around the corner to Grandy's lumber-yard and made a homemade stretcher for Rinor out of three-quarter inch plywood covered with a pad. Then Jocy and Dwight put Rinor on the stretcher, covered him, and carried him from Jocy's apartment to the Iloilo Mission Hospital.

At the hospital a staff worker gave Rinor an I.V. and did a blood workup on him. They found his red blood count was 9.5 instead of 16, which is normal for a boy his age. They told Jocy that Rinor needed blood, so Jocy went to the blood bank and bought a unit. The hospital started administering the blood to Rinor right away.

Rinor improved rapidly, and the next day Dr. Tidon told Jocy that he wanted to operate on him. However, Jocy had been in touch with Toby Wallinberg of the Scandinavian Children's Mission, and Toby told Jocy she should take Rinor to Manila, where he would get better treatment for his wounds. Toby thought the Iloilo Mission Hospital was ill equipped to handle Rinor's serious injuries. Jocy had an appointment that day, and when she returned to look in on Rinor, she discovered that Dr. Tidon had started feeding him through the nose. Dr. Tidon wanted to build the boy up faster so he could operate on him. Jocy told Dr. Tidon not to make plans to operate on Rinor because she had arranged to take the boy to Manila Hospital for further treatment.

Jocy took a Jeepney to town the next day to buy Rinor a toothbrush and some toothpaste as she had promised. When Jocy returned from town, Norma told her two doctors had just left and they planned to operate on Rinor at 1 p.m. the next afternoon. It was believed that the doctors wanted to free Rinor's left arm, but Jocy was very upset by any talk of an operation. She told Norma, "Oh, no, they won't operate on him." "Yesterday I told Dr. Tidon that he was not to operate on Rinor."

In an attempt to stop the operation Jocy called Brother Barcelano a, hospital official, but he was not at the hospital. Then she tried to get in touch with Dwight, but he was staying with a friend, Bob Roberts in Bacolod, and he did not have a telephone. So Jocy called the police and had them go to Mr. Roberts' home and ask Dwight to call her at her apartment, which they did. Dwight returned her call almost immediately and told Jocy he would return on the first-ferry boat in the morning. Bacolod is only a short distance from Iloilo by water. Then Jocy's lawyer let the doctor know there was a sincere concern that the Iloilo Mission Hospital did not have the proper facilities to perform such a complex operation. In fact Jocy was concerned that the operation might kill Rinor.

Jocy's assistant, Angie, stayed with Rinor until the next morning while Norma went home to tell her family that she was going to Manila with him. Norma also took a bath and picked up some clothes for the trip. Jocy planned to obtain permission to transport the sick child, and Dwight came back to Iloilo to accompany them to Manila even though he had been scheduled to teach somewhere else the following day.

When Jocy tried to locate Dr. Tidon, he was nowhere to be found. The flight to Manila was scheduled to leave at 3:00 p.m. sharp, and the time was rapidly approaching. After making a few inquiries Jocy found out that Dr. Tidon was at a meeting at the Amigo Hotel. She called the hotel and told a staff member she had an emergency! They paged Dr. Tidon who immediately returned to the hospital and filled out the necessary paperwork. Then he wrapped the boy for the trip to Manila. Rinor's wounds were still bleeding . By then it was almost time for the airplane to depart.

Jocy rode a motorcycle with a side-car to the main road and then took a pickup taxi to the airport. When Jocy got off the motorcycle, she met one of Rinor's nurses, who agreed to accompany her to the airport and help with Rinor. To help smooth things over with Dr. Tidon Jocy asked him if he would like to accompany Rinor to Manila. Dr. Tidon accepted the offer, and Dwight stayed behind to teach his class. Just before takeoff Norma carried Rinor in her arms up the stairs of the airplane and placed him in the seat next to her.

When they arrived at the Manila airport, Rinor, his mother, Jocy, and Dr. Tidon were met by someone from the Scandinavian Children's Mission. Jocy hoped Dr. Tidon harbored no ill feelings. She also hoped Dr. Tidon would realize that she and her friends were doing what they thought was in Rinor's best interests. Later, she found out that Dr. Tidon was very upset and no longer shared her interest or enthusiasm for her mission's work.

Norma and Rinor spent one night at the mission. Rinor remembers that there were two rooms for children and a small kitchen upstairs. There was a clinic, a larger kitchen, and a chapel downstairs. The next day, July 19, 1990, Rinor was admitted to the National Children's Hospital. One of the first things the doctors did was remove the rest of the heavy scab from Rinor's left side. The periodic cracking of the scab had been one of the main causes of Rinor's bleeding.

When Rinor returned to the Scandinavian Children's Mission, he stayed in an upstairs room for big kids. He also remembers the other room upstairs, were babies were kept. Some of the babies were there for adoption. Other babies were staying there until they were well enough to go home. The main clinic was downstairs.

Because Rinor had constant medical attention at the mission, Norma was able to go to work for a coat factory in Manila. Norma worked seven days a week at the factory, and visited her son on Sunday mornings and evenings. She worked from Monday through Saturday from 7 a.m. to 10 p.m. for 100 pesos a day, or 4 U.S. dollars. She received 80 pesos for regular time and 20 pesos for four hours of overtime. She also worked on Sunday from 7 a.m. to 4 p.m. Her job at the factory consisted of marking lines on the sleeves, facing, and patterns for other workers to follow while sewing jacket parts together. While working in Manila, Norma slept in a loft in a dormitory building near the factory. Other workers also slept on the ground floor and in loft areas. While working in the factory Norma had to pay for her food and clothing.

Rinor's progress improved dramatically at the Scandinavian Children's Mission. Soon he learned how to hop around on one leg and get where he wanted to go in the mission. Rinor also began to pray for himself everyday at the mission church because his mother was no longer around to pray for him. As he prayed for himself, he could feel his strength returning and knew for the first time, he was getting better. The better he felt, the more he ate. Soon he was taking trips with the other children at the mission who were able to travel.

At first one of the clinic nurses helped carry Rinor downstairs in a chair. Once downstairs he could hop to a car, sit in a seat, and go to the zoo or other interesting places with the children. These trips to other places in Manila broke up the daily routine and monotony of the medical treatments.

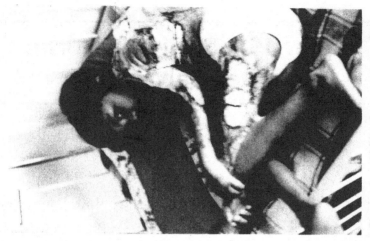

November 1990 - Burns are healing.
White areas - Flammazine for burns.

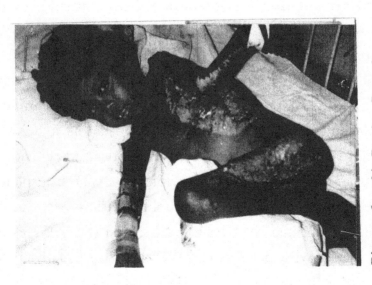

Rinor as found in Bamboo Bungalo
July 1990 - Burns 18+months old.

Chapter 19 – Shriner's Burns Hospital-Galveston

In August 1990 while Rinor was still at the hospital, Jocy flew to Galveston, Texas, to visit the Shriner's Burns Hospital-Galveston. She showed pictures of Rinor to the hospital staff and received tentative agreement from them that they could treat Rinor's severe burns at no cost to the family if someone would pay for his way to the United States.

While at the National Children's Hospital, Rinor was visited daily by a doctor. His treatment consisted of cleaning, scraping, and dressing his burn wounds, just as it was at previous hospitals. He was also given antibiotics and penicillin shots. Rinor was given blood twice while he was at the hospital, but this time the blood and all his medications were paid for by the Scandinavian Children's Mission (SCM). Again Norma stayed with her son and prayed for him daily. Her sister Nenette brought an electric fan to help keep Norma and Rinor cool. This time, none of Rinor's brothers or sisters were able to visit him because he was too far from home, and there wasn't money for them to travel to Manila. Again Norma slept in her son's room.

While in the Manila hospital Rinor tried to hold his left hand up, but because it was not tied up or propped up, it continued to grow to his side. Despite this unfortunate fact, Rinor was well enough to return to the SCM and a lower level of medical care on November 9, 1990, after almost four months. By this time his wounds were healing and his blood count, which had been low, returned to normal. For the first time in almost two years, Rinor was able to wear clothes again.

When Rinor returned to the SCM, he stayed in an upstairs room for big kids. He also remembers the other room upstairs where babies were kept. What he remembers most was that some of the babies there had been given up for adoption. Other babies were staying there until they were well enough to go home. The main clinic was downstairs.

Because Rinor had constant medical attention at the mission, Norma was able to go to work for a coat factory in Manila. Norma worked seven days a week at the factory and visited her son on Sunday mornings and evenings. She worked from Monday through Saturday from 7 a.m. to 10 p.m. for 100 pesos or 4 U.S. dollars a day. She received 80 pesos for regular time and 20 pesos for four hours of overtime. She also worked on Sunday from 7 a.m. to 4 p.m. Her job at the factory consisted of marking lines on the sleeves, facing, and patterns for other workers to follow while sewing jacket parts together. While working in Manila, Norma slept in a loft in a dormitory building near the factory. Other workers also slept on the ground floor and in loft areas. While working at the factory Norma had to pay for her food and clothing.

Rinor's progress improved dramatically at the Scandinavian Children's Mission. Soon he learned to hop around on one leg and get where he wanted to go in the mission. Rinor also began to pray for himself everyday at the mission church because his mother was no longer around to pray for him. As he prayed, he could feel his strength returning and knew for the first time that he was getting better. The better he felt, the more he ate. Soon he was taking trips with the other children at the mission who were able to travel.

At first one of the clinic nurses helped carry Rinor downstairs in a chair. Once downstairs he could hop to a car, sit in a seat, and go to the zoo or other interesting places with the children. These trips to other places in Manila broke up the daily routine and monotony of the medical treatments.

Rinor continued to grow both spiritually and physically at the Scandinavian Children's Mission. Before long he was leading the other children in prayers and songs. Rinor's mobility continued to improve, and he adapted to hopping around on one leg in much the same way that a one-legged bird learns to adapt to his handicap. Rinor could go on long walks and keep up with his peers. He also learned how to go up and down stairs using only a handrail. While at the Rose of Sharon Children's Home in Antipolo, another SCM facility, Rinor completely amazed and inspired the staff by learning how to swim.

Chapter 20 – Rinor's First Trip to the United States

By February 20, 1991, Rinor was healthy enough to travel to the United States. Like most Americans Jocy Johnson had heard of the Shrine and was somewhat aware of their philanthropy. She knew they ran a network of nineteen orthopedic hospitals and three burns institutes. She also knew Shriner's Hospitals provided excellent medical care and treated children under eighteen free of charge. It was only natural that Jocy would contact the Shriner's Burns Hospital-Galveston to see if they could help Rinor walk again. However, except in the case of an immediate emergency, the correct procedure would have been to contact a Shriner or local Shrine Temple on Rinor's behalf. Most of the workers at Shriner's hospitals are employees of the hospital and not Shriners themselves.

Rosa M. B. Chapa, director of the outpatient clinic at the Shriner's Burns Hospital -Galveston, sent the following letter to Jocy on March 1, 1991, after Jocy contacted the hospital.

"Re: Rinor Marcial (Filipino boy)

"Dear Jocy,
    "I received your letter, and am enclosing documents I mentioned in our telephone conversation. Please forward us the pictures of the patient's burn/wound care area(s) (see photography form for positioning of photographs) and return to us."
    "Please feel free to use our fax number .... for further correspondence. You may also contact me by telephone.................if you have questions or concerns."

On March 3, 1991, Rosa M. B. Chapa wrote a second letter to Jocy as follows:

"Dear Jocy,
    "Please be advised that the above named child (Rinor) cannot be considered for evaluation and treatment at Shriner's Burns Hospital- Galveston, Texas until the attached forms are completed."
    "Although all medical treatment is provided free of charge, it is important that you know that the hospital cannot be responsible for any transportation, food, or lodging for the parent/guardian or for any expenses incurred while a child is an outpatient in the United States."
    "During hospitalization we estimate that cost of a parent (room and board) is about $125.00 per week.

Cost for the child/patient during outpatient treatment is about $180.00 per week. Limousine expenses from the airport to the hospital are also incurred and are about $80.00 round trip per child/patient. If accommodation is arranged in Houston, transportation to the hospital for visits and outpatient treatment will be another expense to consider."

"it should be understood that the child's mother will need to accompany the patient to the hospital. This is imperative for treatment/surgical consents as well as emotional and psychological support for the patients during their stay."

"We are looking forward to meeting the child and providing whatever help to the child and family need. Please complete the attached and return to my attention. (Full photographic pictures are not always required, only pictures of the area(s) pertaining to the problem are necessary. Also, please feel free to contact me should you have any questions or concerns."

It was at about this time that Gordon Irwin, the co-author of this story, and his spouse, Irma, first learned about Rinor's plight from their daughter JoAnna, who had married Jocy Johnson's son Carlos.

JoAnna met her future spouse, Carlos, while attending the Southwest Assemblies of God College in Waxahachie, Texas, and working on her bachelor's degree in mission works. Carlos was also working on his bachelor's degree in biblical languages. At first they were so busy working that they barely noticed each other. Finally they realized that if there was anyone in the school they might be interested in, it was each other. In time their interest in each other matured into love and they were married on August 11, 1984.

To get her master's degree in missions JoAnna attended the Assemblies of God College in Springfield, Missouri. After JoAnna completed her master's degree in 1988, she went to work for the college while Carlos pursued his master's degree in Christian education. Carlos hoped a degree in Christian education would help him find a teaching job at a private school.

By early 1990, JoAnna had become Jocy's most important contact in the United States. Jocy gave JoAnna's address for all fund-raisers and entrusted JoAnna with her bank accounts and bills. In effect JoAnna became her volunteer business manager. JoAnna did all the legwork that had to be done in the United States while Jocy was in the Philippines. JoAnna's work included talking to bankers, creditors, and potential donors about Jocy's missionary work.

Jo Anna was especially helpful when Jocy was working with the Assembly of God Church to become an ordained minister in the Philippines. Whenever Jocy returned to the United States from the Philippines, she visited with JoAnna and Carlos at their home.

After six years of marriage and much hard work JoAnna and Carlos felt they were ready for children, and their first child, Robert, was born on August 27, 1990. A short time later Carlos, a chemical warfare specialist, was sent to camp for specialized training before being sent to Saudi Arabia.

Carlos returned from camp to celebrate Thanksgiving with his family. On December 1, 1990, Carlos left for the Saudi Arabian Desert Storm campaign and stayed there until April 1, 1991. JoAnna and Carlos were living in Springfield at the time. They did not return to Texas until August 1994, when they moved to Shertz.

While Carlos was in Saudi Arabia, Jo Anna visited with her parents, who were now living in California. Jo Anna told her parents about Rinor's plight and Irma mentioned that the Ladies' Oriental Shrine might be able to help raise money to bring Rinor and his mother to the United States. JoAnna mentioned this to Jocy, who in turn assumed that Irma was ready to help financially. In reality neither Irma nor Gordon were in any position to be of help at that time.

However on April 2, 1991, Jocy wrote Irma as follows:

> *"I spoke with JoAnna and she informed me that you and the organization you are a member of, the Ladies of the Shrine (L.O.S.), are interested in helping sponsor Rinor and his mother's trip from the Philippines to the Shriner's Burns Hospital-Galveston.*
>
> *"When JoAnna told me this I could hardly believe my ears. I am so very grateful and I am sure I can speak for Rinor and his mother that they too are so very grateful for this wonderful act of kindness. I am sure God is keeping record and He will repay you more than you could ever imagine.*
>
> *"I am enclosing a copy of the expected expenses for parents who accompany their children to the Shriner's*

Burns Hospital-Galveston and a quote from the Philippine Air Lines regarding Air-Fare."

One-way air-fare for an adult was quoted as $934 and one-way and air-fare for a child was quoted as $626. Round-trip for mother and child would be about $3,100, with additional money needed for the mother's room and board while the child was being treated at the Shriner's Burns Hospital-Galveston. However, because of their own financial problems, Irma and Gordon were unable to get actively involved at this time.

One year after founding God's Precious Promises, Inc. Children's Mission, Jocy was successfully operating a feeding program where sixty malnourished children were feed every day but Sunday. The mission also took care of as many emergencies and medical problems as it could afford.

The Irwin's' move to California came about as the result of a contact by an old friend, Tom Sonnonstine of Radio Shack, to help get a new venture started. The plan was to have bookstores at colleges and universities handle Radio Shack electronic and computer products. The plan made sense to Gordon and it seemed to have good wage and profit potentials. Considering his evaluation of the plan, Gordon happily accepted Sonnonstine's offer and moved to Woodland, California, in January 1990, where he rented an apartment.

Irma, who was employed in Austin at the time, followed Gordon to California in February. Gordon was to concentrate on potential clients in northern California, Nevada, Utah, Oregon, and Washington. The greatest numbers of potential clients were in the northern California area, where Gordon centered his attention.

Irma and Gordon had to pay their way from Texas to California, and Radio Shack provided $1,000 per month. Gordon had similar arrangements with Radio Shack from January 1985 until January 1986, when he sold dealerships to small businesses in East Texas, Louisiana, and Mississippi.

Gordon put forth his best efforts for six solid months, calling on prospective managers, buyers, and others. However, he soon became painfully aware that the market was not what he expected, and he found himself going broke. Even Irma's background in manufacturing electronic boards was not in great demand in the area, and she soon found herself visiting local employment offices in search of work. With the help of the California Employment Commission, Irma was able to attend a business school where she learned how to use a number of business-type computer programs. As a result Irma earned herself a "Student of the Quarter" trophy. Despite this success in her studies Irma was still not able to find work in the northern California area.

In the meantime Gordon took a part-time job through Olsten Staffing at the Wells Fargo bank in July 1990, working the night shift in the Home Loan Department as a data entry trainer. Gordon really enjoyed his work, and he considered it a great job. The Home Loan Department was one of the best-run and most profitable departments at the bank. However, someone in upper management at the bank decided it was time to close the department. All Home Loan Department employees were laid off in December 1990. Gordon felt sorry for those employees who had been with the bank for twenty-plus years. They were not offered transfers to other departments-only the opportunity to apply for a job at another location if there was an opening.

Gordon was luckier than most. When Susan O'Neil of ADT, a former employer, learned that Gordon's department at Wells Fargo was closing, she called him on Sunday and asked him to stop by on Monday. Susan hired Gordon immediately, and he went to work in December 1990. Gordon was very lucky and never without work. Once again he was involved with data entry and file maintenance for ADT.

After six months Gordon and Irma both became unhappy with the work situation in northern California and began to look for other work. They missed their family and friends and decided to move to Orem, Utah, in May 1991. In Orem they would be near their daughter Elizabeth, her spouse, Van, and their five grandsons Michael ten, David and Danny nine, Christopher seven, and Garrick, one. Their son-in-law Van Gaffney ran a coupon business selling advertising and promotional coupon books to restaurants, miniature-golf courses, and movie theaters. While in Utah the Irwins rented a house within a mile and a half of their daughter. They stayed in Orem for about three months but were unable again to find suitable work. Because of the absence of work, the lack of money, and a real longing for Texas, Irma and Gordon quit their jobs and returned to Austin, Texas, on August 1991.

Norma's oldest son, Marcial, moved to Manila and landed a job that allowed him to support his family. Marcial made photo copies at a printing facility for about a year and then quit his job for a better paying job. His second job was cutting steel for heavy industrial and building construction.

**Scandinavian Children's Mission worker with Rinor.
Surgery is still needed to free his left arm and left leg.**

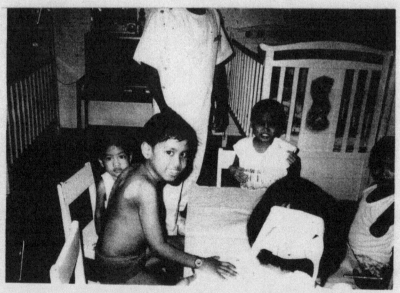

**Rinor is now healthy enough to travel to the Galveston
Burns Institure for further treatment of his injuries.**

Chapter 21 – Preparation and Red Tape Galore!

By mid-October 1991 Gordon and Irma were resettled in Austin. They were determined to do whatever was necessary to help their daughter, JoAnna, bring Rinor and his mother to the United States for his much-needed reconstructive surgery. Gordon became active again in the local Ben Hur Shrine Temple, and Irma became active again in the Ladies' Oriental Shrine (LOS). She returned to her former position of Second Ceremonial Lady of Ben Hera Court 91. This was the same position she had held when she left Texas to join her husband in his new Radio Shack venture in California.

On October 14, Gordon called the Shriner's Burns Hospital-Galveston, and requested a release from the hospital for Rinor's mother to sign and return. Gordon asked that the hospital mail the form to him so he could forward it to the Philippines. Four days later he received the form and mailed it to Jocy Johnson.

Gordon then went to the Divan (officers) of the Ben Hur Shrine Temple to see if they could help in this international effort to help one small boy and his mother. On October 22, Gordon talked to Divan officers Gene Freudenberg, the Oriental Guide, and Bob Emrie, the Chief Rabban. Bob was on the board of directors of the Shriner's Burns Hospital-Galveston. At first Bob thought Gordon's request would require a special fund-raiser and have to be approved by the Imperial Shrine in Florida. Gordon left pictures of Rinor with Gene Freudenberg. For the rest of October and the first half of November Gordon talked with various members of the Shrine about Rinor and his need for surgery.

As a result of these discussions Gordon learned that some funds might be made available through the local Ben Hur transportation fund, but, no decisions were made at this time. On November 20, Gordon picked up the pictures he had left with Gene Freudenberg. Gene suggested that Gordon talk to Ben Hur Potentate Boyce Freitag. Considering previous flight information Jocy had given to him, Gordon estimated that as much as $5,420 might be needed for transportation, room, and board. However, Irma and Gordon planned to save the Shrine some money by providing the boy and his mother with a place to stay after his initial surgery and required hospital stay.

Gordon and Irma had never given any thought as to what could happen when you bring two strangers into your home;- they put their trust in God as they always had. The trailer they lived in had two very small bedrooms, and the Irwin's could barely make the $300 monthly rent payments. Gordon talked to his sister Barbara, who was living in Massachusetts, about what was happening and she offered to pay his next month's rent. Gordon and Irma were in bad financial shape at the time, but they still did not want to take any handouts. Gordon thanked Barbara and assured her he would make out all right even though he did not know how at the time.

Like an answer to his prayers Olsten Staffing came through for Gordon in his time of need. With a computer they pulled his California records and put him to work the same day as a temporary employee at the State Bar of Texas. Gordon's job was to call attorneys and give them the names of people who had called the state bar for referrals.

To save money, Gordon called Continental Airlines, hoping to obtain free air fare for Rinor and his mother. Gordon discussed Rinor's story with Hank Thurstin, a Continental representative who seemed eager to help. Hank asked Gordon to send him all the information he had about Rinor so he could contact the proper authorities at Continental for an evaluation and final determination. Hank estimated that the round trip ticket with seven day notice one-year stay, and return for Rinor and his mother would cost $2,120. This cost seemed reasonable to Gordon based on his previous estimate from Philippines Airlines. Gordon sent the information to Hank Thurstin, c/o Continental Airlines, 9000 E. Smith Rd., Denver, CO 80207.

Hank called Gordon on November 25 to let him know that the information on Rinor had been forwarded to one of Continental's vice presidents who would call Gordon in a couple of days. Gordon's hopes were very high, and he did not think Continental would turn him down on this mission of mercy. After all they furnish airline tickets for game show contestants and athletes. The next day Gordon called the Ben Hur Shrine Temple to find out what information would be needed to get Rinor admitted to the Shriner's Burns Hospital-Galveston. Unfortunately the Ben Hur Shrine had very little information because they had never been involved in an international mission of mercy.

In late November or early December Gordon called Jocy in the Philippines and asked her to forward any information she had about whom she had contacted at the Shriner's Burns Hospital-Galveston. He received the information on December 4 and called the Shriner's Burns Hospital-Galveston on December 5 to talk with Sharon Taylor, hoping to determine the status of Rinor's application for admission to the hospital. Sharon told Gordon that Rinor's application was going to the board of directors on Monday and that she should call back on Tuesday.

Then Gordon called Continental Airlines, but Hank Thurstin was not working. When Hank returned to work, he called Gordon to let him know that Rinor's file had been turned over to a regional vice president. However, Hank had not received any word from him yet.

On Tuesday December 10, Gordon called the Shriner's Burns Hospital-Galveston and requested to see if Rinor's application for admission had been accepted. He was asked to call back the following day about 2 p.m. When Gordon called back the following day, he found out that Rinor's application had been approved. Rosa M. B. Chapa of Social Services was to call Gordon in a day or two. The hospital representative asked Gordon if he would be the Shriner responsible for Rinor. He replied, "Yes, of course I will." Gordon was informed that some additional paperwork would be sent to him. Once Gordon found out that Rinor's application for admission had been approved, he was really inspired. He was more determined than ever to keep the ball rolling on this mission from God.

A couple of days later Hank Thurstin called to tell Gordon that he had still not heard from the Houston office about flying Rinor and his mother to the United States. Hank said that the application was not yet approved but that there was another option available through their Employees Action Group. They had a special program under which they could sponsor charity cases and fly them within the continental United States. In other words, they could provide airline fare for Rinor and his mother from San Francisco to Houston. Hank also quoted round- trip airfare for Rinor and his mother as $1,489 from Manila to San Francisco. Gordon thanked Hank and asked him to stay in touch. At this time, Gordon did not know what direction he was headed in, but he realized he needed all the help he could get.

On December 13, Gordon called Rosa M. B. Chapa at the Shriner's Burns Hospital-Galveston and left a message for her to call him back. This would be the first of a long series of unanswered telephone calls to the hospital. Three days later Gordon called the hospital again and found out that Rosa was in a meeting. Carol from Social Services informed him that the expenses for Rinor's mother would be $10 per day or

$63 per week for an apartment. Carol said the Shriner's Burns Hospital-Galveston would pay Norma a food allowance of $8 per day that would be billed to and paid by the Ben Hur Shrine. Carol asked if Rinor's father had to give his wife a power of attorney because in some countries the wife has no authority. Carol suggested that Gordon check into this aspect of the situation if the mother was going to accompany the child.

Gordon asked the hospital if they could supply a letter saying how long they thought Rinor would have to stay in the United States for his surgery and recovery. He also asked if it was necessary for the mother to be with the child. Finally he asked that the letter be addressed to the United States Embassy in the Philippines but mailed to him.

Gordon was on a roll and did not want anyone or anything to slow his momentum. He called Hank Thurstin at Continental again, but he was out of the office. Hank had given Gordon his home phone number, and although against Gordon's better judgment, he called Hank at home. Hank was very polite and told Gordon he would check with the Houston Vice President again. Gordon urged him to try to get a definite answer by Wednesday.

Next Gordon called his daughter JoAnna inquiring about the legality of the power of attorney documents in the Philippines. Gordon wanted to know if Rinor's mother would be the one to accompany him to the United States. JoAnna said she would call Jocy the next day, but on second thought she went ahead and called Jocy right away. JoAnna found out that a mother has equal rights and that the father's power of attorney was not required. Jocy also said a doctor in the Philippines had recommended that someone from the Philippines escort them since they had never left their village without an escort. Jocy requested a round trip-airline ticket for herself as well, and Gordon said he would try to get enough money for Jocy to come to the United States with Rinor and his mother. Jocy also volunteered to hand carry any letters to the embassy for Gordon.

Gordon suggested to JoAnna that Jocy fax anything from the Philippines to Bob Oakes, a friend of his who owned and operated BVO Motors in Austin. Bob had previously volunteered the use of his fax machine to Gordon especially for this mission of mercy. Later Gordon found out it was not entirely true that Rinor's family had never left the village without an escort. After all, Norma had attended college in Manila for four years. Rinor's family may have been poor, but they were not uneducated or ignorant.

Gordon wrote to Jocy, sending her the consent for medical photography form from the Shriner's Burns Hospital-Galveston and a request for Rinor's immunization records. Jocy forwarded the immunization records and signed the medical photography consent form in early November 1991.

By late December, Gordon was encouraging the Shriner's Burns Hospital outpatient clinic to set a date when they would be able to see Rinor even though the airline tickets were not yet confirmed. Finally on January 3, 1992, Rosa M. B. Chapa of the Shriner's Burns Hospital-Galveston sent a letter to Gordon and asked him to forward it to the American Embassy in the Philippines. The letter advised the embassy that Rinor Marcial had been accepted by the Shriner's Burns Hospital-Galveston, TX for free treatment of his extensive third-degree burns and related injuries. A clinic appointment for Rinor's evaluation in Galveston was scheduled for Monday, July 6, 1992, at 8:30 a.m. It was also pointed out that clinic appointments would be scheduled on a regular basis so Rinor could return for follow-up evaluations and treatments.

Gordon faxed the above information to Jocy in care of the Scandinavian Children's Mission to keep everyone informed on the progress he was making about Shriner treatment for Rinor. A short time later Jocy Johnson wrote to Gordon saying that she had not received a copy of the fax. She asked that a copy be sent to her so she might work on it from her end (in the Philippines), to help get the ball rolling again. According to Jocy:

"This little guy is really looking forward to going to the states for surgery and I am looking forward to seeing him walk again. That will be a wonderful day. His whole family is living in anticipation of that very day, but I need to work on their Visas."

At one point Jocy mentioned to Gordon about bullying her way around the embassy to get some action going. At the time Gordon did not think too much about the comment. Later when he tried to correspond with the embassy himself, he learned to really appreciate Jocy as a person of action.

On January 5, Gordon called Hank Thurstin of Continental, hoping to fill him in on the progress he was making. However, Hank was not in, so Gordon left a message. Gordon never got an answer to his request from Continental Airlines.

It seemed very strange to Gordon that major airlines could furnish free airline tickets for game show contestants and fly celebrity sports stars around, but could not donate a pair of round-trip tickets for one badly burned boy and his mother. In hindsight, it seemed like no one at Continental Airlines had the authority to make this decision for Rinor and his mother. Both Hank Thurstin and Gordon had to give up trying to get free air-fare for Rinor and Norma.

On March 3 Gordon called United Airlines about airfare costs for Rinor and his mother. Airfare was quoted as $2,759 for a round-trip with open return tickets for mother and child. With this most recent quote in hand Gordon called Jack Saul, the business manager at the Ben Hur Shrine Temple, and filled him in on his progress. Jack asked Gordon to bring copies of his paperwork to the office. Gordon jumped in his van and delivered the paperwork immediately. Gordon was asked what it would cost to send a letter to the Philippines. He called DHL delivery service and got a quote of $36. This seemed high to Gordon, but it was close enough for estimating purposes, and he still had time to get other estimates.

At the same time Irma was working with the Ladies Oriental Shrine (LOS) of North American from about mid-October 1991 in hopes of raising money to bring Rinor and his mother to the United States. In early March the women voted on and approved a conditional donation of $1,600 for Rinor and his mother. The condition of the donation was that the Nobles of Ben Hur Shrine Temple would contribute the balance of the air fare and expense funds needed. A brief

149

description of the LOS, their charitable work, and gracious effort on behalf of Rinor and his family follows:

The Ladies' Oriental Shrine of North America is a non-profit corporation that is benevolent, charitable, educational, cultural, social, and fraternal in nature. These women volunteer their time to raise money for the Shriner's Hospitals for Children that include the Shriner's Orthopedic Hospitals and Shriner's Burns Hospitals.

For a number of years before 1991 the ladies of Ben Hera Court 91, the local Austin, Texas, LOS unit, worked at the Erwin Center. They sold hot dogs, soft drinks, candy, and popcorn in one of the food booths. The Erwin Center is a large drum-shaped enclosed auditorium on the University of Texas campus where various sporting events, music concerts and other events are held. For their work the ladies and their husbands earned 10 percent of total sales each night they worked. This money was used by the court to support charitable work. The women earned about $100 to $150 for each event they and their husbands worked.

The Associate Princess is the officer in charge of the fund-raising events for the court. Before an event at the Erwin Center she would call members of the court and ask them if they would be willing to work the event. About six women were needed to work each event, and there were as many as five events a week. Normally, the women each worked two events a week. If your group did not fulfill your obligations to the Erwin Center, the management of the Erwin Center would cancel your contract and promptly locate a more reliable group. It was very demanding work and yet very rewarding because it proved to be a great source of income for charitable groups.

Among the routine faithful workers for Ben Hera Court 91 were Irma Irwin, Louise Barre, Dixie Mix, Gail Carruth, Dolores Mayberry, Milly Oakes, Hazel Forrester, Beryl Oltman, and Barbara James. Many others worked, as well as spouses of the ladies of the LOS. After the Ben Hera Court paid their operating expenses for the year, the remaining funds would be given to the Shrine hospitals in one form or another. The gift could be a check to the hospitals or special equipment requested by the hospitals such as wheelchairs, walkers, and crutches.

Irma first approached the ladies of Ben Hera Court 91 in October 1991 to see if they would be interested in donating some of their hard-earned money to bring Rinor and his mother to this country. In later meetings Irma explained Rinor's tragic accident and his need for reconstructive surgery. After conferring with the Grand High Priestess (international officer) and the court's High Priestess (highest local officer) Coleith Molstad told Irma the Ben Hera Court would donate $1,600 toward the purchase of airline tickets. This was subject to court approval and dependent on the Ben Hur Shrine donating the balance of the funds required. The court approved the donation without hesitation.

On March 9, Gordon brought Gene Freudenberg up to date on his progress. Gene was Gordon's main strength in this endeavor, particularly when it came to dealing with the officers and nobility (members) of the local Shrine. A short time later, Gordon wrote to Jocy that he had been promised enough money to pay for Rinor and his mother's airline tickets on United Airlines. However, he needed to buy the tickets during March to take advantage of the special air-fares. Rinor and his mother would have to leave Manila on or before July 4, 1992, to make a Shriner's Burns Hospital-Galveston appointment on July 6. As it turned out there was no available space on July 4, so Rinor and his mother had to leave before that date to be on time for their appointment.

On March 13, Gordon realized he was getting very close to his goal. He called Continental one more time, but Hank was not in. He did get an airfare estimate of $4,250 from the Continental Airlines representative. Gordon told the Continental representative, "That's not right. Continental gave me a much cheaper rate earlier." However, the Continental agent could not find the original quote and was not interested in negotiating.

Then Gordon called United Airlines again for a firm quote. Airfare was quoted as $2,759 with a $25 prepaid charge. The flight went from Manila to Seoul to San Francisco, and finally to Houston. Gordon told Rinor's story to Ritchie, a United Airlines representative. Ritchie suggested Gordon contact Mr. R. Ruppert of the Friendly Skies Program in Chicago. Gordon knew that time was running out and he needed help fast, but he decided one more try was worth the effort. Gordon received a reply from Mr. Rupert denying his request, but at least he received a reply.

On March 4, Jocy acknowledged that she had received the Shriner's Hospital information about Rinor. She also mentioned that Rinor and his family were very, very thankful and notified Gordon that the name of Rinor's mother was Norma Marcial. She said that Rinor's brother Norman, who is one year older than Rinor, was graduating from grade school on the morning of the 25th. Norman wanted Jocy to be at his graduation ceremony to pin on his ribbon. Jocy and her friend Angie planned to attend the graduation ceremony at 7:30 a.m. the next morning. Activities were scheduled early in the morning because of the oppressive heat during the day.

Jocy desperately wanted to come to the states with Rinor and his mother, and she hoped that God would supply the funds. In a postscript Jocy reminded Gordon that she would need proof that Norma would have a place to stay and that her needs would be provided for while she was in the United States.

Gordon talked to Gene Freudenberg about needing at least an additional $1,200 for Rinor's airline tickets. Gene guaranteed he would get the money. Then Gordon took a break and went to a golf tournament sponsored by the Golf Unit. While eating sausages at the temple Gordon asked Bob Emrie, the current Potentate, about the needs of Rinor's mother. Bob assured Gordon that the Ben Hur Shrine Temple would pay for the mother's keep while she was in Galveston.

On April 10, 1992, Gordon talked to Gene Freudenberg again, who said he had talked to Potentate Bob Emrie about the $1200 needed, but he did not receive an answer. Gordon also left a letter for Jack Saul, the business manager, requesting a letter verifying that Rinor and his mother would be taken care of while in the United States. The requested letter was needed for passport approval. Gordon's letter also informed

Jack Saul that he and Irma would provide a home for Rinor and his mother when they needed a place to stay while Rinor was not being treated by the Shriner's Burns Hospital-Galveston. Gordon left his request letter on Jack's desk.

A few days later Gordon wanted to check on his request, so he called Jack Saul. Jack was not in, so Gordon left a telephone message. Finally, on April 20 Gordon talked with Jack Saul. Jack promised to get the letter Gordon wanted right away. Gordon also talked to Gene Freudenberg about the $1,200 he needed for airline tickets. Gene told Gordon to put in a written request to the Potentate for $1,200 right away.

Gordon called United Airlines to make reservations for Rinor and his mother. The total cost was $2,923. With the $1,600 donated by the LOS Gordon needed $1,323 from Ben Hur or some other source. Gordon tried to arrange their travel on July 3 or 4 so Rinor could make his hospital appointment on July 6. However, seats were not available for those dates. Kathy Nobel, the receptionist, searched backwards and made reservations for June 23, the first date available. Rinor and his mother could stay with Gordon and Irma while Rinor was waiting for his appointment.

Gene Freudenberg told Gordon he needed to meet with the Ben Hur Shrine Temple Divan (officers) and request the money he needed. Gordon met with them at their regular monthly meeting in April and explained the situation. After a brief discussion, the Divan approved Gordon's request for the balance of the airfare, about $1,400, which was donated by the temple's transportation fund. Gordon was excited! He had achieved his immediate goal. He went home and called

Jocy to tell her the good news. Gordon also told Jocy he had made reservations for her if she could come up with the funds needed.

On April 28, 1992, Potentate Bob Emrie of the Ben Hur Shrine Temple provided the following letter:

"To Whom It May Concern …This confirms that Norma Marcial, the mother of the burned child from the Philippine Islands will be cared for while the child is being treated at the Shriner's Burns Hospital-Galveston, Texas by the Ben Hur Shrine Temple, Austin, Texas."

Gordon and Irma had volunteered to provide a home away from home for Rinor and his mother. Gordon faxed the above letter to Jocy with a cover letter saying that he hoped the letter was satisfactory and if it wasn't, to fax him back. Then he confirmed the additional flight information as follows:

> *"Depart Manila June 23 Flight 808 8:10 a.m.*
> *"Arrive San Francisco   9:10 a.m.*
> *"Depart San Francisc   12:30 p.m.*
> *"Arrive Houston   6:11 p.m.*
> *"Confirm departure 3 days prior-*
> *"Manila Phone Monday – Friday 817-73-21-29*
> *Saturday & Holidays 818-54-21-25*
> *"Carry medicine and paperwork with them – not in luggage.*
> *"United Airlines Locator No. 4QD403*
> *"United should have a wheelchair and interpreter available in San Francisco.*
> *"Irma and I will meet them in Houston.*

"Jocy: Your ticket is $971.40 one way same flight. Your United Locator is 0896NN. We have room for you with us anytime during your stay in the United States.

"Norma and Rinor must pick up tickets: 8th floor, Pacific Star Building, Makati Ave., Metro Manila, near Makati Sports Club.

"Look forward to seeing all of you."

The Shrine had supplied the funds they promised, but Gordon and Irma were in no position to help, so Jocy's trip to the United States would have to be postponed until later.

A brief description of the organization of a local Shrine Temple and the charities they support follows:

Shriners or Shrine Masons are members of the Ancient Arabic Order of the Nobles of the Mystic Shrine (A.A.O.N.M.S.). Their charitable work has been called both "one of America's best kept secrets" and "America's greatest philanthropy." These phrases seem to be contradictory. It is hoped that it is not a secret that badly burned children can be treated at no cost to them or their parents regardless of race, religion or creed. If this is a secret then it is one the Shrine would like to dispel. Additional information on the Shrine can be found in the last chapter regarding the Shrine.

The local Shrine Temples are made up of a number of independent units. Typical unit names are Directors Staff, Chanters, Drum and Bugle Corps, Band, Provost Guard, Oriental Band, Greeters, Patrol, Kartwheels, Mini-B's, Lizzyteers, Trailblazers, Golf Unit and Clowns. Each unit engages in activities throughout the year to help raise money for various Shrine charities, such as the blood drive, Shrine Hospitals for Children, and the transportation fund. The blood drive and blood drive funds provide blood for burned children. Hospital donations provide research, care, treatment, and counseling for patients and their parents. The transportation fund provides local transportation from Austin and nearby communities to the Shrine's Orthopedic Hospital in Houston and the Shriner's Burns Hospital-Galveston. The Srekoj Clown Unit supports the Shrine Circus, and usually provides a humorous skit during at mid-time.

People often ask, "What is a typical donation for a clown to entertain for one hour at a child's birthday party?" We remind parents that all clown donations go to our Shrine Hospitals, so whatever you would like to donate is fine. Once or twice a year, the Clown Unit and other Shrine units work a couple of busy intersections during our so-called "Shake the Bucket" campaign to raise money for the Shrine hospitals. Shriner's and their collection buckets are clearly identified. The one point that should be stressed here is that if money is donated for a specific purpose, such as Shrine hospitals, every penny donated must go to that charity. Of course money is also needed for general operating expenses for the local Shrine and individual Shrine units. The Shrine Circus is a good example of a fund-raiser used for the specific purpose of raising funds for operating expenses of the local Ben Hur Shrine Temple.

On May 18, 1992, Gordon tried to send a fax to Rosa M. B. Chapa, R. N., director of the outpatient clinic at the Shriner's Burns Hospital-Galveston. He inquired about

Rinor's evaluation appointment for July 6 at 8:30 a.m. The American Embassy in the Philippines wanted to know the time for Rinor and his mother's stay in the United States for visa purposes. Gordon also wanted to know if Rinor's appointment time could be moved closer to June 23. Gordon was expecting papers from the hospital that he thought he would have to sign, but the paperwork never arrived.

Gordon called Gene Freudenberg to keep him informed. Gene told Gordon that Royce Meyers, a past potentate, had wheel-chairs in his garage if he thought Rinor might need one. Because Gordon knew Rinor could not walk in the normal sense of the word, he called Royce to confirm that he might need a wheelchair. Gordon also called the Shriner's Burns Hospital-Galveston and spoke with Ms. Gonzalez about housing for Norma. She suggested that Gordon call her back on June 26, because by that time he would know whether Norma spoke English and the hospital would have more information on available housing. Ms. Gonzalez pointed out that the Ronald McDonald house would be a better place to stay because the rooms had twin beds and Rinor could stay there with his mother when he became an outpatient.

Finally, the Shriner's Burns Hospital-Galveston sent a letter to Gordon. Gordon forwarded the letter to the American Embassy in the Philippines. The letter advised the embassy that Rinor had been accepted for treatment by the Shriner's Burns Hospital-Galveston and restated that all treatment would be provided free of charge. It emphasized that additional appointments at the hospital would be required for follow-up evaluations and treatments. The letter also said that Rinor was scheduled to visit to visit the Shriner's Burns Hospital-Galveston on June 30. His required length of stay could not be adequately determined until he had an extensive evaluation by a Burns Hospital doctor. However, it was predicted that two or three months might be needed for possible evaluation, treatment, and surgical intervention. Extensive rehabilitation might also be required.

This prediction was very optimistic. However, it was also realized that an extension of the visas could probably be obtained if there were extenuating circumstances. The information was faxed to Jocy, and it was apparently given to the embassy in time for Rinor and his mother to get their trip to America approved.

During the time leading up to Rinor's trip to America, telephone and facsimile communications were excellent between Gordon and Jocy and the Scandinavian Children's Mission. However, communications were practically non-existent between Jocy Johnson and Norma Marcial. After Rinor was admitted to the Scandinavian Children's Mission and Norma went to work for the coat factory in Manila, it was a very long time before Rinor and his mother saw Jocy again. However, Jocy, who was in close contact with the Scandinavian Children's Mission, met with Rinor and his mother again in May when they went to the Bureau of Foreign Affairs to get their passports. Norma was charged a paperwork processing fee of 80 pesos, which she thought was quite extravagant. Besides having to wait for Rinor's paperwork from the Shrine, Norma had to make sure she had her marriage license and Rinor's birth certificate. Norma found the entire process very confusing.

Jocy apparently kept herself well informed about what was going to happen to Norma and Rinor. However, about the only thing Norma knew about her trip to America was that there was a hospital somewhere in Texas that could help her son walk. Norma did not know that her son was going to be treated at a Shriner's Burns Hospital. Jocy told Norma her sister would pick her up at the airport in the United States. She also told Norma she would be staying with three American women at an apartment near the hospital. Norma would stay at the apartment during her son's surgery.

The day before Rinor's and his mother's trip to America, Jocy arranged with her friend Mr. Gunderson to pick up Norma, her luggage, and her sister Nenette. Jocy's plan was to get everyone together at Mr. Gunderson's home, spend the night there, and be ready to leave for the Manila airport early the next morning.

On the morning of June 22, 1992, Norma and Nanette were waiting for Jocy and Mr. Gunderson at the Scandinavian Children's Mission on Santolan Road in San Juan, Metro Manila. Norma was very excited so she was packed up and ready to go by 10:00 a.m. However, Jocy and Mr. Gunderson did not arrive to pick them up until about 3:00 p.m. After Jocy and Mr. Gunderson arrived, they all left in Mr. Gunderson's Ford Fiesta for his home in Antipolo, Metro Manila about an hour and a half away. At this time Rinor was staying in another Scandinavian Children's Mission building that was very close to Mr. Gunderson's home.

At about 7:00 p.m., Jocy, Norma, and Nanette left Mr. Gunderson's home to pick up Rinor and his luggage. Rinor was told he was going to the United States, which meant absolutely nothing to him. He had no idea what or where the United States was, but that was all right with him, and he was willing to go. He thought he was going to the United States so that American doctors could treat his burns. He had no idea they planned to free his arm and leg so that he could have full use of them again. Rinor had been in and out of so many hospitals by this time that he thought he would never walk again.

About thirty minutes after they returned to Mr. Gunderson's home, a pastor from the Scandinavian Children's Mission came by with papers for Norma to sign. The papers released Rinor from the care of the Scandinavian Children's Mission. The pastor kept one copy of the papers and gave the other copy to Jocy. Norma wondered why she was not given a copy.

Everyone hoped to get a good night's sleep before getting up early the next morning to go to the Manila airport. However, Rinor was far too excited to go to sleep. How long will it take to get to America? What will they do to me when I get there? Will the people be nice to me in America? A hodgepodge of thoughts and images raced through the little boy's mind. He was very excited, a little frightened, and had no idea what to expect.

At 5:00 a.m. the next morning, everyone got up and dressed. Jocy gave Norma her airline tickets, and they all headed for the Manila airport as the sun was rising. The traffic was very light, and they noticed only a few cars and a Jeepney bus on the way to the airport. Norma's first impression of the Manila airport was that she would be able to manage just fine by herself. She told her sister Nenette that if she and Rinor had any problems, she would just ask for directions. Norma became a little frightened when she realized that she and her son had never traveled so far from home before. She had no idea what to expect in America and kept telling herself to "be brave."

When Norma and Rinor passed through Philippine customs, an officer asked Norma who had packed her two very small travel cases. She replied, "I packed them myself." "They contain clothing and nothing more. " Apparently her answer satisfied the customs agent and he let her pass without opening up her travel cases. A short time later Norma and Rinor passed through the metal detectors and headed toward a medium-sized waiting room. No one offered Rinor a wheelchair; he merely hopped along beside his mother and followed the other people in the airport who were headed for the same waiting room. The metal detectors and customs agents were also new experiences for the boy and his mother. Their fantastic flight to a strange new world was about to begin!

Chapter 22 – A Strange, New, Wonderful World

The first leg of Rinor and his mother's fantastic journey to the United States was aboard a medium-sized commercial jet traveling from Manila to Seoul, South Korea. When the boarding call was made, Rinor and his mother got in line and the boy hopped his way through the boarding tunnel into the aircraft. The flight crew was very friendly and welcomed everyone aboard. They knew they were in a United States airplane that was painted white with red and blue stripes. They had no idea how many jet engines the airplane had or how long it would take to fly to America.

Rinor and his mother sat in the front of the airplane, with Rinor sitting next to the window. The airplane took off from the Manila airport around 8:00 a.m. and began climbing immediately. After the airplane reached its final altitude and leveled off, the flight attendants demonstrated the safety features of the aircraft in case of an emergency.

Norma was happy that the flight was very smooth because she and Rinor were able to relax a little bit until the flight landed in Seoul. The flight to Seoul seemed short, taking about three and a half hours. However, the landing in Seoul was very rough because the plane hit the runway hard and bounced several times. Rinor and his mother were scared because they did not know what was happening. They had a two-hour layover in the Korean airport and the whole experience was quite frightening to them. Norma and Rinor were overwhelmed by the number of big airplanes, cars, and taxis that came pouring into the airport. It was the first time they had seen so many big airplanes with so many different destinations and loading gates.

It was a very crowded and busy airport. When Norma asked the Koreans for directions or help, no one could or seemed to want to help her. Most of the time, no one even answered her. Like most young boys, Rinor made matters even more hectic for his mother by constantly asking her, "Where are we going next?" After she had all the frustration she could stand, Norma decided to seek out someone who spoke English to help her with her questions and concerns. She finally found one gentleman who was very helpful and kind. The Korean layover was the worst two hours Norma and Rinor experienced on their long flight.

For their trip from Seoul to San Francisco, they boarded a United Airlines 747 jumbo jet. Once aboard Norma and Rinor were dazzled by the spaciousness of the aircraft. They learned there was a first-class section upstairs somewhere and that the airplane had several restrooms. The aisles in the airplane were very wide, and Rinor had no trouble navigating them. However, the airplane was so large that Rinor and his mother had to ask directions to find the rest-rooms the first time. When Rinor used the rest-rooms, he did not flush the toilet because he did not know how.

The takeoff from Seoul was also very scary because the plane climbed very rapidly and seemed to be going straight up into the sky. Once the plane leveled off, there were plenty of things to do, but Norma could not keep her mind off the trip. There were several magazines like *Ladies Home Journal* and the airline flight magazine in the magazine compartments on the seat backs. There were overhead TV sets throughout the cabin and radio jacks in the arms of the seats. The flight attendants passed out sterilized headsets to each of the passengers. Norma glanced at the television set a few times but she could not really get interested in it. There was some sort of sports program and Norma did not understand the rules of the game, so she quickly lost interest in it.

During the flight the passengers were fed regular meals at mealtime and snacks in between meals. Some of the items served during the flight were coffee, orange juice, coke, peanuts, chocolate candy, and other snacks. One meal Rinor remembers eating consisted of a green salad, chicken, and fish. It was also the first time he drank Coke out of a can. In the Philippines he always drank Coke out of a bottle. He did not eat the salad because it looked like grass and was too dry. With that one exception, Rinor thought he was in heaven with all this strange and wonderful food.

Unlike his mother, Rinor understood very little English and even less talk that was going on around him. The boy was frightened when the airplane hit turbulent air. He was frightened by anything that could cause a bumpy ride in such a big "cool" airplane. Rinor enjoyed looking out the window and watching the clouds below that were so beautiful. He looked through the magazines, but they were all in English and he could not read them. Once when he looked at the television, he saw an Arnold Schwarzenegger movie, but he could not understand English, so he quickly lost interest. Most of the time he looked out the window while listening to music through his headset.

Norma was constantly worrying about the next step she would have to take to get to her destination. To pass the time, she tried to close her eyes and rest, but she was too excited to sleep, and too curious about what was going on around her. She kept her eyes and ears open, and listened intently to all the sounds around her. She had no idea that her flight from Manila to her final destination in Houston would take twenty-two hours.

One of the highlights of Norma and Rinor's trip to America was their arrival in San Francisco. The first thing they noticed was that it was very cold in California. At first Rinor thought San Francisco was the end of his trip. When his mother told him there was one more flight to go, he was disappointed because he was not yet to his destination but happy that he was getting another airplane ride. Both Rinor and Norma were very happy because they knew this was the last leg of their fantastic journey. Shortly after their arrival in San

Francisco, Norma and Rinor had their passports inspected. Norma picked up her small traveling case and filled out the custom's form. Norma and Rinor were very thankful that there were no long lines or delays going through customs. It had been a long ten-hour flight from Seoul to San Francisco. As they went through the terminal, they noticed that the buildings and shops inside the airport all looked very different from the buildings and shops in the Philippines.

The only unusual thing that happened in San Francisco was that Norma forgot that her ticket for her last leg of the trip to Houston was in her purse. When the flight attendant asked her for her ticket, she was afraid she did not have one. Then she quickly looked through her purse and found it. Norma was so happy and excited to be in the United States that she lost most of her fear about her and Rinor being so far away from home.

Boone Dowdy was the volunteer driver for the Ben Hur Shrine on the day Rinor's flight arrived. He picked Irma and Gordon up in the hospital van at 1:00 p.m. and the trio headed for the Houston airport. They arrived at the Houston terminal at 4:35 p.m. and Norma and Rinor's plane landed at 5:57 p.m.

When Norma and Rinor arrived in Houston, Norma was even more excited because she knew she had reached her goal at long last. She began looking for Jocy's sister, whom she had never met. However, Gordon and Irma, who had never met the Marcial's, were there to pick them up. After their arrival at Terminal A, Gordon spotted Rinor and Norma and went up to Norma and asked, "Are you Norma?" Norma was quite surprised. "He knows my name," she thought to herself. She imagined that this person in the bright yellow golf shirt must be an employee of the hospital. "Do you speak English?" Gordon asked. "Yes," Norma replied. "Good," said Gordon. Norma imagined that the woman with Gordon must be Jocy's sister.

Gordon's first impression of Rinor and his mother was that they were very good people. When Rinor saw Gordon and Irma greet his mother at the airport he was very happy. His first impression was that they had met someone who would take care of him and his mother. The five of them left the Houston airport in the hospital van at 6:20 p.m. and paid the $2.00 ticket for two hours at the parking lot gate-house. On the van ride to the Irwin's trailer home, Norma asked Irma, "Are you Jocy's sister?" "No," replied Irma, and she explained to Norma and Rinor that they would be staying with them while Rinor was an outpatient of the Shriner's Burns Hospital-Galveston.

Because it was already past their normal supper time, everyone agreed to stop at a Mexican restaurant on the way home. The restaurant had a buffet line, and Irma had to explain to Norma what type of food it was. Then Norma explained what the food was to Rinor and they settled on chicken fajitas and rice. Finally Gordon, Irma, and their two new friends arrived home at 10:00 p.m. After their arrival Irma called Bonnie Stanley, a very good friend, to let her know that everyone was home. Bonnie came over immediately and brought Rinor a toy and a radio with headphones. Rinor was very, very happy.

Norma and Rinor thought the Irwin's little trailer was spacious and well equipped because it had bedrooms, a bath room, a shower, and a refrigerator. However, Rinor and his mother would spend only one night in the little trailer. The next morning Rinor enjoyed a breakfast of honey-nut toasted oat cereal without milk. Rinor watched as Gordon drank a glass of orange juice. He had never tasted orange juice, but he decided to try some and did not like it!

Norma and Rinor were quite surprised the next evening when all the neighbors came over and moved the Irwin's household into a newer, bigger, double-wide trailer. The move was made possible by the kindness of the trailer park management, who agreed to forgo the balance of the lease for the little trailer. Gordon planned to help with the move, but the neighbor's who knew of the Irwin's good deed recruited other neighbors who showed up and moved the household in a very short time. Gordon was at work. By the time he returned home, the neighbors had moved his household goods into the larger trailer.

The next day Gordon and Rinor went swimming in the trailer park swimming pool and Irma taught Norma how to use a microwave oven to cook. This was the first microwave oven Norma had seen, and she was fascinated by how it worked. Because Rinor could not straighten his left leg or use his left arm, Gordon thought the boy could not swim. Gordon thought they would just sit near the edge of the pool and visit. Perhaps they would take a dip a little later. Gordon was surprised when Rinor took to the water like a fish! Rinor could not swim on the surface of the water, but he could propel himself eight to ten feet underwater and was having a great time. Gordon thought to himself, *"This boy has great courage and he will make it!"*

In a June 1992 newsletter from her mission in Iloilo, Jocy Johnson recapped Rinor's plight. Rinor was admitted to the Iloilo hospital in July 1990. He stayed there for two and a half days and was transferred to the Scandinavian Children's Mission in Manila. He remained there until June 23, 1992, when Rinor and his mother left Manila on United Flight #808 at 8:10 a.m. She credited the Scandinavian Children's Mission in general and Toby Wallenburg in particular for helping to save Rinor's life.

Then she thanked her son's in-laws, Irma and Gordon, for their endless hours of help and extraordinary hands across the waters efforts. Finally, she thanked the Ben Hur Shrine in Austin, the American Embassy in Manila, and the Shriner's Burns Hospital-Galveston, who had all worked so diligently on behalf of Rinor and this unified effort.

On June 26 Gordon made numerous calls to the Shriner's Burns Hospital-Galveston, trying to confirm the plans for Rinor's surgery. He was unable to reach Mrs. Gonzales, who was out of the office, then out to lunch, and finally, busy. Gordon was told to call back after 3:00 p.m., but he had to go to work himself and told the receptionist he would call back Monday. When he called the following Monday, he found out that Mrs. Gonzales was out because of illness. Finally on June 30, Rinor was taken to the hospital in the Ben Hur Shrine van. Boone Dowdy and Gordon accompanied Norma and

Rinor. Doctor's evaluated Rinor's condition and immediately admitted him to the hospital.

As strange as it seems, Rinor had no idea that the American doctors at the Shriner's Burns Hospital-Galveston planned to operate on him to free his arm and leg. "I thought I was coming to the United States to have my burns treated again. I never thought I would walk on both feet. I was very excited and happy when I learned I would be able to walk again after I had surgery!"

The reader is probably wondering why Rinor did not fully understand the impact of his planned surgery. It should be remembered that Rinor was a small, frightened eleven-year-old boy who did not understand English. He had not attended school since he was burned when he was in the third grade. Most of the conversations between Jocy, his mother, and others about his medical problems and treatments were in English. Even if Rinor heard his family and friends talking about him walking again, he never realized they meant walking on two feet without the aid of crutches or a walker. His left arm had grown to his side and his left leg had grown to his thigh, and he had resigned himself to living that way for the rest of his life!

After getting Rinor admitted to the hospital and settled in for the night, Gordon returned home in the van. Norma stayed in Rinor's room for two nights, the night before his surgery and the night after his surgery. She slept on a small pull-out bed at the hospital after Rinor's surgery. Before Rinor's surgery Norma had to sign a hospital release acknowledging that the Shriner's Burns Hospital-Galveston was a teaching hospital. Shriner's Burns Hospitals are pioneers in burns research and surgery. The family also promised not to hold the hospital responsible for any possible complications arising from surgical treatments.

Just before his surgery a medical technician took a sample of Rinor's blood and gave him some medicine to put him to sleep. He was not given an I.V. or shots because the surgery was not invasive. Rinor was put to sleep in the operating room and went into surgery at 7:00 a.m. The operation freed his arm and his leg, and he returned to his room at 3:00 p.m. When he returned to his room, he was sick and in a great deal of pain. He threw up once and the sick feeling subsided. The pain stayed with him much longer, however. Rinor looked like he had been run over by a truck. He had a catheter for urine, and blood was being administered to him through an I.V. tube. His left arm stuck out at a right angle. His arm, chest, and legs were bandaged and braced. At about 6:00 p.m. a nurse brought Rinor some crackers and milk. Rinor was still a little sick, weak, and groggy. Eating was the last thing on his mind.

Rinor's operation would eventually allow him to use his left arm, walk, and run normally. His expected length of stay in the hospital was four to six weeks. Nurses cleaned and dressed his wounds every day. At times the pain was excruciating! However, in less than a week Rinor was eating normally.

Gordon called the hospital on July 7 and talked to Nurse McGowan. Gordon found out that the hospital staff had removed Rinor's dressing and the surgical areas looked good.

Because Rinor was healing nicely, the hospital doctors planned to remove the surgical staples. The surgical staples were used to hold Rinor's skin together under his left arm and behind his left leg. About a week after his surgery Rinor was getting out of bed and starting therapy aimed at getting him up and moving again.

About two weeks after surgery Rinor felt safe putting some weight on his newly freed left leg. Another hospital van driver, Greg Trejo from Ben Hur, stopped by at this time to check on Rinor's condition. Greg found out that Rinor was doing fine and called Gordon to let him know. Gordon immediately called the hospital and talked to Nurse McGowan again. While talking to the nurse Gordon learned that Rinor would need additional surgery to close up a few open gaps on his body. These open gaps or areas were nothing new to Rinor. On the brighter side, Gordon learned that the hospital was going to try to get Rinor to walk for the very first time the next day. Gordon was elated! With the use of his leg braces and by holding on to someone, Rinor was able to walk.

On July 19, Gordon and Irma went to the hospital to visit with Rinor and his mother. After visiting them for awhile, Gordon took some pictures of Rinor. Because of Rinor's physical appearance, Gordon felt like the boy still needed a great deal of medical attention. He had numerous unhealed areas on his body, but of course Gordon was not a doctor. Rinor was not well enough to leave the hospital at this time. However, Gordon, Irma, and Norma left the hospital for a few hours. They stopped at a K-mart store where Irma bought Norma some yarn because she knew Norma loved to crochet.

Later they stopped at Long John Silver's for lunch. Gordon remembers that Norma ate chicken and liked it but that she carefully removed the thick, fried batter crust that she did not like. After lunch they returned to the hospital.

When they arrived back at the hospital, what to their wondering eyes should appear but old Saint Nick without any reindeer. A group of Shriners from the Houston Shrine Temple were visiting the hospital and brought Santa Clause with them to cheer up the patients! It was Christmas in July at the Shriner's Burns Hospital-Galveston. This was the very first time Rinor had seen Santa Clause. At eleven years of age he became a real believer in the jolly old elf. Santa and the Shriners gave Rinor a package of goodies, a "Walkman" radio, a cap, and toys. What more could any kid want?

Gordon and Irma spent about five hours with Rinor, his mother, and the hospital staff. Rinor made it a point to tell his mother, who in turn told Gordon, that he wanted to go to school in Austin. The boy's request caught Gordon by surprise because he had not given much thought toward Rinor's future schooling. Gordon and Irma were more concerned with Rinor's state of health. Doris Hall, a registered nurse at the hospital, assured them that Rinor was doing well and progressing normally.

Two days later Leslie Cypert of the hospital's Physical Therapy Unit called Gordon about the possibility of Rinor's getting physical therapy in Austin and going to school there. Leslie said Rinor would need five hours of physical therapy a week. While at the hospital Rinor was tutored by Rubin

Infante through the Galveston Independent School District (GISD).

Gordon went to work again on behalf of Rinor. He called Austin's Brackenridge Hospital's physical therapy unit in hopes of finding a local source of free physical therapy for the boy. Gordon found out much to his displeasure that he could not arrange for free physical therapy for the boy unless he remained in the United States or was an illegal alien. Diane at Brackenridge said Rinor's PT would cost $88 per hour or $440 per week. There was no way that Gordon or Rinor and his mother could afford to pay the weekly bill. Gordon knew he had to find another way to get Rinor his much-needed physical therapy.

Next Gordon called Jan Martin of the Pflugerville ISD Special Education Department that was closer to home. Jan said they would need paperwork from Galveston ISD to put Rinor in a special education and PT group. Gordon notified Leslie in Galveston and asked Rubin to contact Camile Hopper of the Pflugerville Special Education Department. Another week passed and nothing happened. Rinor's PT and special education were at a standstill.

In early August Gordon decided it was time to get back "on the ball" again and try to arrange some free PT for Rinor. Rinor was scheduled to be released from the hospital in a week or two. He called Seton Northwest Hospital in Austin and asked to talk to Penny, who was in charge of the physical therapy department. Penny referred him to the Seton Medical Center Mission Affairs office and Sister Mary Ann. Sister Mary Ann promised to check on what could be done to get Rinor approved for PT. First she needed additional information from the Shriner's Burns Hospital-Galveston. Gordon told Sister Mary Ann how to get in touch with Darcy Stormer, Rinor's physical therapist at the Shriner's Burns Hospital-Galveston.

Gordon then talked with Cindy at Dessau Elementary School, who agreed to enroll Rinor there. Gordon met with Cindy and Principal Pat Reuter (pronounced Ritter) and told them about Rinor's accident, medical history, and current reconstructive surgery at the Shriner's Burns Hospital-Galveston. Both school officials were very cooperative and eager to help Rinor in any way they could.

The following weekend Gordon and Irma returned to see Rinor and check on his progress. Rinor was now able to walk with the help of leg braces and by holding on to someone. His legs were stiff and he could not bend his knees. To give Rinor a break from his hospital routine Gordon and Irma took him out to a park for the first time. Rinor saw many animals and a large pool, but the weather was too hot for him even though he was being pushed around in a wheelchair. Burns victims are very sensitive to heat, because the sweat glands on the left side of his body were destroyed. Rinor was very uncomfortable. The heat hurt his burns and the lack of sweat glands made him feel itchy, wanting to scratch the left side of his body. They returned to the air-conditioned comfort of the hospital.

After they arrived back at the hospital, Dr. McCauley had good news for Norma and the Irwin's! He thought Rinor could be released from the hospital if Norma and Gordon could oversee his physical therapy. Dr. McCauley informed Gordon and Irma they would have to watch a slide program on the care of burn patients; the program was presented only on Fridays. While Darcy the physical therapist was in Rinor's room, Gordon mentioned she would be getting a call from Austin about Rinor's physical therapy. Gordon will never forget her answer: "Oh, you mean from Seton?" "We have already heard from them and everything is set." What a great surprise for Gordon! He had talked to Sister Mary Ann only on Friday morning, and the same afternoon she called the Shriner's Burns Hospital-Galveston and arranged for Rinor's PT in Austin! With a little bit of luck and a great deal of help Gordon had fulfilled another important goal he had set for himself about Rinor. About the same time, the Shriner's Burns Institute-Galveston gave Gordon and Irma a copy of Rinor's Immunization records so that he could enter school.

On the following Friday Boone Dowdy drove Irma, Jocy, and Gordon to the Shriner's Burns Hospital-Galveston to get instructions on Rinor's general burn care. The program for the day was as follows;

"Schedule for Mr. and Mrs. Gordon Irwin, August 14, 1992

8:00 a.m. to 9:30 a.m. Bathing and Wound Care – Rm. #306 (3rd floor)

9:30 a.m. Coffee Break – 7th floor

10:00 a.m. Meeting with Catherine Morgan, Child Life Specialist, concerning school reentry – Rm. #333 (3rd floor)

1:00 p.m. Meeting with Darcy Stormer in Rehabilitation Department in Rm. #418 (4th floor)"

Everyone learned a great deal about burn patients and burn care. Jocy was so wound up she that talked and talked. She talked until she went to bed that night. Gordon and Irma brought Rinor and his mother back home with them on the return trip. It was a very long day for Jocy and the Irwins; they had left Austin for the Shriner's Burns Hospital-Galveston at 3:30 a.m. and returned to the Irwin home in Austin at 10:00 p.m.

While at home Norma helped Rinor with his baths while Gordon helped him get into his Jobst suit: a special compression suit that helps reduce the healing time. As the patient grows a larger suit is needed. Norma also helped Rinor exercise his left arm and leg. Gordon thought that although Rinor's physical therapy at home was progressing, he needed to do more PT work on his own. Gordon called Gene Freudenberg at the Ben Hur Shrine Temple and brought him up to date on Rinor's progress.

Gordon called Seton Northwest Hospital on August 17, and made an appointment for Rinor at 11:00 a.m. The appointment went well and the hospital agreed to admit Rinor on an outpatient basis for continuing physical therapy. The hospital gave Rinor a walker and he loved it! He still walked stiff-legged, but he walked! The hospital also suggested to Gordon that he get Rinor a large ball to exercise and play with, which he did.

For all practical purposes Rinor began his intensive PT program at Seton and started school at the same time. Rinor entered Dessau Elementary School as a fourth grader. He had been a first and second grader in the Philippines, but he was now eleven years old and about three and a half years behind in school. Because of his small size the difference in his age was not obvious. This was the first time Rinor had attended school since his Christmas accident more than two and a half years earlier when he was barely nine years old.

To make his school experience a little easier the Shriner's Burns Hospital-Galveston made a video tape of Rinor and mailed it to the school. The tape showed Rinor walking, explained his surgery, described his accident, and outlined the medical care he still needed. However, Rinor started school before the video arrived. When the tape did arrive, the school showed it twice during assembly periods, and the children all wanted to help Rinor. After showing the tape the students became very interested in Rinor and the Philippines. So Ms. Rector conducted a short, impromptu geography lesson showing the students where Rinor lived and talked about the people of the Philippines. Soon the children found a great way that was full of fun to help Rinor. Because Rinor could not walk on his own, they pushed him from room to room and class to class in Ms. Rector's chair, which had wheels. The children even argued mildly among themselves about whose turn it was to push Rinor to his next class.

When Gordon found out about Rinor's free taxi service at school, he called Ms. Rector. "Rinor has to be encouraged to use his arms and legs more and walk," he advised. "Oh, I know, but it's so hard to be tough on him," she replied. That was just about the way everyone felt about Rinor. He had a splendid disposition, and everyone loved him. The teacher's chair was Rinor's main mode of transportation around the school for about a month. After that Seton's therapy had improved his mobility and he was able to get around on his own with the aid of a walker.

Rinor had to learn English and he was very eager to do so. He learned by listening and watching the other students and by asking questions. Ms. Rector was very patient and always happy to help Rinor, and she gave him as much individual attention as she could. One of Rinor's favorite subjects was math, the universal language. Rinor was very good in math, and his English rapidly improved. He was honored with the "Student of the Week" award once in his first year at school and awarded an "Honor Badge" every day of the week. The Honor Badge was given to well-behaved students who did not cause trouble or disrupt the class in any manner.

At first Gordon took Rinor to Seton for PT at 9:00 a.m. five days a week, Monday through Friday. On August 19 Barbara Barton at Seton said she wanted to have one physical therapist and one occupational therapist OT work with Rinor for an hour and a half a day starting the following week. Gordon agreed to the intensified schedule, believing it would help Rinor. The OT helped Rinor with his hands, improving his dexterity; the physical therapist worked mainly with his legs, helping him bend his legs and improve his flexibility. After switching to the new PT schedule, the OT at Seton asked Darcy, Rinor's therapist at the Shriner's Burns Hospital-

Galveston, about taking Rinor's arm splint off and getting him a new Jobst garment.

The arm splint was intended to keep Rinor's left elbow from bending backwards but the contoured molded splint could easily be put on backwards, and it was not doing its job. Darcy agreed to take the arm splint off, but notified Seton that they were not planning to give Rinor a new Jobst garment. The right leg of the garment was not needed; it was too tight and caused Rinor's leg to swell. Darcy also notified Seton that the Shriner's Burns Hospital-Galveston was being evacuated because of Hurricane Andrew.

As Rinor's physical conditioned improved, his physical therapy schedule was reduced to three times a week at Seton. Before his physical therapy ended at Seton, the Sisters of Charity there had donated services valued at over $25,000. Their charitable works helped ensure that Rinor would learn to walk and run again.

One occupational therapist at Seton cleaned up and painted a scooter for Rinor. With Gordon's help Rinor tried very hard to learn to ride the scooter, but he never really mastered it. He had to try to steer the scooter with his right hand because his left arm was stiff. He had to balance the scooter and put his weight on his right foot. Then Rinor had to push and propel the scooter with his left leg and foot. At first it bothered him that he could not master the scooter, but once Rinor decided it was a lost cause, he turned his attention to other challenges he could master.

Gordon took a personal interest in Rinor's rehabilitation and wanted him to become involved in and enjoy as many different physical experiences as possible. On Saturday mornings Gordon took Rinor to the Pharr Tennis Center in Austin, where a gentleman named Rubin gave him tennis lessons for $5 per hour. The first week they gave Rinor a "junior-sized" tennis racket that was furnished by the United States Tennis Association through a program to help underprivileged kids. Rinor was very excited about this gift and he still has it! Rinor did very well, considering he did not yet know how to run and couldn't bend his left arm at the elbow.

Gordon also took Rinor and a couple of his friends bowling in the summer. Showplace Lanes, a large bowling alley, gave the boys free bowling passes. The bowling was free, but Gordon had to rent bowling shoes for the boys. Gordon did not pay any attention to the scores Rinor bowled and did not want Rinor to worry about his scores. Gordon just wanted Rinor to learn how to throw the bowling ball and have a good time. Naturally Gordon and the three boys had a great time. Gordon had taken a course through the Youth Bowling Association that came in handy for helping Rinor with his bowling.

In October Rinor wanted to attend a Halloween party at school. The Halloween party was in the morning, and so were his physical therapy treatments. Gordon called the hospital and arranged for Rinor to take his treatments at 3:00 p.m. Rinor kept the afternoon schedule until the end of his physical therapy treatments.

In November, Jeanne Williams, a member of the Ladies Oriental Shrine wanted to do something for Rinor, so she donated $25 for him to buy a used bicycle. Gordon and Rinor shopped the pawn shops and flea markets and finally bought a good used bicycle at the Highway 290 flea market for $30. Gordon took Rinor to the tennis courts at the Dessau Trailer Park, but he just could not seem to master riding the bicycle.

In December the Irwins moved from a trailer home in Dessau Park to a rental home in Lamplight Village. Irma was tired of her comfortable trailer home and looked forward to moving into a house. An old friend, Bonnie Stanley, told Irma about a Housing and Urban Development home that a friend of hers had bought. However, the friend had never moved into the house. It seems she had asked the next door neighbor to trim two beautiful trees she had in the front yard, and the next thing she knew, the man had cut them down. After that she lost interest in moving into the house and decided to rent it for $850 a month with a $500 security deposit.

Even though the Irwins could not afford $850 a month, Bonnie talked Irma into taking a look at the house. The screen porch and laundry room with washer and dryer sold Irma on the house. Gordon drove by the house and thought it was great. However, his price range was more like $600 a month. The security deposit was another problem.

When the owner of the house learned from Bonnie that the Irwins were interested in the house and Bonnie vouched that they would take good care of it, the owner called Gordon. She wanted someone who would take care of the yard and keep the house in good repair. Gordon agreed he could make the required minor repairs. In return the owner dropped the rent to $650 a month and the deposit to $250. Gordon agreed he could afford that.

There was still one big surprise for Gordon and Irma. During their telephone conversations with the owner she mentioned, "And I will fix the pool." Gordon's jaw dropped, but no one could see it. Neither he nor his wife had realized the house had a large backyard swimming pool! They took a look at the back -yard and saw the eight-foot-deep in-ground swimming pool covered with black plastic. The plastic cover was supported by two-by-twelve planks, and the pool was full of pitch-black water.

When Gordon first moved into the house and was unloading his van, Nicholas and Elliot, two boys who lived next door, came over. They were a couple of rough-and-tumble kids who were younger than Rinor and in the first and second grades. They asked Gordon if any kids lived there. Gordon told them there was one boy that would be going to Dessau Elementary School, not the local school. Nicholas and Elliot told Gordon they were going to Dessau Elementary School also. When Gordon asked the boys how they got to school, they told him their dad took them when he got up in time.

Lou, the boy's father, did not have a job. The family held garage sales once or twice a month at their home. After the Irwins moved into the house, Gordon went next door to see if Lou would take Rinor to school in the mornings. Gordon hoped he could get a little more sleep in the mornings because his work ended at 1:00 a.m. In return Gordon offered to pick the boys up after school. The two-man carpool to school worked well except for a few times when the neighbor's kids forgot to wake up Gordon.

Gordon picked the kids up in the afternoon before going to work. There was one small problem in the afternoon as well. Lou's kids probably never earned an "Honor Badge," and they were frequently kept after school and got out late. Soon Gordon found himself acting as a substitute father, disciplining the boys on their behavior and warning them not to be late when he came to get them. A stern warning from a new neighbor was more than enough to make the boys toe the line. After his stern little lecture the boy's were seldom late!

After moving into the house Rinor was more eager than ever to learn how to ride his bicycle. There was a sidewalk in front of the house and a quiet street with little traffic. Gordon would run along next to Rinor, helping him balance the bike. When it seemed as if Rinor was beginning to get the knack of balancing the bike, Gordon let go. Rinor was suddenly riding the bike by himself without knowing it. Gordon ran up beside Rinor and shouted, "Look what you're doing!" Rinor and the bike fell over immediately. After another try Rinor took off riding the bicycle on his own and no one could catch him. Although there are plenty of bicycles in the Philippines, this was Rinor's first bike. He was very proud that he had learned how to ride the bike, and it was a major accomplishment for hm.

Gordon frequently sold various odds and ends at the Austin Flea Market, which was open only on weekends. One weekend while Gordon and Rinor were at the flea market, a fellow vendor gave Rinor a pair of roller skates. Gordon had to teach Rinor how to roller-skate, but it turned out to be much easier than teaching him how to ride his bicycle. Rinor held onto Gordon for a few times but quickly mastered the sport of roller skating.

While attending Dessau Elementary School, Rinor had relearned how to walk. Later he learned how to run. One day while the students were having physical education outdoors, Rinor noticed that the other boys leaned forward and synchronized the swing of their arms with the movement of their legs when they ran. Rinor could not run in the upright position, but he learned that if he bent his knees and shifted his weight forward a little; he could run, and run he did! Rinor was very excited the day he learned how to run; he could hardly wait to tell Gordon. When Gordon arrived to pick the boys up in his van, Rinor came running and shouting, "Tito Gordon, Tito Gordon, I can run, I can run!" Running was a great thrill for him. At twelve years of age Rinor had accomplished more than he had ever dreamed!

Rinor and his mother arrive in the United States of America.

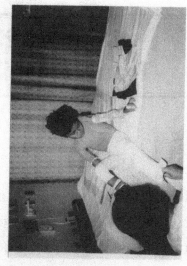

The Shrine Burns Institute frees Rinor's left arm and leg.

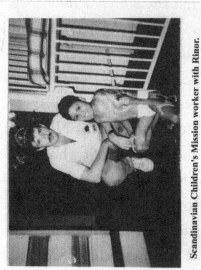

Scandinavian Children's Mission worker with Rinor. Surgery is still needed to free his left arm and left leg.

Rinor is now healthy enough to travel to the Galveston Burns Institute for further treatment of his injuries.

187

Chapter 23 – Trouble, Trouble, Boil, and Bubble!

Shortly after Rinor and his mother came to America, storm clouds began to gather on the horizon. Norma's teeth and gums had been bothering her for a very long time, but the Irwin's were not aware of it. First she suffered in silence at home in the Philippines because she knew her family could not afford a dentist. Then she continued to suffer in silence because she did not want her personal pain to ruin Rinor's chance to come to America for surgery.

To live with the pain in her teeth and gums Norma cut her food into very small pieces and swallowed it whole. If the food was soft enough, she mashed it into mush so she could swallow it without chewing. However by August 18, 1992, she could no longer stand the pain. She told Irma about her mouth and teeth problem, and Irma could not sleep that night. "Honey, I wonder what we've got ourselves into she said to Gordon." When Gordon asked her what she meant, she explained that Norma had complained to her about severe pain and her teeth hurting. Gordon and Irma did not have a dental insurance plan for themselves, and the thought of a huge dental bill for their new friend was frightening.

In desperation Gordon looked in the Austin telephone book in hopes of locating a local dental school, but there was none. Then he called the local Dental Association and found out that the nearest dental school was in San Antonio; they gave him the number. In desperation Gordon called the University of Texas Health Center Dental School and talked to a young woman named Karen who worked in the dean's office. Karen put Gordon in touch with Dr. Billy Rigsby, the associate dean of clinical affairs. After talking with Dr. Rigsby, Gordon realized it would not be worth the time and effort involved in taking Norma to San Antonio for her dental work. First he would have to take her to San Antonio and back. Then he would have to wait for her while her dental work was done by students and checked by the staff.

Dr. Rigsby suggested that Gordon call Dr. Jim Orr's office. Gordon found out from his receptionist, Becky, that Dr. Orr did charitable dental work at a clinic named Manos de Christo (Hands of God). Becky suggested that Gordon talk to Leah, who worked at the clinic on 1201 East First Street.

Gordon called the Manos de Christo clinic and made an appointment for Norma on September 3, at 11:00 a.m. Gordon took Norma to the clinic for her scheduled appointment. When Norma was examined, the dentist told Gordon and Norma that her mouth was so infected that there was no way he could work on her teeth. He gave Norma a prescription for penicillin and told her to take it as prescribed and come back in one week.

One of Jocy's good friends, a Filipino nurse named Faith, lived in Irving, Texas. She worked for two local hospitals and was a big supporter of Jocy's mission. On September 7, Jocy brought Faith with her while visiting Austin to see Norma and Rinor. Faith brought clothes for Norma and Rinor, and then they all went out to eat. Gordon did not join them because he sensed the women wanted to visit and get to know each other a little better.

Gordon took Norma to the clinic for her appointment on the 10th, and her mouth was healthy enough for the dentist to pull one badly decayed tooth. Norma returned to the clinic several times during the next few months and ended up losing a total of four teeth. Today, Norma's teeth and gums are still in very bad shape and she takes an over-the-counter pain-killer to ease her discomfort. Eventually all of her teeth will probably have to be pulled before the pain and discomfort ends.

On September 11, Jocy picked up Norma and Rinor at 7:15 a.m. for a TV interview. The interview was intended to give Jocy a chance to tell Rinor's story and create general interest in her mission and her work. Gordon remembered that Rinor missed both school and physical therapy that day. A couple of days later Norma received information that her daughter had a spot on her lungs or chest with possible bone involvement. Norma was very worried and tried to call her daughter. Sidney was still in school when Norma called, so she called back the following day. Sidney was scared and wanted to see her mother. The following day Jocy called Gordon at 6:30 a.m., wanting to know if he was planning to do anything about Norma's daughter. Gordon replied that he was not, mainly because he did not know what he could do about the situation under the circumstances.

Then Jocy asked Gordon if he would like someone to pick up Norma and Rinor on weekends, perhaps thinking this might give Gordon and Irma some sort of break. Gordon told Jocy that whatever Norma wanted to do was fine with Irma and him. Gordon also let Jocy know that he and his wife treated Norma and Rinor like family. Norma and Rinor were no problem, and the families enjoyed their weekends together. Later that day Gordon called Ann Chavarria at the Shriner's Burns Hospital-Galveston. He wanted to know when Rinor would be well enough to return to the Philippines with his mother so she could be with his sister Sidney. Ann was not in, so Gordon left a message. Ann called back and they discussed Norma's situation. Ann said she would check with Dr. McCauley about Rinor's going home early. Dr. McCauley said Rinor's next appointment was on October 6.

On September 17, Jocy called Gordon to say that she would like to take Rinor and his mother to the Philippine Festival in Copperas Cove, on September 19. She also said she wanted to go with Rinor and his mother to the Shiner's Burns Hospital-Galveston in the Ben Hur hospital van on October 6. Gordon said that was fine with him.

Unfortunately Rinor was still having trouble with his contoured arm brace. It was the same old story;-it was easy to put the brace on wrong or in the reverse direction, and it rotated easily on his arm. Barbara Barton at Seton wanted to do more for Rinor, but she did not want to interfere with his treatment or upset the personnel at the Shiner's Burns Hospital-Galveston. Barbara thought Rinor should be x-rayed and under the care of a local doctor. She said she would check with her advisor, Sister Mary Ann, to get her opinion on these recommendations.

On Saturday, September 19, Rinor and his mother went with Jocy to the Philippine Festival in Copperas Cove. After returning home Norma told Irma that she did not want to go with Jocy anymore because Jocy treated her like a child. Jocy told Norma what to do and when to do it and never asked Norma what she wanted to do. Both Norma and Rinor were treated like family at the Irwin's, and they resented Jocy bossing them around.

On September 27, Gordon talked with Faith about Norma's daughter Sidney. Gordon read her a report that Ricardito had sent to Norma. It described calcification in the lung area with possible bone involvement. Faith was concerned about the report and Gordon assured her that Norma would be talking with her husband to determine what should be done for Sidney.

On October 5, Gordon called Ann at the hospital, but she was not in so he left a message with Jenny, the receptionist. Gordon left a message that Rinor and his mother would need a letter from the hospital to extend their visas, which were about to expire. Later that day Boone Dowdy called Gordon to let him know the Ben Hur hospital van would be full on the 6th and there would not be enough room for him and

Jocy. Gordon called Jocy to let her know that the van would be full on the 6th and she promptly hung up on him.

October 10, 1992 was a great day for Rinor. He was twelve-years-old and awoke at 5:00 a.m. to see the Ninja Turtle birthday cake that Tita Irma had baked for him. Later that day Tito Gordon took him to the Ben Hur Shrine Circus. Gordon's friend Bob Oakes gave them tickets because Gordon had already given his away to other deserving friends. One of the highlights of the circus for Rinor was the elephant ride. Children and parents buy tickets for a ride on the elephant before the circus, and at intermission. A handler and clowns with the aid of a portable ladder helped load eight or more youngsters into a large, specially-made basket that was tightly strapped to the elephant's back.

The children sit down and hold onto the handrail as the elephant was led around the ring several times. The elephant ride is a great thrill for youngsters, although some of them have been heard to exclaim to their parents, "Elephants stink!" Both Rinor and Gordon thoroughly enjoyed the circus with its lions, tigers, clowns, acrobats, trapeze artists, and elephants. For those of you who do not know it, elephants are considered "good-luck, "symbols by circus performers and clowns are considered "good-luck" by the Mexican people. Many parents want to have a picture of a clown with their child. Rinor was so excited on his birthday that it was 11:00 p.m. before he settled down and went to bed. Then he slept until 11:05 a.m. the next morning.

On October 12, Rinor was taken to Seton for physical therapy. The next day Kathleen talked to Dr. Strock, who worked with Dr. McCauley, and Rinor's therapy was scheduled for the mornings. The same day Norma complained about her mouth being sore and bleeding. Gordon took her to the Manos de Christo clinic, where the doctor informed her that bleeding was normal, considering the condition of her teeth and gums. Norma was advised to brush her teeth and gums daily until her gums had a healthy pink appearance. She was told that her gums should not bleed when brushed.

October 17 was another big day for Rinor. Gordon took him to his first auction. The auction was held by Bill Boulter, a friend of Gordon's. Rinor kept trying to imitate Bill, but he spoke so softly that only Gordon could hear him and tell what he was trying to do. At 6:30 p.m. that evening Gordon, Irma, Norma, and Rinor went to a reception dinner and dance for Imperial Potentate Everett Evans of Tyler, Texas, at the Ben Hur Shrine Temple. The temple was also celebrating its 100th year in Austin. Norma, Rinor, and the Irwin's had received a formal invitation from Ben Hur Potentate Bob Emrie and they could hardly wait for the big event. Guests at the reception ate at 6:30 p.m., and danced until about 9:00 p.m. Norma did not dance, but Rinor danced with LaDell Freudenberg, Gene Freudenberg's wife. Everyone had a great time!

On October 21, Rinor became sick with a sore throat and headache. Seton gave him Tylenol when he showed up for his physical therapy, but the cold had to run its course. Rinor went home early and was kept out of school for the next three days. By the end of October he was back to normal and ready for his scheduled appointment at the Shriner's Burns Hospital-Galveston on November 4.

It was at this time that Gordon decided to talk to Norma about Rinor's progress or lack of progress, depending on how you looked at it. Gordon expressed his concern that Rinor would never be completely well and have full use of his left arm. As strange as it may seem, Norma had never thought about the possibility that Rinor might not be fully healed until Gordon talked with her. She always assumed because of her faith in God that Rinor would be fully healed in every sense of the word. She was disappointed but at last faced the possibility.

On November 3, Ann called to let Gordon know that the hospital letter requesting visa extensions was ready. Ann said she would give the letter to Norma that day. She also promised to check on Rinor's arm and arm brace. Gordon pointed out to Ann that there seemed to be a communications problem between Seton Northwest Hospital and the Shriner's Burns Hospital-Galveston. Seton had called the Shriner's Burns Hospital-Galveston, but their calls were not returned. The real problem seemed to be that Seton did not want to do anything without the Shriner's Burns Hospital-Galveston approval and they would not return Seton's calls. Ann promised to work on improving communications between the two hospitals.

Woody, another hospital van driver, picked up Norma and Rinor at 7:30 a.m. to take them to their Galveston appointment. When Norma and Rinor returned, they had a new leg splint that was the same as the original one and no written instructions on when to wear it. Gordon assumed the leg splint should be worn at night. They also returned the Jobst garments, top and bottom, with no written instructions for Rinor, his mother, or Seton. At this point Gordon concluded there was still a communication problem. Both he and Kathleen at Seton decided they would call Ann at Galveston the next day.

The following day Darcy Stormer called and said she would call Seton. Five days later the Shriner's Burns Hospital-Galveston called Norma early in the morning and told her that Rinor's left arm extension was good. Darcy told Norma that she would call Seton, but she did not. At 9:00 a.m. Kathleen at Seton tried to call both Darcy and Dr. McCauley, but she was transferred around and never got to talk to anyone. She left a message asking Dr. McCauley to call her. At 10:45 a.m. Gordon talked with Kathleen at Seton; she said Dr. McCauley's secretary had called and said that he had not seen any reports sent by Seton. Kathleen told Dr. McCauley's secretary that Seton had been trying to get cooperation with them about the fact that Rinor's elbow was not responding to physical therapy.

Darcy at Galveston then talked to Ed, another physical therapist at Seton, and requested that Rinor be given extensive therapy for his elbow with the splint casting. Ed told Darcy that Seton was not set up for that type of work, but Darcy did not offer any assistance. At 10:53 a.m., Gordon called Ann at Galveston again and told her about these continuing communications problems. Ann said she would show Dr. McCauley the Seton reports and have Darcy call Kathleen.

At 11:00 a.m. Gordon talked to Norma and asked her to talk to Dr. McCauley to find out if Rinor would ever be able to bend his left elbow again. At 11:15 a.m. Gordon called Barbara Barton of Seton and brought her up to date on the morning activities. Barbara told Gordon that she thought progress could be made on Rinor's elbow. At the end of a very frustrating morning there was hope that at least Rinor would regain some use of his left elbow. Perhaps that was all that anyone could expect.

Three days later Kathleen at Seton had an orthopedic technician look at Rinor's elbow. In turn the technician talked with one of the Seton doctors who at times worked with the Shriner's Orthopedic Hospital-Houston. Kathleen called Darcy in Galveston, but she was not in, so Kathleen left a message that Seton would like to have an orthopedic doctor look at Rinor's left arm and elbow. Darcy called back, but when she could not reach Kathleen, she left a message informing Kathleen that Dr. McCauley did not think it was necessary to have an orthopedic doctor brought into the case. Considering what Dr. McCauley said, it appeared that Dr. Strock at Galveston did not take X-rays of Rinor's arm nor have an orthopedic doctor look at his elbow. This was very disappointing to Gordon, but at least Darcy and Kathleen were now communicating with each other.

Gordon called Ann to thank her for acting as a mediator in his attempt to improve communications between the Shriner's Burns Hospital-Galveston and Seton Northwest Hospital in Austin. During their conversation Gordon learned Ann had given Dr. McCauley Seton's reports and asked him to read them. Gordon also found out that it was Dr. McCauley who vetoed Dr. Strock's recommendation to bring in an orthopedic doctor for consultation and treatment of Rinor's elbow. Ann said she would continue to talk with Dr. McCauley in an attempt to resolve any differences of opinion about Rinor's treatments.

Rinor was still suffering with some open sores and infections. On his last trip to Galveston he had been given an antibiotic to help knock out the infection. Ann asked Gordon how Rinor was doing with his new medication. Rinor had to apply the medication before putting on his Jobst suit. Ann suggested that if Rinor's wounds were not healing properly, he should let them air out more. The best time to air out his wounds would be before going to school in the morning and before going to bed at night. Ann also recommended that Rinor apply the medication to gauze pads and wear them under his Jobst suit, especially if he sweated a lot during the day.

On the evening of November 19, Rinor cried a lot before going to bed. The next morning Gordon asked Norma why the boy was crying; she told him he did not want to take a bath. Later Gordon talked with Rinor and asked him why he did not want to take a bath and why he was crying. After hesitating a little, Rinor told Gordon that the cold water hurt his burns. After that Norma took more care when adjusting the temperature of Rinor's bath water to minimize his pain. Gordon made a mental note to talk to Dr. McCauley about why Rinor was so cold. Was it the burns, the Jobst suit, the medication, or what?

It was also at this time that Irma got some comments at the November Ladies Oriental Shrine meeting. Some of the ladies at Ben Hera Court no longer wanted to sponsor Rinor and his mother because of a recent newspaper article that implied that Jocy's mission was paying for their care. Irma assured the court that the mission was not paying for Rinor and his mother's care. Irma asked Jocy to print a retraction or correction to the article, but it was never done.

Jocy called Gordon to let him know that she had arranged for Norma and Rinor to talk to Ricardito at 8:00 a.m. on Friday, November 20. She wanted Irma and Gordon to be ready at 7:30 a.m. for this family conference call. The call was sponsored by radio station B93, and Gordon reluctantly skipped work that morning to be there. Jocy and Gladys, a Filipino friend from Killeen, and Mr. McNeil with radio station B93 showed up on time, but the expected TV coverage never arrived.

The phone call reunion was a happy event for the Marcial family. Jocy tried to take charge of the event and direct the conversation, but her plan did not work. Norma, Rinor, and Ricardito talked about the things that were important to them, such as Sidney's condition, and forgot about the media hype. When the conference call ended, Jocy and Gladys wanted Norma and Rinor to go home with them. However, Norma got sick because of the 500 mg Veetids medication she was taking for her dental problems and had to leave. Her morning medication had made her sick and nauseated. Gordon called the doctor for Norma. The doctor told Gordon to have Norma cut her medication in half and take one capsule in the morning after eating and one capsule in the evening after eating. That seemed to do the trick.

Rinor was admitted to the Shriner's Burns Hospital-Galveston on November 23 for physical therapy observation and X-rays. Norma returned with Boone Dowdy, the Ben Hur hospital van driver, when she realized that Rinor would be in the hospital for several days. Everyone thought the appointment was for a day visit, and therefore Norma had not packed any extra clothes. Gordon called Jocy and told her not to come down before Thanksgiving to pick Rinor and his mother up because Rinor would be in the hospital. Jocy said she would stop and visit Rinor on the 24th since she was headed that way. Jocy tried to urge Norma and Rinor to take a bus and spend Thanksgiving in Kileen. However, Norma dug in her heels and refused to take Rinor out of the hospital or go anywhere.

On Wednesday December 2, Dr. Donna L. Bedonia of the Western Visayas Medical Center in Iloilo notified Ricardito that Sidney was suffering from a lung problem and needed additional tests. She was to be admitted to the medical center for treatment and possible surgery; the doctor thought Norma should be there. According to the doctor, "The success of treatment will depend on a concerted medical effort and family support." The same day Ricardito sent a letter to Jocy as follows:

"Dear Sis. Jocy,

"My wife is needed at home. Our daughter Sidney is going to the hospital and she needs her mother. Our daughter has been

separated from her mother for a long time now. Sidney needs her mother at her side since she is facing possible surgery."

"Please Sis. Jocy let my wife come home - our daughter needs her mother. Sidney will be admitted to the hospital on Dec. 4."

From the urgency of the letter Gordon thought Sidney's condition must be serious, so he called David at United Airlines to check on a flight for Norma to return to the Philippines. At first they told him there were no flights to the Philippines available in December. Then Gordon talked to Jackie Jones at United, who said Norma's ticket was non-refundable and could not be used with other airlines.

Finally Gordon talked with Iris Jones of United who, because of the urgency of the situation, was able to schedule a return flight for Norma on December 15. Norma was scheduled to depart from Houston International Airport on Flight 1853 at 8:05 a.m., arrive in San Francisco at 10:23 a.m., and take Flight 807, which would arrive in Seoul at 7:35 p.m. on the 16th. Norma would then depart from Seoul on Flight 807 at 8:55 p.m., arrive in Manila at 11:45 p.m., and check out through customs at 6:15 the next morning. Gordon also signed Norma and Rinor up for United's Friendly Skies Program. Then Gordon called Ann at Galveston and told her about the reservations.

At about 1:15 p.m. Norma called Gordon collect. Jocy had called her and she was very upset. She was upset about being asked to sign over power of attorney for a family in Houston to take care of Rinor while she was gone. Norma did not want that to happen. She wanted the Irwins to take care of Rinor while she was gone. Gordon told Norma not to sign a power of attorney form until he and Irma could talk to her on Saturday. Gordon asked Norma if she had decided whether go home, and she said she had decided to go. Gordon told her to relax and stop worrying.

On Friday, December 4, Gordon called Ann in Galveston to check on Rinor. Ann told Gordon that Norma had received a letter from Ricardito asking her to come home. Sidney was thought to have cancer in the breast area, and Ricardito thought that Norma should come home soon.

On Saturday Jocy called to check on Norma's flight reservations. She was trying to make plans to return to the Philippines on the same flight. Gordon gave her all the details. On Sunday Jocy called Gordon again at 7:15 a.m., saying that Norma was balking at going home. Jocy told Gordon she would be on the same plane with Norma to make sure she did not get off in San Francisco. Jocy tried to get Gordon to promise that Norma would get on the plane for her scheduled flight home. Gordon told Jocy he could not force anyone to do anything but that he would be firm with Norma and encourage her to return home. After this call Gordon thought Jocy would let Norma alone and let her get used to the idea of returning home.

However, Jocy called back around 9:00 a.m. after talking with her friend Gladys. Jocy called back again at 9:30 a.m. and asked what she had done to make Norma mad at her. Gordon told Jocy that she never asked Norma to do anything; she always told Norma what to do. Jocy did not want to hear that explanation and started to argue her side of the story with Gordon. At that point Gordon told Jocy he was tired of the conversation and suggested that they end it on a friendly note. He told her he would call her back after he talked with Norma.

A couple of days later, Ann at Galveston called Gordon and told him Norma was quite upset. Gordon told her what had happened and explained why Norma was so upset and confused. On one hand she wanted to stay with Rinor, and on the other hand she wanted to go back home to be with Sidney. Ann told Gordon that Rinor's surgery might have to be postponed. Dr. McCauley planned to do a large skin graft on Rinor's arm. The graft would have to remain wrapped for ten days and he would be in the hospital for at least two weeks. At that point Irma and Gordon began to wonder if it might not be better for Norma to stay with Rinor.

Ann also mentioned that the people at Seton Northwest appeared to be tired of carrying Rinor in their physical therapy program. Gordon told her the Seton people were frustrated because the Shriner's Burns Hospital-Galveston would not communicate with them and Dr. Strock had apparently lied to them. Ann said she would bring these problems up at their daily meeting and call Gordon the next day.

On December 9, Gordon called Immigration to apply for Rinor's visa extension; his visa was set to expire in fifteen days. Gordon got a form from Representative Jake Pickle's office, filled it out, and sent it to Irving, Texas. Gordon also called Ann who said that Rinor's surgery might be scheduled for Friday the 11th. She did not know if they would try to free up Rinor's left elbow or just do a skin graft and leave enough room to free up his elbow or to free his elbow later. Gordon also talked to Norma. Norma wanted to talk to Ricardito without anyone else listening in on their conversation. Gordon mentioned this to Ann, and Ann said she would try to make arrangements where Norma could talk to her husband in private.

Later that evening Ann called Gordon and told him that Rinor's surgery would be postponed for at least three months. They planned to take some muscle from Rinor's chest, but his wounds had not healed enough at this point. Ann asked Gordon if he could make arrangements to pick up Norma and Rinor, so he said he would pick them up the following morning. The next morning Gordon left home at 6:30 a.m. in his car and arrived at the hospital at 10:00 a.m. Gordon discussed Rinor's therapy with Kimberly at Galveston and then Rinor and his mother. Gordon left the hospital at noon and arrived back in Austin at 4:20 p.m. On December 10, Norma signed her authorization for medical treatment and power of attorney over to Gordon.

On December 11, Norma called Sidney and told her she would be coming home. Norma tried to get the telephone number of her aunt and sister, but the Philippine operator was unable to get it. Jocy called Norma to find out when she would be leaving Austin and arriving at Houston International Airport. Norma said she did not know. Jocy asked Norma to take something back for her. Norma said no. Two days later Jocy called Irma to find out when they were leaving for the airport and Irma said she did not know. The next day, December 14, Irma was able to get the telephone number of

Norma's sister. Norma talked with her sister about coming home.

On Tuesday, December 15, Bob Oakes came by and picked up Gordon, Irma, and Norma at 2:30 a.m., and they arrived in Houston at 5:30 a.m. Norma and Gordon got in line to get Norma checked aboard her flight. Gordon noticed a young man and his daughter standing in front of them. Gordon talked with the man and found out they were also going to Manila. He asked the young man if he would like to help Norma if she needed any help and he said he would. Then Gordon gave Norma $45 and a big hug and left. Bob, Gordon, and Irma left the airport at 6:20 a.m. and arrived back home at 9:20 a.m.

Later that day Ann called from the hospital and asked if Norma had left. Gordon told her she had. Ann told Gordon that Lorna Adams of Immigration had called several times in the last four days. Lorna wanted to know why the visa extension was for Austin rather than Houston. Gordon had no explanation, so he told Ann to have Lorna call him if she had any further questions.

On December 17 Lorna Adams called Ann again. This time she was concerned because she noticed that Rinor's time was almost up. Ann asked Gordon to call Lorna, which he did. Lorna said Dr. Strock's letter had been sent to Austin and then to her. She was concerned with Rinor's paperwork being filed on time. After talking with Gordon, Lorna concluded that there shouldn't be any problems.

On December 19, the Irwin's along with Rinor left Austin at 6:00 a.m. heading for Bedford, Texas to celebrate Christmas early with their long-time friends Jan and Johnny Moreland. They stopped at the Irving Community Hospital to see Faith, who had a gift for Rinor. She had some shoes and pajamas for him. Then they stopped to see Gordon's sister, Barbara Bearse, and her husband, Lawrence, who were visiting with their daughter, Diane Jarrett, her husband Steve Jarrett and their family. While Lawrence, Steve, and Gordon played golf at the Grapevine Golf Course, Rinor, Irma, Barbara, Diane, and her two daughters went to see A "Muppet Christmas" at a movie theater. This was the first motion picture that Rinor had seen at a movie theater, and he was very excited.

Then it was on to the Morelands', for their early annual Christmas party. For Christmas Rinor received a Yak, a model car, the card game Uno, an Etch-A-Sketch, and several Matchbox cars. If you brought a friend with you to the Moreland's Christmas party, they always made them feel at home even on short notice. They always made sure there were Christmas presents for everyone. Because of the large number of people who showed up for the party, Rinor slept on the floor that night. During the night Jan got up several times to make sure Rinor was covered.

On the morning of the 20th, Rinor and the Irwin's ate breakfast at the Moreland's. Rinor ate Rice Krispies for breakfast and loved them. The Irwins left and had lunch with the Bearse's before heading home to Austin. Rinor slept almost all the way home; it was a three-hour ride. Rinor was a very tired young man, but he was also a big hit that weekend. As usual everyone who met Rinor loved him.

On December 22, Rinor left in the Ben Hur Hospital van with driver Greg and his wife, Stella, at 6:45 a.m. for his checkup at the Shriner's Burns Hospital-Galveston. Gordon called United Airlines to verify the name he was given for the Friendly Skies Program. He also checked on the cost of a round-trip ticket for Norma. Cindy Medina, the UA representative, said the cost of Norma's ticket would be $1,417 if the ticket was purchased the first of March for a return in June.

On December 23, Rinor and the Irwins left to spend Christmas in Springfield, Missouri, with JoAnna, Carlos, and Robert. They spent one night in a motel in Oklahoma and then went on to Springfield the next morning. On Christmas Day Rinor saw his first snow and ice. Gordon and Rinor played outside in the snow even though it was only 24 degrees, with a biting cold wind chill factor of minus 4 degrees. Rinor loved being in the cold weather, but the next day he was ready to return home to Austin. After they arrived home, Gordon received a letter from Immigration asking him to send Rinor's request for a visa extension to the San Antonio office.

On December 27, Norma wrote to Gordon, Irma, and Rinor. Rinor's sister Cindy added a note to her mother's letter to Rinor. The letter's read as follows:

"Dear Gordon and Irma,

"How are you doing? Great I hope. Rinor is doing great too isn't he?

"Gordon, Irma you just left about 2 minutes before Jocy appeared in the airport. She read a Bible for me

there and asked me if I had any money. Then she wanted to get my passport and my ticket but I did not give them to her. She said that she will not go to the Philippines if she cannot take Rinor with her. Please do not give her the Power of Attorney. She frightened me when she said she would go to the American Counsel and she did not leave me alone until the airplane took off.

"I arrived in Seoul at about 12:45 p.m. Thursday and my sister and son met me at the Manila Airport. Then we took a ship to Iloilo. We arrived in Iloilo at about 10:00 a.m. Friday and got home safe and comfortable. Some of the travel was a little hard but it was okay.

"About my passport-the custom's officer did not take my visa; he just stamped it Extension.

"And then I went directly to the mission with my husband. I talked to Angie and she gave me my daughter, who was the only child left in the mission. I am happy I got my daughter but before that they asked my husband to sign papers that Jocy was their guardian. My husband did not sign it.

"On Monday we went to the hospital in Western Visayas Medical Center at Iloilo City and Sidney was X-Rayed again. I paid 150 Pesos and the doctor said that Sidney will be admitted on December 24 but the female surgical ward is already filled up. We are on the waiting list. Gordon, Irma please help pray for Sidney on Monday December 28th. I will go to the hospital again if there is a vacancy in the female surgical ward.

"Bye regards and sweet kisses to both of you.
"Love Norma.
"Merry Christmas and a prosperous New Year!!!"

Norma's letter to Rinor read as follows:

"Dear Nonay,
   "How are you Rinor? It is great isn't it?
   "Your father, mom, brothers, sisters miss you very much. We all love you. We hope you are happy there. We are happy too that you are with Gordon and Irma.
   "You know I told your father, brothers, and sisters, everybody that you are very happy staying with Gordon and Irma, and I also said, "They are very good."
   "Okay always pray, study hard, and be good. Love your Tito Gordon and Tita Irma.

   "Bye sweet kisses.
   "Love father, mother, brothers, and sisters."

To the bottom of Norma's letter sister Cindy added:

"Dear Tito Nonoy,
   "Hi, Hello, How are you? I hope that you are in good health. How about your schooling? Enjoy yourself as well as your Tito Gordon and Tita Irma. Noy, did you learn how to speak English? Noy, did you pray to God every day, and before your meal, and especially before you go to sleep? When will you go back to the Philippines because

we really miss you so much. Noy, I am sorry that I have no gifts for you because I have no money. I told Nanay when they go back there to please write me okay? Before I stop my short letter, I give my warmest regards to you, Tito Gordon and Tita Irma.

"Noy, study your lessons everyday and don't forget to pray to God."

"Always, Nanay Cindy."

Chapter 24 – Return to the Philippines

On January 3, 1993, Gordon was concerned because Rinor still had a rash and sores on his lower left leg. It was a reoccurring problem that disappeared when the rash was treated but reappeared when Rinor wore his Jobst suit. The Jobst suit was being washed with a soft detergent as directed. Gordon called the Shriner's Burns Hospital-Galveston to discuss Rinor's rash problem and find out if Rinor still needed to wear a medicated silicone pad under his arm. Gordon pointed out that Rinor was a very active twelve-year-old and that the silicon pads never stayed put. Rinor was still wearing his arm and leg braces to bed at night, and Gordon wondered if that was still necessary. The doctor's answer was yes to all his questions.

The next day Gordon wrote United Airlines explaining Norma, Sidney, and Rinor's situations. Norma had to return to the Philippines to be with her sixteen-year-old daughter, who had a mass on her lung. Gordon knew the odds were against him, but he hoped American Airlines might donate round-trip airfare for Norma to return to the United States to be with Rinor for his upcoming surgery.

On January 5 Gordon went with Rinor to the Shriner's Burns Hospital-Galveston. Rinor was taking Penicillin VK antibiotic orally to treat his sensitive bacterial infections and applying Mercurochrome to his silicone pads. The doctor's prognosis was that Rinor was doing fine and the hospital staff intended to fit him for a new Jobst vest on his next visit to the hospital, which was scheduled for the 26th. Rinor's left arm required further healing; it was still too tight and tough. There was very little elbow flexibility. The doctor's would still have to take skin from the right side of his chest for an arm and elbow graft. The skin on his arm and elbow needed to be loosened so the stiffness in his elbow could be released. The doctors planned to do the skin graft in March.

On January 9 Gordon took Rinor to a middle school near the house to practice riding his bike. The weather was mild, and Gordon thought the temperature would be neither too hot nor too cold for Rinor. Rinor rode his bike around the one-eighth-mile track several times. He really loved to ride his bike. However, the next day Rinor's leg was very sore, probably from riding the bike too much. That evening the Irwin's took Rinor to the last half of the University of Texas basketball game against Southern Methodist University at the Erwin Center. Rinor loved basketball, and it gave him a chance to rest his sore leg.

Toward the middle of the month Gordon tried to call Norma several times. Supposedly Norma had access to the telephone of a neighbor in the Philippines who said she would get Norma if anyone called. However, the neighbor didn't answer the phone; they never seemed to be home. After numerous attempts to call Norma, Gordon wrote to her on the 19th inquiring about Sidney's health and informing her that Rinor was doing fine. Gordon asked Norma when she thought she would be able to leave Sidney and return to Texas. He also advised Norma to do whatever was necessary so she could return to Texas. He asked Norma to let him know if she needed anything from him or Irma. Gordon told her he would call her on February 8th at 7:00 a.m. his time, or 8:00 p.m. her time.

As an interesting side note Gordon let Norma know that Rinor was riding a bicycle by himself for the first time. He also mentioned that Rinor liked to play with the two boys next door and spend as much time as possible outdoors.

Gordon went with Rinor to the Shriner's Burns Hospital-Galveston on the 26 th for his next scheduled appointment. After examining Rinor, Dr. McCauley told Gordon he did not think he could use Rinor's right chest skin for his upcoming skin graft. The doctor thought that further healing was needed for Rinor's left chest and rib area. He was unsure when skin could be grafted to the open areas.

Dr. McCauley was pleased with Rinor's arm and leg progress and wanted to have Rinor's elbow checked weekly. Gordon told Dr. McCauley that he would try to set up routine elbow examinations for Rinor. Then Rinor was measured for a new Jobst garment, and the doctor told Gordon that the garments would be sent to him. Rinor's next appointment was set up for April 27 th.

At the same time that Rinor was in the hospital, his sister Sidney was having X-rays taken at the Medical Imaging Center in Iloilo. Dr.Barronds's diagnostic X-Ray report read as follows:

"Chest PA view shows osteolysis involving the angle and posterior portion of the 3 rd rib left side associated with soft tissue mass adjacent to the area of bone destruction. The remaining visualized lung field appears normal. The heart is not enlarged. The diaphragmatic leaflets are smooth with intact ostophrenic sinuses.

"Comparative study with previous film taken 12/18/92 shows no significant change in radiographic appearance of the left upper hermithorax findings.

"Findings may be due to:
- *Primary or metastic bone tumor, 3 rd rib, left.*
- *Pleural neoplastic process with bone involvement.*
- *Pulmonary tumor with bone involvement."*

On the same day Gordon received a discouraging reply to his United Airlines inquiry on behalf of Norma. The letter read as follows:

"Thank you very much for your recent letter to Mr. Ruppert and for giving United Airlines the opportunity to consider your request for a complimentary airline ticket from Manila to Houston for Norma Marcial.

"United Airlines receives numerous requests for free travel for worthy causes like yours and I regret we are not

214

in a position to provide assistance. Until the financial performance of our company improves, we will not be considering any expansion of our corporate or foundation donation programs.

"We appreciate your interest and enclose a copy of our mission and guidelines for your file. I am sorry we cannot be of assistance and hope that you will understand..."

By the end of the month Gordon was very upset with both Dr. McCauley and the Shriner's Burns Hospital-Galveston. He expressed his feelings in a letter to Bob Emrie, a member of the Shriner's Burns Hospital-Galveston board of directors. First Gordon pointed out the apparent lack of communications between the Burns Hospital staff and Seton physical therapy staff. Seton had sent detailed physical therapy records to the hospital. They were hand-carried by Norma but ended up being filed and not brought to the attention of Dr. McCauley.

In desperation Gordon asked Bob to intercede for him and find out how long it would be before skin could be grafted to Rinor's left arm and chest area. He also questioned if a graft or additional surgery was needed. Finally Gordon questioned the need for frequent Seton physical therapy since it didn't seem to have any effect. After talking with Bob Emrie, Gordon found out that Bob had the utmost confidence in Dr. McCauley's judgment. At this point he felt it would be futile to mail the letters. Gordon had to admit to himself that Dr. McCauley was the one who determined Rinor's treatment, even if some people disagreed with him.

On February 4, Norma wrote the following letter to Irma and Gordon.

"*Dear Gordon, Irma,*

"*Hi! Hello there! I hope you are great. How is Rinor doing? I hope it's great.*

"*Well, you know Sidney was not admitted to Western Visayas Medical Center because it was full, so we went to Dr. Barronda about 3 kilometers from Zaraga. Sidney has not taken any medicine since she was hospitalized in the Western Visasyas Medical Center. Dr. Barronda gave her three kinds of medicine and bottle of vitamins.*

"*Then we went for a checkup four times and Dr. Barronda said we needed to go for another x-ray again; the results are enclosed. Gordon, Irma, please help Sidney even if I cannot return to Texas. Please help her get the medical treatments she needs. I do not know what to do. It's OK if I cannot come back to Texas, but please help Sidney.*

"*You know I am crying as I write this letter because I do not know what I can do. You are a person who can help us. I used all my money for Sidney's medicine. If she needs to be operated on I have no money for hospitals or medicine.*

"*When will Rinor be operated on? Anyway I have told you and Irma about Sidney's problem. I hope you can be of help because I do not know what to do. But, if I could come back to Texas I would be very happy to. "Sweet kisses for both of you and goodbye, Love Norma.*"

She also wrote a short note of encouragement to Rinor reminding him to do well in his studies at school and to be good. She admonished him to treat Irma and Gordon like his own parents because they were good-hearted people for helping to care for him in her absence. She signed her letter to Rinor with sweet kisses from mother, father, sisters, and brothers.

After receiving Norma's letter Gordon called a cancer center to see if he could send Sidney's X-rays to them along with a brief medical history for possible evaluation. The center seemed very disinterested in trying to help out in this manner and merely suggested that Gordon "bring the girl in and we'll see what we can do for her." Gordon had hoped against hope that the girl's X-rays and letter from her doctor might be used by the cancer center's doctors to help evaluate her condition. Gordon thought that if doctors in this country had some suggestions for her treatments, he might be able to raise some money to bring her here. He knew there was no way that either he or the Ben Hur Shrine could afford to bring her to this country when her medical condition was unknown and undetermined.

Later Gordon talked with both Sidney and Norma on the telephone. He asked them what they wanted him to do. They really didn't have an answer. As it turned out, doing nothing at this time was the correct thing to do, as her medications eventually solved the problem.

On February 5, Rinor went to see the Harlem Globetrotters play basketball with Janice and Scott Sandler and their son Scott who was about seven years old. Janice was a friend of

Irma's from work. Basketball was one of Rinor's favorite sports, and he thoroughly enjoyed it. The next night when Gordon put Rinor to bed, Rinor told him he wanted to stay in the United States and not go back home to the Philippines. Rinor feared with just cause that there might not be enough money to bring him back to the United States. Gordon comforted the boy the best he could without making any promises he might not be able to keep.

The following day the Channel 7 TV News team visited the Irwins at noon for a television interview. They asked Gordon to tell Rinor's story, so Gordon started at the beginning and told Rinor's story one more time. It was a great testimony to the boy's courage and determination and the work of the Shriner's Burns Hospital-Galveston. Gordon hoped to say more about Seton's help with Rinor's physical therapy, but only a fraction of the interview was aired at 5:50 and 10:00 p.m.

On the 8th Gordon also called Ann at Galveston and tried to make an appointment for Rinor, whose foot was hurting. Ann said she would get in touch with Dr. Line one, of Dr. McCauley's assistants, and call Gordon back. Gordon was so frustrated by the12th that he sent a letter to Norma, hoping to get in touch with her. He asked Norma to write and let him know how Sidney was doing. He wanted to know if she wanted to come back to Texas to be with Rinor. Gordon also informed Norma that Rinor's surgery would be postponed for six months to a year.

The same day, Ann called back trying to set up an appointment for Rinor. However, the notice was too short, and Gordon could not make arrangements for an appointment on Saturday, which was the next day.

By February 16, Gordon had found out from Norma that Sidney's condition was improving. Medication was dissolving the calcium spot near her lung. Norma wanted to return to the United States to be with Rinor in case his March surgery wasn't postponed. Immediately Gordon called Ms. Mathers at United Airlines and started working with her to get a return flight for Norma.

Rinor turned twelve in October, and while his mother was gone, Irma and Gordon decided it was time for him to do his own chores. Irma had Rinor make his own bed and clean his room and bathroom. Rinor never argued about doing this work; he just did it. Sometimes Rinor's room and bathroom didn't pass Tita Irma's inspection, but he tried and he did the best he could. It should be remembered that Rinor had never had to do anything like this before and barely knew one end of a toilet brush from the other. But he did learn!

On February 23, Norma called Gordon collect at 1:10 a. m. Sidney was much better and Norma was ready to return to the United States. She was just waiting for someone to send her the tickets, which she couldn't afford to pay for. That evening the Ben Hur Shrine Temple was having its annual Circus Fish Fry, an event to raise money to send children who were poor or had disabilities to the annual Shrine Circus. Gordon planned to talk to Gene Freudenberg to discuss ways to raise money to bring Norma back to the United States. The Shriners passed the hat that night and collected $600 toward Norma's airfare. Then Potentate Sammy Powell donated matching funds from the temple's transportation fund. Sammy told Gordon that the temple's transportation fund would continue to match any funds that Gordon could raise. After receiving the good news Gordon called Norma and told her to make arrangements to return to the United States on March 13, 1993.

On Monday, March 1, Gordon wrote to Faith to let her know he had heard from Norma, who was eager to return to the States and no longer deeply concerned about Sidney's condition. Gordon mentioned he was sending a copy of Sidney's X-ray report, although he didn't know what it meant. Gordon also informed Faith that $600 had already been raised for Norma's flight and he was planning a backyard sale to raise money. He also sent out a letter to several friends asking for donations. Gordon told Faith he could raise the needed funds so he could make advance reservations with United Airlines for Norma's return on Saturday, March 13th.

The next day Gordon went with Rinor to his appointment at the Shriner's Burns Hospital-Galveston. The doctor looked at Rinor's sore foot and leg. He was given instructions on physical therapy, bathing, and applying his external medications. Rinor's prescription for Penicillin VK 125 mg was refilled. Rinor took his penicillin pills three times a day to help fight the persistent bacterial infection that seemed to constantly plague him. The trip also gave Gordon the chance to talk with Dr. McCauley about future plans for Rinor's treatment. Gordon also brought Dr. McCauley a sealed letter from the Seton physical therapy unit in Austin.

. Dr. McCauley followed up on Gordon's expression of concern with the following letter:

"In follow up to our conversation at the Shriner's Burns Hospital-Galveston on 3-2-93, I am writing you this letter to confirm and document the findings on Rinor Marcial. This Filipino boy is recovering from reconstruction of his burn injuries to his left arm, chest and lower extremity. His reconstructive surgery should be followed by a period of rehabilitation and intensive occupational therapy as his scars continue to mature. He will require further reconstructive surgeries after his scars mature and further rehabilitation is achieved.

"The following procedures are expected to be planned in about one year. In the meantime the patient is followed by our service and is under our care in Galveston. After future reconstruction to his elbow and chest area we anticipate additional rehabilitation will take at least six months. We will continue to follow Rinor as scheduled on a regular basis. Please contact my office for any further details or questions."

On Saturday the 6 th the Irwins had a garage sale at their home. Irma sold her prized clown collection and a lot of other items the Irwins had in their home. Bonnie, Milly, and Irma ran the sale. Gene Freudenberg, Joe King, Greg, Bonnie, and Milly donated other items. The sale raised an addition $231, but the group didn't raise as much money as they'd hoped to because a lot of donations that were promised never materialized. However, Potentate Sammy Powell donated enough money from the Ben Hur transportation fund to purchase Norma's round trip ticket which cost $1,513.25. Gordon purchased Norma's tickets on Monday, March 8th. The round trip tickets would be good for one year.

Later that month Gordon went to the installation of officers for the Ladies Oriental Shrine and talked with Gene about the possibility of getting a refund on Norma and Rinor's return airline tickets. His plan was to put money back into the Ben Hur's transportation fund until it was needed.

By Thursday March 18, Rinor's favorite mode of transportation finally broke down and had to be repaired. Gordon took the well-used bicycle to Cothran's Bike Shop on Burnet Road and paid $16.74 for new bearings and a new rear wheel hub. A short time later the Irwins had another garage sale. This time they sold a refrigerator for $25. The money was given to the Transportation Fund for Norma's return tickets.

On Easter Sunday, April 11, Rinor and the Irwin's went to Houston to visit Irma's sister Bertie. The day was too hot for Rinor, and he ended up with a headache. The following Friday Gordon talked with Isela Sanchez in Senator Lloyd Bentson's office about visa extensions for Rinor and his mother. Isela told Gordon that as long as the immigration form was extended, visa extension was unnecessary.

On April 27, Rinor had another routine checkup at the Shriner's Burns Hospital-Galveston. This time the news was good. Rinor's infection cleared up, his foot and leg were healed, and there were no open wounds. Rinor received some rehabilitation and photos were taken. His next appointment was made for two months later, June 29 at noon. When Gordon talked with Norma about refunding her airline tickets, she was uncertain about any conditions that might apply. After talking with the airline company Gordon found out that the unused portion of Rinor's ticket was fully refundable.

On Thursday May 6, *Austin American-Statesman* carried a story "Austin Couple Opens Home to Filipino Victim of Burns." In a typical family picture, the Irwin's, Rinor, and his mother sat together in the living room of their rented home. The story told how the Irwins first met Rinor and his mother at the airport. Then it told how the Irwins volunteered to provide a home for Norma and Rinor while Rinor was in the country being treated for his burns. The story also told how Rinor had been burned in December 1988 and gone eighteen months with minimal treatment before being flown to the Shriner's Burns Hospital-Galveston by the Ben Hur Shrine organization.

Finally the story told how Rinor's first surgery freed his arm from his chest and his leg from his thigh. As a result of this surgery Rinor could walk and run for the first time since he was eight years old. The article went on to explain about the twenty two children's hospitals nationwide including the two hospitals in Texas – the Shriner's Orthopedic Hospital-Houston and the Shriner's Burns Hospital-Galveston The article was timely because the Shriner's were having a "Shake the Bucket" drive on Saturday, collecting donations at about twenty main intersections in town. The funds donated help pay for hospital operating expenses and burn's research.

In a related interview Potentate Bob Emrie, a Ben Hur Shriner since 1967 and a member of the board of director's for the Shriner's Burns Hospital-Galveston said, "This is an annual fund raiser. We have to support our hospitals. These hospitals are making a difference and giving children a second chance."

On June 6, Gordon requested a refund on Rinor's ticket and wrote to United Airlines for information about a refund on Norma's ticket. Norma's return ticket was for a non-stop coach trip from Houston to San Francisco leaving at 8:40 a.m. and arriving at 10:55 p.m. This leg of the trip included two meals, dinner, and a movie.

Rinor went to the Shriner's Burns Hospital-Galveston on June 29 for a checkup and rehabilitation work. More photos were taken and he was scheduled to return for another visit two months later on August 24, at 1:00 p.m. On August 6, Gordon called United Airlines about Norma's refund. He was told that someone would call him the following Monday.

Rinor went to the Shriner's Burns Hospital-Galveston on September 7, and given instructions on skin and wound care. He was also scheduled to return later in September for a CT scan and examination by an orthopedic consultant. On September 16 a postcard was sent to Norma scheduling Rinor for surgery at the Shriner's Burns Hospital-Galveston on September 19, 1993. The CT scan examination by an orthopedic consultant and surgery scheduled for September 19 never took place. These were just other examples of confusing information sent out by the hospital at this time. Rinor did return to the Shriner's Burns Hospital-Galveston on September 21 and was given instructions with regard to wearing his new Jobst suit.

On September 16, 1993 Jocy Johnson wrote to one of the Past Imperial Potentates of the Shrine. She recapped her role in Rinor's story and complained that Rinor and his mother were originally scheduled to stay with a Filipino family in Killeen. In the rest of the letter she attributed Norma's rebellion against her to some sort of direct or indirect brainwashing by Gordon. Nothing could have been further from the truth.

Despite Gordon's earlier gentle admonition, Jocy refused to accept the fact that Norma rebelled against her because she didn't want to be treated like a child. Norma didn't want to be told what to do and when to do it. Norma didn't want to be exploited and didn't want her son to be exploited. All Norma and her son wanted were the same degree of freedom they enjoyed with the Irwins.

In a reply letter dated September 28, 1993, the executive director of the Shrine informed Jocy there was absolutely nothing the Shrine of North America could do toward solving her problem. He pointed out that Rinor Marcial was in the United States with his mother, his legal guardian, and that all decisions about where he went and what he did were hers and hers alone.

On October 26, the Shriner's Burns Hospital-Galveston told Norma that it would be two years before they could operate on Rinor again. The doctors at the Burns Hospital thought it would take that long for Rinor's chest and rib area to heal well enough to consider additional grafting.

Immediately Gordon started to make reservations for Rinor and Norma to return to the Philippines. They left for the Philippines on October 31 on a United Airlines flight. Rinor's return flight cost $1,344 and Gordon deeply regretted getting a refund on Rinor's ticket. When Gordon bought Rinor's ticket he was eleven years old and the $600 fare seemed reasonable. Rinor was now thirteen years old and had to fly as an adult.

On November 8, the Shriner's Burns Hospital-Galveston sent a "consent for treatment" form to Gordon for surgery to release Rinor's left elbow. They pointed out that infection, bleeding, damage to adjacent structure, and the need for future procedures were possible risks and hazards regarding Rinor's medical treatments. Because Rinor had left for Manila a week earlier, the form was never signed. This was one more example of poor communications on the part of the hospital.

On November 10, 1993, Norma wrote as follows:

"Dear Gordon and Irma,

"Hello how are you doing? Rinor is doing great. He started school Monday, November 8, 1993. Our trip was very hard but fine because when we arrived in Manila there was a typhoon. It was very stormy and we all got wet. Rinor was crying and yelling. We took a taxi to my son's house which he is renting and we arrived around 2 p.m. Tuesday. The plane arrived at Manila airport at

12:00 p.m. midnight. We stayed at my son's house two nights because there was no ship to Iloilo.

"We got on a ship at 4:00 p.m. Wednesday and my son went with us to Iloilo. It was an easy trip because all we had was my son's carry-on luggage. My son returned to Manila 2 days later. My husband and Angelo met us at the pier.

"All my children are here together. We are very happy. One of Rinor's Jobst garments is already torn. We love you all.

"Love, Rinor and Norma"

On December 1 Rinor wrote the following letter:

"Dear Tito Gordon and Tita Irma
    "Hi! How are you?"
    "I'm really fine but my arm has sores and my mom will put the medicine I bought on them. Don't forget my Jobst suit has torn and don't forget my silicone because the burns on my chest have sores too. I miss you all. Thank you for helping me. I love you!!!
    "Good luck to all.
    "Love Rinor
    "Love Norma"

The December 1993 Vol. LX, No. 11 issue of *The Chariot*, the Ben Hur Shrine Temple's magazine, printed the "Thank-you" letters from Rinor and his mother. Norma thanked the Shriners for bringing them to the United States and for providing hospitalization and surgery for Rinor along with the medications and other services for them at no cost to them.

Next she thanked Gordon and Irma for providing her a home, food, clothing, and Rinor's schooling, again at no cost to them. Then she thanked as many people in the Shrine as she could remember. She especially thanked Bob and Milly Oakes, Gene and LaDell Freudenberg, Boone and Lorraine Dowdy, Potentate Sammy Powell and his wife Judy, Joe King and Bonnie Stanley. She also thanked Ben Hur's Greeters Unit and Ben Hera Court's Demolition Unit.

She also thanked Hope Faith Mava, and Craig and Inez Franklin, and finally, she thanked everyone again and said she would never forget what everyone had done for her and her son. Everyone was special to her and she loved them all.

In Rinor's letter he thanked all the Shriners for helping him with his burns. He gave special thanks to the Freudenberg's for all their help and to the Dowdy's for driving him to the Shriner's Burns Hospital-Galveston in the Ben Hur van. He also thanked Greg Trejo, another Ben Hur van driver, and his wife Stella, for driving him to the hospital.

Then he thanked Joe King and Bob and Milly Oakes for helping him. Finally he thanked all the ladies of the Shrine and Bonnie Stanley, a good friend.

He signed his letter "Love Rinor" and made a smiley face on top of the "R".

On December 21, Gordon received notification that Norma's application to Extend/Change Nonimmigrant Status had been extended to March 13, 1994. Of course it was not needed because the Marcials had already returned to the Philippines.

At Christmas-time Gordon, Irma, and their daughter JoAnna and her family went to Utah to visit with family and friends. Gordon knew it would be just a matter of time before Rinor would be returning to the United States for further treatment.

Chapter 25 – Reunited at Last

Norma and Rinor left for the Philippines on Sunday October 31, 1993 about 8:00 a.m. The plane arrived in Manila about midnight. Shortly after the plane landed, a typhoon struck. The weather turned dark and stormy, bringing strong winds and torrential rains. Norma had hoped her sister Nanette would meet them, but no one showed up at the airport. After Rinor and his mother waited for Nenette until about 2:00 a.m.-they decided to hire a taxi and have a driver take them to the home of their oldest son, Marcial. Marcial and some former neighbors from Negros rented a small single story residential house in the Rizal Park area.

When Norma and Rinor arrived in the neighborhood, it was still dark and raining. They could not remember what Marcial's house looked like. Rinor and his mother got out of the taxi and began looking for the house. Soon they were soaking wet and Rinor began crying. It was dark, and he was lost and miserable. Norma told Rinor to sit down while she began going door to door trying to find Marcial's house. Rinor got tired of waiting and went to one of the houses and knocked on the door. When a man answered the door, Rinor asked him if he knew where his brother Marcial lived. The man did not, and Rinor waited on the porch for his mother to return.

When Norma finally located her oldest son, Marcial, he told her he hadn't been expecting her to arrive so soon. After a brief hug and kiss they rushed back to get Rinor. Marcial was so happy to see Rinor that he picked up his little brother and gave him a big hug. Then Marcial began to carry Rinor as he had done before his surgery. "Put him down. Put him down. He can walk now. He can walk now!" exclaimed Norma. Marcial was so happy to see his little brother walk again after five long years that he cried. When they arrived at Marcial's home, everyone was happy to see that Rinor could walk again. It was a miracle of modern medicine, Norma's faith, and Rinor's determination.

Norma and Rinor were tired and wet but also very happy. Marcial and his friends insisted that Norma and Rinor tell them all about America. When Rinor showed Marcial and his friends his walkie-talkies, they were fascinated by them. It was like a group of children discovering a new toy for the first time. Indeed the walkie-talkies were luxury toys from America. Few Filipino children would ever get to see or play with a set of walkie-talkies.

The next morning Norma's sister Nenette came by to pick up Marcial. She was planning to go to the airport to meet Norma and Rinor's flight. Nenette was shocked but pleasantly surprised to discover that Norma and Rinor had already arrived. Norma and Rinor stayed with Marcial for two nights while they waited for a ship to carry them home to Iloilo. At first Marcial hesitated to go with Norma and Rinor to Iloilo, but Norma talked him into going back home with them for a few days. Marcial lent his mother and brother some carry-on luggage to make their trip a little easier. Norma bought tickets for the trip, and Norma, Marcial, and Rinor boarded the ship for Iloilo on Wednesday morning. The ship traveled non-stop from Manila and arrived at the dock at Iloilo the next afternoon. Rinor was very happy that his entire family was together again, and the family was very happy for Rinor because he could run and play as a normal boy again. After spending two days with the family in Zarraga, Marcial returned to Manila.

Rinor's Jobst vest tore shortly after they arrived in the Philippines. The tear started as a small hole under his armpit. The tear became larger and larger until the Jobst suit was so loose that it wasn't doing him any good. Rinor was active and growing very fast, and he quickly outgrew his Jobst garments. However, he was still very small even at the age of thirteen. Norma wrote to Gordon telling him about the torn Jobst garment and Gordon notified the Shriner's Burns Hospital-Galveston. A short time later the Shriner's Burns Hospital-Galveston sent a new Jobst garment to Rinor.

Rinor was enrolled in the fifth grade when he entered elementary school at Zarraga. Sometimes he would take his lunch to school and sometimes he would take enough money to buy something to eat there. However, there was no cafeteria at the school. After school Rinor would run across the freeway near the school and walk about a mile and a half to his grandmother's house. Ricardito would pick Rinor up after work and take him back to Zarraga and fix dinner for the family.

Sometimes Rinor went on fishing trips with his father. They would fish along the inlet and bays and in small lakes. They used shrimp, small minnows, and worms for bait. Sometimes they would catch their bait with small nets. Usually they would fish from the banks with bamboo poles and fishing lines. Between the two of them they caught many fish for the family. In a way the fishing trips made up for some of the lost time between father and son. Rinor and his father spent some quality time together for the first time in about six years.

In January 1994 three typhoons struck the Marcial's small bamboo home in Zarraga. Water rose in the rice fields until it was waist-deep in the Marcial home. The strong winds blew palm branches off the roof and damaged the structural integrity of the house. The typhoons virtually blew substantial portions of the bamboo house down every time they struck. When the water rose, the Marcial family could not see the Jetmatic pump in their backyard. They had to rely on rain water to drink, and sterile water was not available to cleanse Rinor's wounds.

When the rains subsided, clean water was available from a deep-well Jetmatic pump about half a mile away. The Jetmatic pump in the backyard of the Marcial home pumped water from a shallow well. The use of this water was very limited because it was salt water. When times were rough and money was scarce, there was always something to eat in the Marcial home. One vegetable meal consisted of green bananas, young bamboo shoots, and other green leafy vegetables. The vegetables were soaked in salt water and then cooked or boiled.

Ricardito's bamboo bungalow was moved once and destroyed a number of times in Zarraga. The first bamboo bungalow was built on Carlos's land. It was destroyed a number of times by typhoons. In the late summer and early fall of 1992 the original bamboo bungalow was moved from Carlos's land to land owned by Ricardito's brother-in-law Isko. Ricardito's family and Isko's family literally picked up the bamboo bungalow and carried it to Isko's land a short distance away.

Isko gave Ricardito and his family half a hectare of land, which is equal to 5,000 square meters or about 1.3 acres. In return Ricardito helped work the land and the rice fields. Ricardito was free to plant whatever he wanted on his half hectare. During the off-season Ricardito planted many vegetables and shared them with Isko and his family. Eventually the original bamboo bungalow was damaged beyond repair and replaced by a larger, sturdier bungalow. However, the new, sturdier bungalow was also subject to the ravages of typhoons.

That same month someone came to Rinor's school and took photographs of him. Rinor didn't know who the person was and really didn't care if his picture was taken. However, when Rinor told Norma about it, she became very upset and angry. Norma went to school with Rinor the next day to talk to his teacher. Norma didn't know why someone had taken pictures of her son. As Rinor's mother she thought this person should have at least asked her for permission to take the pictures. Norma then asked Rinor's teacher and principal not to allow other people to take Rinor's picture in his classroom.

As it turned out, the person who took the pictures worked for Angie Aragon, according to Cindy and Sidney. She was the same person who went with Sidney when Sidney had X-rays taken at the Western Visayas Medical Center. Apparently Jocy wanted pictures showing that Rinor's left arm and leg were freed and that he had returned home.

While attending school in the Philippines, Rinor studied English, science, social studies, math, art and home economics. In home economics he learned table manners, sewing, crafts, and cooking. These subjects are similar to those studied in the United States, although U.S. students often have music and physical education as well. The reason for this is probably that few Filipino families can afford musical instruments and the weather in the Philippines is often too hot for sports and other strenuous activities.

Rinor's brother Norman, who was one year older than Rinor, was living in Iloilo City with his father's aunt. Norman worked in a small flea market store where they sold fish, rice, and other food staples. The food store was an open yard with many other food stores constructed of wood frames and tent material. Ricarditio's aunt Lucing and her friend Pakha owned the food store and the Jeepneys that Ricardito drove. For his work Norman earned his room, board, and tuition to the Sacred Heart Academy High School. Norman graduated from the Sacred Heart Academy in 1996 when Norma and

Rinor were in the United States for Rinor's continuing medical treatments.

In February Norma took Rinor to town to have photographs taken. Rinor cried because he didn't want to take off his Jobst garment in front of so many people. There was a large window at the studio. Outside the studio many people were staring at Rinor through the window. After reading a letter from Gordon, Rinor also pitched a fit for ice cream and pizza. Norma told Rinor that there was no ice cream or pizza in the city. She suddenly realized how spoiled Rinor had become by the food and his experiences in the United States.

In early February Gordon tried to obtain United Airlines United Mileage Plus credit for Norma and Rinor's return trip to the Philippines. However, his request was denied by Sam Lewis, a customer service representative. The reason for the denial was that retroactive credit in Mileage Plus was limited to mileage earned in the past twelve months. Norma and Rinor's travel to the United States had been about twenty months earlier.

In late March Norma wrote to Gordon to let him know that she had received a package the Shriner's had sent. The Ben Hur Patrol Unit had chipped in along with other individual Shriners to purchase supplies of alcohol, silicone pads, Neosporin, and soap. However, the package did not contain any cotton balls, which Norma was expecting. She informed Gordon that Rinor was taking a bath twice a day and had no open sores. She also mentioned that she had received a new Jobst garment form the Shriner's Burns Hospital-Galveston in early March. Norma commented on the weather, noting that it was now summer in the Philippines and very, very hot. The heat was especially hard on Rinor.

In April while Rinor was still in school, Norma and Cindy went to work at Balintawak. Balintawak is in east Manila and part of Quezon City, the former capitol of the Philippines. Norma put Sidney in charge of cleaning and dressing Rinor's damaged skin. Everyone in the family knew how to care for Rinor, and they all helped him at one time or another after he took his bath. First Rinor's silicone pads were cleaned with cotton balls soaked in alcohol and dried. Then Rinor had to let his damaged skin air and dry. Finally Aquaphor was applied to the healed areas and Neosporin was applied to the remaining open areas. Aquaphor is for severely dry skin. It provides a moist, uniform coating. Norma also had Sidney take pictures of Rinor at four-month intervals and sent them to the Shriner's Burns Hospital-Galveston. Doctors there hoped to evaluate Rinor's progress based on the photographs and physical measurements.

On June 19, 1994, Norma wrote to Gordon to let him know that Cindy had been working with her in Manila since April 13. Norma and Cindy were sending money back home to the rest of the family who were still living in Iloilo. Toward the end of June, Rinor wrote to Tito Gordon and Tita Irma, informing them that he was in the sixth grade at Zarraga Elementary School. He also mentioned that his old Jobst garment was damaged and he didn't like the new Jobst garment the hospital had sent him. Rinor said he could hardly wait to come back to America because he missed Texas and especially Tito Gordon.

In late August Norma wrote a short note to Gordon and Irma telling them that Rinor had received his new Jobst garment on August 1. Rinor was very happy and really liked the new Jobst garment. Norma also mentioned that Rinor was in the sixth grade and doing well. She also sent a note to the Shriner's Burns Hospital-Galveston at the same time.

A couple of weeks later in early September Norma wrote to Gordon again , mentioning that Jocy had been to Zarraga trying to pick up Rinor. Ricardito was caught by surprise, but he did not let Jocy take Rinor to Cebu without Norma's permission. Jocy took some pictures of Rinor, probably for use in her mission's newsletter, and left. Ricardito wrote to Norma, letting her know that Jocy wanted to take Rinor to Cebu for additional medical treatments. Norma wrote back, letting Ricardito know that she didn't want Rinor going anywhere with Jocy. Norma wrote that she planned to return home to Iloilo and tell Jocy herself. Because of Norma's refusal to let Rinor go with her, Jocy told Norma she was "very bad."

Norma also let Gordon know that Rinor was out of medicine again and needed more silicone pads. She sent her thanks to the Shriners and especially the Irwins for their help and support.

In early January 1995 Gordon began making plans to bring Norma and Rinor back to the United States for surgery to gain some flexibility in Rinor's left elbow. On January 5, 1995, Gordon wrote to Ann Chavaria at the Shriner's Burns Hospital-Galveston asking her a series of questions. Had she been getting the pictures of Rinor as requested? Did Rinor's skin show any signs of healing progress? Had the Shriner's

Burns Hospital-Galveston and Dr. McCauley expressed an opinion about whether or not Rinor should be operated on when he returned in October? Apparently Ann never received Gordon's letter, or it was misdirected or ignored. Gordon's letter was never answered, and it caused him great concern.

On February 7, Gordon wrote to the U.S. Embassy on behalf of Norma and Rinor. His letter read as follows:

"In Zarraga, Iloilo is a young man by the name of Rinor Marcial. Rinor came to the U.S. in June 1992 with, according to information we have, a lady by the name of Jocy Johnson signing the paperwork there at the embassy and therefore being responsible for Rinor and his mother, Norma Marcial.

"While in the U.S. Rinor and his mother stayed with us and this was noted each time we requested an extension of their visas (twice). In October 1993 Rinor and his mother returned home as the medical staff of the Shriner's Burns Hospital-Galveston, concluded that Rinor would need at least two years of healing before another operation could be performed. This operation could release his arm which cannot now be bent.

"It is now getting close to the time when they should return so that:

A.   We can evaluate the skins condition, and if need be, insure proper expeditious care.

B.   His arm can be operated on to be released so that he can bend it.

"We respectfully request from you any assistance that you can give us to insure that:

A.   Jocy Johnson's name is taken off the records and our names be inserted.

B.   Informing us of any paperwork that we will need to send to you, either from the Shriner's Burns Hospital-Galveston and/or ourselves.

C.   Rinor and his mother, Norma, be allowed to return to the U.S. no later than June 15 of this year.

"As you can tell we are novices at dealing with our embassy and your assistance and guidance through this will be greatly appreciated. If you feel a fax is warranted please feel free to fax us at (512) 873-0016."

This time the embassy did not answer the facsimile. Finally Gordon wrote to Norma, telling her about his unsuccessful efforts with the embassy. Ricardito forwarded Gordon's letter to Norma at her work address in Manila. Norma personally took Gordon's letter to the U.S. Embassy and they gave her an application for a visa. However, the embassy staff told Norma that they would hold her and Rinor's paperwork until they received a letter from Dr. McCauley. At this point Norma was very confused and she wrote to Gordon on March 10, asking his help in contacting Dr. McCauley.

On March 20, Gordon sent a facsimile to Nancy at the Shriner's Burns Hospital-Galveston. It was a new, retyped version of the January letter asking the hospital to contact the U. S. Embassy. Again Gordon's request went unanswered. Three weeks later Gordon sent another facsimile to Nancy at

Galveston. Gordon reminded Nancy that he still needed a letter from Dr. McCauley addressed to the American Embassy in the Philippines. The letter was needed to bring Rinor back for his proposed surgical procedures. Again the hospital failed to acknowledge or respond to Gordon's facsimile.

Totally frustrated, Gordon sent a facsimile to Frank Wisner II at the U.S. Embassy in Manila a month later. He repeated much of what he said in his earlier facsimile. One additional excerpt read as follows:

"It is my understanding from Norma's recent letter that she made a trip to the embassy. From her letter I am not really sure what you need to give for them authorization to return to the United States. My wife and I will be happy to sign any papers and send any documentation you need. We would like to have them here this summer so that he can be evaluated and if need be take the necessary actions to insure he is physically ready to have the operation. The total time required on this trip would be approximately six months."

Again Gordon's facsimile was not answered. In anticipation of their return to the United States Norma had Rinor join her at the coat factory in Manila in May 1995. The name of the coat factory was Rick's City Apparel. She wrote to Gordon to let him know that Rinor had received his new Jobst garment from the Shriner's Burns Hospital-Galveston. She also mentioned that Rinor's silicone pads were torn again and that he had one open area that hurts him when he wore the Jobst garment. Norma asked Gordon if he knew anything about her visa applications. At this point no one could possibly know that it would take almost another year to bring Norma and Rinor back to America for his final medical treatments.

For the first three months Rinor was in Manila, he stayed with his sisters Cindy and Sidney and his mother at the coat factory where they all worked. Nenette also worked at the coat factory. Cindy was in the service department and brought cut goods to the sewers. Nenette was one of the many sewers who made the garments, using the heavy industrial-type sewing machines. The Marcial family shared an upstairs living and sleeping area in a warehouse. The warehouse had been converted into a number of upper and lower living and sleeping areas. Some families lived and slept on the bottom floor, and other families lived and slept on the upper floor. A ladder went up to the second floor that was made of thick plywood. There were no beds so the families slept on the floor.

Rinor counted jackets at the factory and was paid 500 pesos every other week, but he spent most of his money on food and clothing. He liked to go to a nearby strip shopping mall with his sister. Rinor bought loose-fitting, comfortable clothing designed for young teenagers.

On May 21, 1995, Norma wrote to Gordon and Irma, informing them that she was still sending pictures of Rinor along with his chest and hip measurements to the Shriner's Burns Hospital-Houston. Norma and Rinor make plans to visit the U.S. Embassy again to inquire about their visas. Norma was hoping that permission would soon be granted for her and Rinor's return to the United States.

In June Gordon called one of Senator Kay Bailey Hutchinson's aides and told her about the difficulties he was having communicating with the U.S. Embassy in the Philippines. The aide told Gordon that everyone had problems communicating with the U.S. Embassy in the Philippines, even the senators. She said she would not be able to help Gordon.

Gordon did not know that Dr. McCauley was beginning to believe that Rinor did not need further surgery. Apparently Dr. McCauley was so impressed with Rinor's photographs and measurements that he thought the surgery was no longer needed. The photographs clearly showed a healthy-looking boy with outstretched arms. What the photos didn't show was that Rinor's left arm was still too stiff to bend at the elbow. He had very little use of his left hand and could not bend his left elbow.

On July 10 Dr McCauley wrote to Bob Emrie in Austin, staying that it no longer appeared that major surgical procedures were needed at that time. Dr. McCauley raised the question of whether Rinor's elbow functioned properly. For some unknown reason Bob Emrie did not forward Dr. McCauley's letter to Gordon until August 29.

On July 22, Gordon wrote to Norma, thanking her for her letter and the copies of Rinor's pictures. Gordon asked Norma what sort of help she needed and lets her know he was expecting a letter from the hospital. Gordon told Norma he would send the letter to her when he received it. Gordon advised Norma to let the embassy know she would be returning to Iloilo soon after Rinor's next surgery.

On August 20, Norma wrote to Gordon from Balintawak where she worked. Norma planned to send her visa application to Gordon to check that it was filled out properly. She also planned to fill out another one for Rinor if hers was correct. Norma lets Gordon know that Rinor had been with her since May and asked Gordon to send her $200 for travel expenses. She also mentioned that Rinor's silicone pads were bad, and that he had a fever as well as swelling problems where he was burned. As a side note she told Gordon that the landowner wanted to demolish the bamboo bungalow in IloIlo. Ricardito and Norma began to make plans to move to Manila.

After working for three months in the coat factory and waiting for information about his return to America, Rinor quits his job. He wanted to live with his brothers Marcial and Angelo. Rinor's brothers shared a rented apartment with Ricardito's brother Allan and Allan's girlfriend. They all lived together in a rented upstairs room of a small house and slept on the floor. The only bathroom was downstairs, and they shared it with the owner's family. The rent for the room was 1,000 pesos, which included water and electricity. The Marcial's did not have a refrigerator upstairs, but they were invited to use the home owner's refrigerator downstairs.

Allan and his girlfriend had wanted to move for some time, and shortly after Rinor came to stay, they did so. After Allan and his girlfriend left, Rinor cooked rice for his brothers in the mornings except for days when he slept late. During the day Marcial would give Rinor money and a food list, and Rinor would buy food from the street vendors, mainly fish and rice. When Marcial came home from work, he would cook the evening meal. Meals were cooked on a portable two-burner kerosene stove. The kerosene fuel was pressurized and vaporized with a hand pump. By this time only Rinor's father, Ricardito, was living in the bamboo bungalow in Zarraga, with many chickens and a lot of ducks.

On Saturdays Norma and the girls visited with Marcial, Angelo, and Rinor. They would bring them food to eat and visit with each other. Rinor really enjoyed having his family together again. When he lived with his brothers, he enjoyed watching TV or going outside where he would sit and listen to other people talking. Sometimes he would hear people talking in English, and he was very happy that he could understand what they were saying. Rinor would not talk to the people he heard. He would just listen and learn.

On September 1, Gordon wrote to Bob Emrie, a member of the Board of Director's for the Shriner's Burns Hospital-Galveston, and lets him know that the embassy might not release Rinor for further surgery. Initially Dr. McCauley believed two years were needed for Rinor's healing and possible future skin grafting. Now apparently he did not believe Rinor needed elbow surgery at all, after the pictures he had seen.

At this point Gordon realized that something had to be done. As a desperate attempt to get Rinor the surgery he still needed, he contacted Jack Saul, the business manager of the Ben Hur Shrine Temple. In turn Jack wrote to Dr. McCauley, expressing concern about Rinor's large open wound areas, bad silicone pads, and the swelling that Norma had mentioned in her letter of August 20. Again, Dr. McCauley and his staffed failed to respond to Jack Saul's letter.

On October 17, Norma wrote to Gordon, telling him she was sad because she had not heard anything about her and Rinor's return trip to the United States. Norma sent more pictures of Rinor taken by her daughter Cindy to Gordon and the Shriner's Burns Hospital-Galveston. Rinor's open wounds were small again. However, the silicone made Rinor sore and he no longer had any Aquaphor.

Finally Dr. McCauley changes his mind and wrote to Bob Emrie. On January 7, 1996, Gordon sent Norma a copy of Dr. McCauley's letter to Bob Emrie. The letter said that Rinor should return to the United States for final evaluation. Rinor's elbow movement or lack thereof was of major concern. On January 15, Gordon reminded Jack Saul that Norma and Rinor needed a $200 travel advance and asked Jack to send him a check for that amount.

On February 26, Norma wrote to Gordon that she was she looking forward to their return to the United States. Rinor's measurements were now as follows:

chest , 25 inches;

hips, 26½ inches.

Gordon wrote to Norma on March 6, and sent a money order for $200 to help with her travel expenses.

On March 28, Gordon informed Potentate Steve Rye that Rinor and his mother had their visas for Rinor's return for another operation. The Potentate asked Gordon to work closely with Jack Saul on the plans for their return to this country. By the end of March Gordon informed Jack Saul that the lowest airfare from the Philippines to the United States was $1,593 per person. On April 4, Sandy of Oak Hill Travel provided an itinerary for Norma and Rinor's return. She also noted that passengers must pay an alien tax of 125 pesos when departing Manila.

On April 14, Gordon alerted Buzz Grabo, the temple's publicity chairman, that Rinor and his mother would be brought back to the United States. In a couple of days doctors planned to re-evaluate Rinor's condition and possible need for surgery on his left elbow to gain some flexibility. On April 16, Rinor and his mother arrived in the United States. The Ben Hur Shrine released the following press release to local newspapers:

"Local Shriner's Return Rinor Marcial from the Philippines."

"In December of 1988, Rinor (REE-NOR) Marcial was severely burned over most of his body with fourth degree burns. He came to Gordon and Irma Irwin in May of 1992 with no use of his left leg and arm and very limited use of his left hand. Then Gordon and Irma Irwin contacted the Shriner's Burns Hospital-Galveston. Rinor was admitted for treatment. He was operated on in July 1992 and after a lengthy recuperation period and therapy, he returned home to the Philippines in October 1993 to allow time for the scars on his chest to heal. All of Rinor's expenses were covered by the Ben Hur Shrine. After a long period of negotiations and healing the local Ben Hur Shrine and their Potentate Steve Rye authorized the payment of travel expenses in excess of $3000 to return Rinor to Austin for further evaluation at the Galveston Burns Hospital. It is hoped that Rinor will have

an operation to his left arm which now has very limited mobility and usefulness. Rinor is returning to Austin by American Airlines on Wednesday April 17, 1996. Once a patient has been accepted for treatment in a Shriner's Burns Hospital they remain under their care until they are returned to health or age 18."

Ricardito continued to live in the bamboo bungalow in Zarraga until June 1966. By that time his eyes were beginning to bother him and he needed to see an eye doctor. Years of driving an open vehicle had dried his eyes. His eyes had also changed through the normal aging process, and he needed eye glasses to see clearly.

Rinor's brother Norman graduated from the Sacred Heart Academy High School in 1996. He returned to the bamboo bungalow in Zarraga and lived there for a few months. In August Norman also moved to Manila. Now all the Marcial family lived in Manila and no one lived in Zarraga. Ricardito signed over his half hectare of land, the bamboo bungalow, and the Jetmatic pump to his brother-in-law Isko, who also had a large family. Another chapter was closed in the life of the Marcial family.

Chapter 26 – Cool and Friendly

Norma and Rinor arrived back in the United States in mid-April 1966. This time there was no stopover in Seoul and no change of planes. The flight was smooth and uneventful. The flight went from Manila to San Francisco, Dallas, and finally Austin. During the flight Rinor had a window seat again and listened to the radio through the aircraft's headset. This time he understood the English he heard on the radio. Rinor was very happy to be returning to Austin. He looked forward to seeing Tita Irma and Tito Gordon again. This time he knew the doctors would be operating on his elbow so that he would finally be able to bend his arm. Rinor was very excited about the possibility of getting the full-use of his left arm.

About a week after his arrival Rinor had a routine checkup at the Shriner's Burns Hospital-Galveston. In May hospital staff wrote a "To Whom It May Concern" letter intended for the American Embassy in the Philippines. The intent was to authorize visa extensions for Rinor and his mother and let the embassy know the expected length of their stay in America.

The June date for Rinor's next scheduled surgery left Gordon and Irma with a minor predicament. They planned to visit with their daughter Lisa and her family in Orem, Utah in May. Gordon asked a few Shriners who had offered their help in the past if they could open their hone Rinor and his mother for a week. However, these friends were quick to come up with excuses why they were unable to have Rinor and his mother in their home while the Irwin's went on vacation. Gordon made the best of the situation and left for his vacation with Irma, Norma, and Rinor,

It was a very long drive to Orem-about 1,333 miles. The first day they traveled about 800 miles and ended up in Gallup, New Mexico. They rented a motel room in Gallup for the night. The next morning they got up early and traveled through the mountains of New Mexico, Colorado, and Utah. Norma and Rinor were amazed by the size of the mountains compared with the mountains in the Philippines. The mountains were very tall with a little snow and ice on top of the tallest peaks. The trip to Orem took two days, leaving only four-five days for a visit with Lisa and her family. Gordon was amazed that Norma and Rinor sat in the back seat and barely spoke a word during the long journey.

When they arrived in Orem, Norma and Rinor made friends easily with Lisa and Van Gaffney and their seven children. With six other boys around, there were plenty of activities for Rinor. Norma made herself at home by helping Lisa with her home day care center. Norma loved to pick up the little children, hold them, and care for them. Like all vacations the time seemed to fly, and soon it was time for the long drive back to Austin.

Toward the end of May, Gordon helped Norma apply to the U.S. Department of Justice for an extension of immigrant status. Norma and Rinor's visas were paid for by the Ben Hur Shrine and extended until November 16, 1996. Rinor was admitted to the Shriner's Burns Hospital-Galveston on June 5, for additional surgery. He reported to the reconstructive surgery unit on the third floor, where his home care progress in the Philippines was evaluated. On June 7, surgery was performed on Rinor's left elbow. After the surgery Rinor was able to bend his elbow about 5 degrees. This probably seems like an insignificant amount of movement to the reader, but Rinor was very happy with his progress and eager to show his friends that he could finally bend his elbow! Later at the Ladies Oriental Shrine dance and barbeque Rinor proudly showed everyone that he could bend his left elbow and he enjoyed dancing with several of the ladies, especially LaDell Freudenberg.

Rinor stayed in the hospital for about a month, and he and his mother returned to the Irwin home on July 9. Rinor went back to the hospital in August for a routine checkup. Then someone on the staff wrote a note on the bottom of Rinor's medical report saying that he would not return for additional surgery for one year. Gordon was disappointed to say the least. He had hoped that this surgery would be Rinor's last. Additional surgery would be required in a year, and there would be some recuperation time. The Irwins both loved Rinor and his mother, but they certainly were not looking forward to such an extended stay. At this point Gordon decided he had better review and explain the options as he saw them to Norma. Gordon told Norma:

1. She and Rinor could return home to the Philippines. In this case, he would probably be unable to bring Rinor back for additional surgery.

2. She could return to the Philippines and stay there, and Rinor could stay in America until he received his next surgery.

3. Both she and Rinor could stay in America until he had his next surgery.

Gordon advised Norma to think it over and let him know her decision.

Norma made her decision in an instant. She immediately let Gordon know that she would like to stay in America with Rinor until his next surgery. She was very, very happy at the prospects of staying in the United States. Gordon had expected that this would be Norma's reply, so he found himself with another important problem. How could he find a free private tutor or classroom-type atmosphere where Rinor could feel at home? Rinor was now fifteen years old and had only five out of ten years of schooling. He had attended the first, second grade in the Philippines and part of the fifth grade in the Pflugerville, Texas, school district. Rinor was way behind in school, and it would not do him any good to go back to a public grade school. He was not ready for a public high school.

In the meantime fourteen-year-old David Gaffney and his baseball team had become Utah All Stars, and he and his mother had flown to California for the baseball playoffs. Gordon called Lisa to congratulate David and find out how he did in the baseball playoffs. Gordon just happened to mention that he was looking for specialized educational training for Rinor. Lisa remarked, you know they say that "God works in mysterious ways." Then she related the story of how she had shared a room with a lady at the tournament to help save costs. The lady happened to work for a specialized learning center in Orem. To Lisa it sounded as if the learning center would be ideal for Rinor. She told her father she would check into the matter and call him back. When they talked again, Lisa told her father that the Alpine Life and Learning Center would be perfect for Rinor that it cost only $100 a year. Then Lisa offered to let Norma and Rinor stay in their home while he was going to school.

Gordon said, "Darling, that's great, but you know you have seven children." "I cannot ask you to take on two more people." "It's expensive." Lisa replied, "Oh daddy, two more people aren't going to make any difference." Then she jokingly mentioned something about "cheaper by the dozen." In reality Lisa is the type of person who cannot refuse to help anyone in need.

Gordon replied, "Well, okay, we will send them there for a year or until Rinor finishes school." Routine pictures could still be taken of Rinor and sent back to the Shriner's Burns Hospital-Galveston for evaluation. There was also a Shiner's orthopedic hospital in Salt Lake City. After Rinor was in Utah for awhile, Gordon hoped that Rinor's final surgery might be performed there. Initially the Salt Lake City hospital confirmed that it was a definite possibility.

Rinor was very excited when he learned he would be going to a special school in Utah. He thought about the fun he might have and wondered about what new experiences he might have. He already knew the Gaffney family and Gordon's seven grandchildren. However, after he arrived in Utah, he began to have second thoughts about going to a new school for the first time. The Alpine Life and Learning Center in Orem was both exciting and frightening to him. He was a little frightened by the unknown and afraid that he might not make new friends at school.

At first Chris Gaffney went to school with Rinor and taught him how to use local bus transportation. There was a bus stop in front of the Gaffney house and a nearby shelter with a bench. The bench was used only on windy, cold and just plain nasty days. The boys took the first bus to Valley State College and hopped a second bus there. The second bus took them directly to the Alpine Life and Learning Center. After a few days Rinor knew the bus routine by heart and was on his own. Rinor also discovered he could save time and catch a bus that went directly to his new school if he walked one block to the next bus stop.

Members of the Gaffney family are dedicated Christians and Mormons. Shortly after Norma and Rinor's arrival missionaries from the Mormon church visited and talked with Rinor and his mother at the Gaffney home. The missionaries invited Norma and Rinor to visit and attend the Mormon church and Sunday school. Norma and Rinor were happy to attend the Church of Latter-day Saints (LDS) regularly with the Gaffney family. Church activities became an important part of their lives while living in Utah.

By early October 1996 Norma and Rinor were settled in with the Gaffney family in Orem and Rinor was making friends and doing well at his new school. Gordon contacted Teresa Pickett at the Shriner's Burns Hospital-Galveston and asked if Rinor's medical records could be transferred to the Shriner's Hospital in Salt Lake City. Gordon hoped that any additionally required surgery for Rinor could be handled there. Gordon also pointed out that Norma and Rinor's visas would be expiring in November and that another letter would be needed from the hospital to extend their time again in the United States.

Soon Rinor's list of friends at school grew to include Erika, Misty, Brandy, Sabrina, Nick, Kevin, and Tiffany, just to mention a few. Rinor reluctantly admits he liked Erika. On one occasion they went to a movie together but Rinor claims it really wasn't a date. The movie they went to see was *Jurassic Park, the Lost World*. Rinor's description of the movie was that it was "awesome." Rinor also enjoyed bowling and playing baseball with Danny Gaffney. At other times the boys played basketball in the back yard. Danny's brother Michael shared his Nintendo 64 game with Rinor, and the two boys enjoyed playing Mario's Car, Basketball, Toruck, and Hockey. Mario's Car is a racing game, and in Toruck the object of the game is to kill the man-eating dinosaurs before they kill you.

One night after leaving Blockbuster Video, Rinor and Michael decided to stop at the Arctic Circle ice cream store for some ice cream. The store closed as they were leaving. A young couple pulled up to the drive-through speaker and began hollering into the speaker. "Is anyone there? Can you hear us?" Then the young couple went to the door, and were told that the ice cream parlor was closed. Rinor and Michael finished their ice cream while sitting on the curb. Suddenly Michael shouted "I left my CD player inside!" At first Rinor thought Michael was just joking, but he wasn't. Michael hurried back to the store while Rinor waited for him; he was able to get his CD player before the employees left for the night. Then Rinor and Michael laughed all the way home about the young couple who were hollering into the dead drive-through speakers.

Sometimes Rinor and Chris Gaffney would go to a movie, and at other times they would just go to the store or hang out with friends. Rinor liked action, adventure, and comedy movies the best. Tom Cruise and Will Smith were two of his favorite movie stars. Rinor and his friend Kevin also liked to hang out at the Movies 8 arcade games without going to the movies. Another one of Rinor's favorite stores to hang out at was Media Play, where he could check out his favorite compact discs.

Rinor and the Gaffney boys frequently enjoyed eating pizza. However, Rinor likes CiCi's pizza in Austin the most because it's an "all-you-can-eat" restaurant. What more could a teenage boy want? Rinor's favorite was a combination pizza with mushrooms, pepperoni, and cheese.

Danny became one of Rinor's best friends, and he taught Rinor how to roller-blade in the driveway of the Gaffney home. Roller-blading was hard for Rinor to learn at first. Danny held Rinor's hand until he got the "feel" for the skates. Soon Rinor was roller blading at Classic Skating with Danny, David, and kids from his Sunday school class. Rinor fell down only three times, and that was when the kids were playing "Crack the Whip." In this game the youngsters hold hands, skate in a circle, and try to stop suddenly or reverse direction. Rinor was determined to learn how to roller-blade well, and he soon did. Sometimes he and his friends would take off and go roller blading at Kevin's house. Rinor enjoyed roller-blading in mild weather and ice skating in the winter. These were new experiences for him. Danny, David, and Rinor also liked to go to parties with their friends, listen to loud music, eat junk food, and drink sodas. Once the boys slept overnight at a friend's house after all the girls went home.

While in Utah Rinor learned to cook pancakes, scramble eggs, and make chocolate chip cookies. Chocolate chip cookies were his favorite. He also learned how to use an automatic dishwasher. The Gaffney family was large, and each child, including Rinor, had two daily chores to do. They each had to do a kitchen chore and another chore. The chores included cooking, washing the dishes, cleaning the kitchen counters, cleaning the bathrooms, and vacuuming the halls and living areas.

Everyone had to keep their bedroom clean and tidy. Rinor and Michael slept in the same bedroom. Rinor slept in the top bunk and Michael slept in the bottom bunk. Michael's room also had a TV and VCR. The two boys enjoyed watching rental movies from Blockbuster Video and Cougar Rental.

The Gaffney family did not own any videos. Michael and Rinor enjoyed sleeping in until noon when they thought they could get away with it.

At school, Rinor would go to his assigned room and pick up his work packet. Each work packet was worth one eighth of a credit. Rinor wore an identification badge with a bar code ID when he went to school. The badge was scanned to verify his student status and authorize him to pick up his work packets. He received one full credit of work for every set of eight student packets completed. While in school, he worked his packets as fast as he could so he could earn as many credits as possible. Every time Rinor finished a work packet, the teacher would assign him a project. The project tested his knowledge of the packet's subject matter and enabled him to summarize what he had learned. Teachers were available to answer any questions the students might ask. Rinor would then take his project to a computer room and type a summary of the subject. Then he would take a test on the packet's subject matter.

Some of the subjects that Rinor studied were English, math, science, keyboarding, theatrical makeup, astronomy, and art. In keyboarding Rinor learned how to type and use a computer. Some subjects such as English, math, and science, were required, whereas others such as art and theatrical makeup were electives. Rinor was given a list of subjects and allowed to choose his electives. One of the subjects Rinor studied was art. Credit for art was based on the following:

1. The packet assignment had to be completed and corrected by a teacher.

2. The packet review questions had to be completed and reviewed by a teacher.
3. The packet vocabulary matching had to be completed and reviewed by a teacher.
4. A final project of your art-work using the elements and principles, in your own original composition, had to be turned into the teacher with a written description of how you planned your composition.

Topics covered by the packet were as follows:

The Definition of Art

Ways to Look at Art

The Elements of Art (line, shape, form, space, value, color and texture)

The Principles of Design

Rhythm Balance, Symmetry, Radial Balance, Symmetrical Balance

Proportion, Emphasis, Unity

Final Review

Rinor's favorite elective was Theatrical Makeup. In this course, Rinor learned how to use different makeup to make hisself look gory, scary, and gross. Step by step he learned how to change his appearance at will. With the teacher's encouragement and his imagination, Rinor learned he could transform himself into anything he wanted to be like magic. Rinor's theatrical supplies consisted of brushes, grease paint, cosmetic wedges, skin-toned latex, ping-pong balls, baby-bottle nipples, chicken bones, and tissue paper.

Rinor learned how to use various makeup bases and other cosmetics. He learned how to blend colors to match his skin tones and further enhance the look he was striving to obtain. For example, he learned how to create the appearance of a bullet-hole wound using fake blood. He also learned how to simulate a big, nasty, open wound with the flesh peeling away and his skull showing.

Finally Rinor learned how to use latex to simulate cuts, bruises, skinned knuckles, and broken bones. He was amazed by how easy it was to use a chicken bone and a little makeup to simulate a broken arm with startling reality! Rinor quickly learned the importance of stage makeup and being a good makeup artist. The makeup artist creates the illusion of reality.

Rinor's favorite special effect was the simulated eyeball. The trick here was to make it look like your eyeball had been gouged out and was lying on your cheek. To accomplish this illusion you need a ping-pong ball, brush, and simulated bruises. First you put the tissue over one of your eyes to protect it. Then you covered the tissue with skin-tone latex and blended it into the surrounding area. To make it look as if your eye has been gouged out, you add red to the fake eye socket and blue to the top of the socket. Then you cut a ping-pong ball in half and paint it to look like an eye. You can paint a blue or brown iris and black pupil. Then you add a little red to make the eye look bloodshot. Then you cement the fake eye to your cheek with latex, and add latex bruises all the way from the fake eye to the fake eye socket. According to Rinor the effect is gross but very cool!

By mid-October 1996 after completing his courses in theatrical makeup and astronomy, Rinor developed some abscesses and open sores on the scar tissue on his chest and under his left arm. The Gaffney family made an appointment for Rinor to see an orthopedic surgeon at the Shriner's Salt Lake City Hospital. Van Gaffney took Norma and Rinor to the Shriner's hospital in Salt Lake City. The orthopedic surgeon took one look at Rinor and panicked. He advised the Gaffney family to send Rinor to the Shriner's Burns Hospital-Galveston right away. Gordon checked into getting airline tickets in a hurry and found out that a one-way ticket would cost $400. However, if the trip could be postponed for a couple of weeks, Gordon could get one-way airfare for $85. Gordon called Lisa and they decided to have a local doctor who was a burns expert give them a second opinion.

Doctor Dell P. Smith observed the burns to the entire anterior lateral half of Rinor's chest, burns to his upper and lower arm, elbow and arm constrictors. He also noted a one-centimeter-deep ulcer in Rinor's left chest area. The area was red, but not increasingly painful. Rinor showed no signs of fever, chills, nausea, vomiting or malaise. Dr. Smith had blood samples taken and a Neosporin and Telfa dressing placed over the ulcer. The doctor gave Lisa a ten-day supply of Augmentin 500 mg, an antibiotic. The doctor told Lisa that Rinor's condition was serious but that his trip to Austin could be postponed for a couple of weeks.

Rinor was re-examined by Dr. Smith two weeks later. The ulcer was reduced to about 0.5 cm and had healed down to a small fistula tract. The doctor credited the healing to the

Augmentin and Neosporin dressing. Rinor's blood count was normal and Dr. Smith saw no reason to postpone Rinor's elbow surgery. The doctor told Lisa that Rinor needed a chest X-ray and basal pathology but it could be done at the Shriner's Burns Hospital-Galveston.

On the following Saturday, November 2, Rinor was on a one-way flight back to Austin. Shortly after his arrival in he was on his way to the Shriner's Burns Hospital-Galveston in the Ben Hur Shrine Hospital Van. Greg Trejo drove the van, and Gordon and Stella Trejo accompanied Rinor. The doctors examined Rinor and admitted him to the hospital on the same day. Rinor spent two weeks in the hospital alone. First his infection was cleared up and then his skin was scraped and skin from a cadaver was grafted to his chest and arm. At first it formed a blood clot and half of it was removed. The cadaver skin allowed the healing to begin. Later Rinor's skin was grafted over the same area.

Rinor was comfortable at the Shriner's Burns Hospital-Galveston. By now he knew all the regular staff, and they tended to cater to his whims. He thought nothing of going to the seventh floor cafeteria and asking Carlos, the Filipino cook, for his favorite food. Rinor likes pork chops, hamburgers, rice, beans and corn. However, he never has liked green vegetables or tomatoes. Naturally, Carlos gave Rinor whatever he wanted.

When Rinor's two weeks were up, he was very eager to get back to school in Utah. He liked school very much and was beginning to miss his new friends. Rinor's final instructions from the Shriner's Burns Hospital-Galveston was to clean his chest wound areas with warm water once a day and apply Bacitracin and Adaptic two times a day for one week. He was also to clean and apply Adaptic to his burned leg daily. Burned areas were to be wrapped with ACE bandages to apply pressure and minimize scarring. Although Rinor was eager to return to school, he had to have a follow-up visit to the hospital and did not return to Utah until December.

As Greg Trejo and Gordon were taking Rinor back for his December follow-up visit, Gordon asked Rinor if he wanted to return to the Philippines. Rinor said "no." Then Gordon asked Rinor if his mother wanted to go home. Rinor said "no." Gordon reminded Rinor that all his life someone else had been taking care of him. Now Rinor would have to find out on his own how to stay in America. Gordon asked Rinor if he knew anything he could do to stay in America. Rinor said, "Marry an American," but he knew that was not possible at this time. Gordon laughed with Rinor at his answer.

Gordon told Rinor that he would have to use all the resources he had at school to find a way to stay in this country. Gordon reminded Rinor to use his computer to check out the Internet for immigration rules and regulations. Rinor could also talk with his teachers and some of his Filipino friends in Orem. Gordon told Rinor he would have to figure out a legal way to stay in the United States. If Rinor did anything illegal, Gordon would be the one responsible. If Rinor could not figure out a legal way to stay in the United States, he would have to return to the Philippines and try to figure out a way to return. In either case Rinor would have to work on this goal on his own.

During Rinor's follow-up visit Gordon talked to Dr. Evans and asked him if it would be okay for Rinor to wait until he finished the school year before he had his next surgery. Dr. Evans agreed that it was okay and Rinor's next surgery was scheduled for June 1997. Apparently the Shriner's Burns Hospital-Galveston staff was originally under the impression that Rinor and his mother were going to return to the Philippines rather than the Irwin home.

For one school project Rinor compared *life in the Philippines with life in America*. This is a rather stark description of life in the Philippines.

"People work in the Philippines to make enough money to buy food for their family. Some people have no work. Some people collect cans and recycle them to get money to buy food. Some places are really bad because people throw garbage in the streets."

"There are many people walking in the streets because many people cannot afford to ride a bus or buy a car. Some people work in the construction industry and build stores and other buildings. Some people sell food in the streets because they do not have enough money to build a store. Some children don't go to school because they don't have enough money to pay for school."

"Food in the Philippines is different from American food. People in the Philippines buy food in the street because it is too expensive in the store. Some Philippine food is the same as American food but the main food in the Philippines is fish and rice."

"The weather in the Philippines is similar to the weather in America. In the Philippines there are typhoons and in America

there are hurricanes. *In America there is snow, but in the Philippines there is no snow. In American there are many cars and buses. The heavy traffic is a leading cause of accidents."*

About language, Rinor wrote the following:

"In the Philippines we have a different language. I live in Manila. Manila is a big city and we speak Tagalog. Other people speak other languages. Other people live in other countries like Cebu, Davao and Iloilo. People speak other languages in America too, but the differences in languages do not seem to be as great."

Other elective subjects that Rinor studied in school dealt with cashing a check, driving a car, planning a wedding, and protecting the environment. Students were free to select any subject matter of interest. The next six paragraphs tell some of the lessons Rinor learned in these elective subjects.

Author's Note: The thoughts expressed here are Rinor's, but the exact wording has been changed a little for better clarification.

Rinor learned that it was easier to cash a check at the bank where you had a checking account. He also learned that you needed to sign a check on the back and show the teller some form of identification. By showing tellers your ID, they can verify your identity and cash the check. He also learned that you should make sure you receive the same amount of cash as is written on the face of the check. Then according to Rinor you can go and spend the cash.

Rinor concluded that learning to drive a car was not easy. There were many things that you had to learn first. One way to learn was to take a drivers' education course. After you learn how to drive a car and pass a written exam and road test, you can get your driver's license.

When learning to drive you need to look where you are going. When turning left or right you need to use your turn signal. This lets other drivers and pedestrians know when you are about to turn. You have to be very careful and drive the posted speed limit. You also have to obey traffic lights and stop signs. You have to be observant and look in all directions when you are driving a car. There could be children playing in the road or other traffic around you. You have to be aware of traffic signs and people walking on the edge of the roads. When driving at night you need to turn your headlights on so you can see where you are going.

People who do not know how to drive a car should go to driver's education to learn the proper techniques. Driving a car is important to people. It lets people go where they need to, like work, the store, or to visit with their family.

Planning is an important part of a wedding. As part of your wedding plans you need flower girls, food, dresses, and a reception for the people who come and participate in the wedding. You need to buy wedding rings for the bride and groom. You need to buy enough food and drinks for the wedding party and guests. The future bride will have to be measured for her wedding dress along with the bridesmaids. You may need to buy a new suit or rent a tuxedo for yourself. You also need to decide how to decorate the reception area. How many flowers, ribbons, balloons, wedding signs, wedding bells, and candles will be needed, and how much will they cost?

Everyone should make a resolution to save the forests and keep them safe and clean. You can help save the environment by protecting trees and animals. You can save the earth by recycling trash and not throwing trash in the rivers. The smoke from big factories pollutes the air and causes plants and animals to die. Saving the earth from danger is very important to people.

At 2:30 p.m. Rinor would catch a bus back to the Gaffney home. On the way to their home he could change buses again or walk. Because there was a relatively long time between buses, Rinor usually walked. Sometimes after Rinor got home from school, he would sell promotional coupon books in the nearby Smith Store parking lot to earn a little spending money. At other times he would sell coupon books door to door. The books sold for $10 each and Rinor would pay Van Gaffney $3.50 for each book. He saved some of his money for future needs.

Every Sunday the Gaffney family, Norma, and Rinor went to the Church of Latter-day Saints and Sunday school. They also enjoyed many other church activities. It was the first time Rinor and his mother had ever attended a Mormon church. Every Sunday Rinor took communion at church and then went to Sunday school.

Norma and Rinor spent their first Christmas in Utah in 1996. During the Christmas season they went shopping, had plenty of food to eat, and enjoyed life with the Gaffney children. On Christmas Day gifts were handed out and everyone took turns opening their gifts. Everyone enjoyed everyone else's happiness that wonderful Christmas Day.

Some of the gifts Rinor received were roller-blade skates from the Ladies Oriental Shrine, a CD from the Irwins, and a CD player from Lisa and Van Gaffney. He also received boots from Leslie and Brian Low, and snow pants from Becky and Brad Caldwell. Michael, David, Danny, Chris, and Garrick Gaffney all had presents for Rinor.

Some of Norma's gifts were a nightgown from Gordon and Irma, jacket and pants from Lisa and Van, and various shampoos and perfumes from Leslie, Rinor, Brian, Becky, and Brad Caldwell. Rinor and his mother also received cookies and other treats from members of the church.

Thanks to Louie F. Caputo, Jr., a neighbor who lived across the street from the Irwins, they were also able to go to Orem for Christmas. Louie was so impressed by what the Irwins had done for Rinor and his mother that he gave the Irwin's round-trip tickets to Orem. While Gordon was in Orem, he asked Rinor if he had found out what he would have to do to stay in the United States. Rinor told Gordon that he hadn't done anything yet, and Gordon assumed that Rinor was not trying to get the information he needed. Later after the Irwin's returned home, Gordon called Lisa several times and asked if Rinor was doing any research on immigration. Lisa's reply was always "I don't think so, Dad." Gordon began to think that Rinor was just looking for an excuse to go back home to the Philippines.

Some of the new experiences that Norma and Rinor enjoyed were seeing snow for the first time and visiting the "Trail of Lights" holiday display in the park. The adults also watched as the children went to sleep under the Christmas tree on December 24. The Christmas dinner and huge amount of food that was served was a memorable sight on Christmas Day. On New Year's Eve the Gaffney family along with Norma and Rinor went to a massive fireworks display. Norma and Rinor were impressed that fireworks were set off by other people in their front yards, backyards, and streets in America. They thought they were very noisy and dangerous. However, bamboo bazookas are still used extensively in the Philippines, and Rinor knows how dangerous they can be.

Rinor enjoyed both the snow and cold weather in Utah. At age sixteen he made his first snowman and an igloo. With the first snow an inch or so deep on the ground Chris taught Rinor how to build his first snowman and Igloo. Chris showed Rinor how to make a large snowball and gently roll it in the moist snow. The snowball rapidly grew in size as it was rolled. The first snowball for a snowman had to be a very big one. Then a medium-sized snowball was needed for the middle. Finally a smaller-sized snowball was used for the head. The next step was to round off the corners of the rolled snow to give it a real ball shape. To decorate the snowman the boys used small tomatoes for the eyes and a carrot for the nose. Then they put a baseball cap on his head for a "very cool" look. To build an igloo Danny, Garrick, and Rinor made a huge pile of snow. Then with small shovels they hollowed out a cavity just big enough for two teenage boys. Now there was a private place for two of the boys, but it was still very cold!

Rinor continued his schooling at the Alpine Life and Learning Center in Orem until June 1, 1997, when he and his mother returned to Austin. He was listed as being in the 10th grade and his student transcript read as follows:

Pre-Algebra B
English   A and B
Theatrical Makeup A and A-
Drawing   A and A
Business Management   A
Foundations/Tech. A and A
Information Process 1   A-
Physics   B-
Weather/Meteorology   A
Keyboard 1 B+
Theatrical Production/Direction A
Total Credits Earned = 7.125; Grade Point Average = 3.721

Chapter 27 – Thank You and God Bless You

When Rinor and his mother returned to Austin for their June appointment, Gordon learned that Rinor had tried to find some information about staying in America. However, no one in Orem was able to help or guide him. Rinor did not know how to get the information or where to get it. Gordon tried to show Rinor how to look up the information about immigration on the Internet, but Rinor seemed content to watch TV and play computer games. At this point Gordon told Rinor and Norma there was no way he could afford to hire a lawyer to help keep them in the United States. They would just have to return home to the Philippines after Rinor's final surgery.

On June 3, Rinor had a checkup at the Shriner's Burns Hospital-Galveston. Gordon asked that Rinor be able to see Dr. Evans. Greg and Stella Trejo drove Rinor and his mother to the hospital in the Ben Hur Shrine hospital van. Norma and Rinor took some of their clothes in case Dr. Evans decided to operate on him right away. Later that evening the Irwins planned to attend the installation of officers at Creedmoor Chapter 607 of the Order of the Eastern Star. As they were preparing to leave the house, Norma and Rinor returned because Dr. Evans was off duty for the rest of the week. Gordon was upset to say the least. This was another classic example of poor communications between the hospital and the parents or guardians of their patients. Irma and Gordon invited Norma and Rinor to go with them, and they did. Norma and Rinor dressed up, looked great, and had a chance to visit with Eastern Star friends they had not seen for some time.

The next day Gordon called the Shriner's Burns Hospital-Galveston several times. He was unable to get in touch with Teresa Pickett. Gordon refused to leave a message and told the receptionist it would not make any difference because the hospital staff never returned his calls. Apparently Gordon's message finally got the hospital staff's attention. Ms. Pickett called Gordon at work on Thursday afternoon, but he had already left for home. She left a message that she had called.

On Friday morning Gordon called the hospital and was able to talk to Ms. Pickett. She told Gordon she was unaware that Dr. Evans was not going to be at the hospital. She told Gordon that Dr. Evans was in now and that she would discuss Rinor's case with him on Monday. Gordon asked her to talk with him right away. He also reminded her that everything had to be done by September 15, unless they wanted to pay for Rinor's and his mother's return airfare to Manila. The following Monday someone from the hospital called back and said they would set up an appointment for Rinor on Tuesday, June 17.

Rinor's elbow operation was scheduled for June 18. Ms. Pickett informed Gordon that Norma and Rinor would be at the hospital for at least two weeks. The timing seemed great for Gordon, because Irma was scheduled for a heart catherization on June 20. Irma was having angina problems. The doctors also found a spot on one of Irma's breasts, so Gordon and Irma did not want any company for awhile and looked forward to a little time alone. Thank God Irma's problems disappeared and everything turned out fine. Irma needed to continue to take her heart medicine, and the spot on her breast disappeared on the next set of X-rays.

Rinor stayed at the Shriner's Burns Hospital-Galveston for one week. Ms. Pickett called Gordon on Wednesday, June 27 to let him know that Rinor was ready to go home. Someone at the hospital also called the Ben Hur Shrine Temple office and arranged for transportation. Greg Trejo picked up Rinor and his mother and brought them home.

The hospital inserted four steel rods in Rinor's left arm and attached them to a rotating external fixture. Rinor used a dial on the fixture to determine the position of his arm. Initially Rinor was supposed to bend his arm 5 degrees a day. However, Rinor chose to bend his arm 10 degrees a day because there was not too much pain. His goal was to bend his arm gradually from the straight position to the 90-degree position. By bending his arm in 10 degree increments it took nine days to bend it to the 90-degree position and nine more days to straighten it. Then Rinor was to bend and straighten it in 20-degree increments, taking five days in each direction. Finally he was to bend and straighten his arm in 30, 45, and 90 degree increments, taking three days, two days, and one day respectively.

By moving his elbow and arm in this manner Rinor was strengthening muscles he had not used for five years. Rinor was instructed to clean his arm twice a day with applicators a 50-50 mixture of peroxide and water. He was also allowed to take Vicodin every six hours for pain if needed. While Rinor wore the external fixture, he had to keep his arm elevated so he propped his arm up with three small pillows when he was sitting or lying down. Doctors at the hospital wanted Rinor to keep his elbow elevated always. For a while the poor boy couldn't do anything but watch TV or lie in bed and listen to his tapes or the radio. Maybe this sounds like fun, but it wasn't long before both Rinor and his mother started getting claustrophobic.

Norma was so eager to get outdoors that she could hardly wait to take out the daily garbage. Meanwhile the weather was just too hot for Rinor. Rinor did not enjoy sitting on the patio or going to the pool. It was difficult for him to go anywhere because he had to lug three pillows around everywhere he went. However, when Bill Boulter scheduled an auction on July 19, Gordon asked Rinor and his mother if they wanted to go. Gordon reminded them that it would be hot outside but said Rinor could sit in a lawn chair. Rinor and his mother jumped at the chance to go to the auction.

At this kind of auction, items are kept in rows of storage sheds. The items are taken out of the storage sheds and auctioned. The auctioneer goes down the row, auctioning each item, and then moves on to the next row of items. While the auction was in progress, Norma moved Rinor's lawn chair around for him so that he could see what was being auctioned. While at the auction a kind stranger gave Rinor a large number of baseball, football, and hockey cards. In turn Rinor shared his good fortune with his friends Thomas and Robert Gaffney. Rinor gave his friend Thomas the hockey cards and his friend Robert the football cards. Rinor's favorite sports and the ones he liked to watch and play were baseball, golf, tennis, and roller-blading. He also liked to play catch with a baseball and football.

After the auction everyone went to Kyle, Texas, where they looked at some property. Then they drove to Wimberly and on to Dripping Springs to get some German pastry. It was a long and tiring day for Rinor and his mother, but they were very happy just to get out of the house. Norma also went shopping with Irma just to get away from the house for awhile.

Rinor returned to the Shriner's Burns Hospital-Galveston on Tuesday August 19, and had his elbow fixture removed the next day. While Rinor was at the hospital, an appointment was set up for a return visit and final checkup in three weeks. Gordon told Ms. Pickett that Rinor's visit on September 9 would be his last. Rinor was returning to the Philippines sometime after September 15 and before September 20. Ms. Pickett said she would check with Dr. Calhoun to see if two visits could be worked into Rinor's remaining time. She never called back.

Gordon wanted Rinor to have a chance to meet some of his Shrine friends so that he could say goodbye to them before returning to the Philippines. Gordon talked to Ron Harrison, the Potentate of Ben Hur, and arranged to address the members at their regular September meeting. Gordon spoke to the group toward the end of their meeting on September 13. During his talk Gordon updated the Shriner's on Rinor's progress. The little Filipino boy who could not walk or use his left arm had made remarkable progress and regained full use of his left leg and most of the use of his left arm. He could run, play, and roller-blade just like any other teenage boy his age. Rinor would be seventeen years old in less than a month. As Gordon recapped Rinor's story, his voice cracked and tears came to his eyes. He was losing two members of his family, Rinor and his mother.

Then Gordon invited the Shriners to meet with Rinor and his mother in the Divan Room after the meeting. He also mentioned that a money tree had been set up to help restore the Marcial family to the way they were before Rinor's tragedy. Gordon had also rented a slide projector with the intent of showing Rinor's story in chronological order, but he never got beyond the first two heart-wrenching slides. As the Shriners came into the room, they were fascinated by the pictures of Rinor. The pictures were laid along one side of the large wooden table in the Divan Room. The photographs provided mute testimony to Rinor's eight years of suffering and six years of remarkable healing. The little Filipino boy had endured a lot and matured into a young man with a bright future.

Rinor and his mother greeted each of the Shriners with big hugs and sincere "Thanks" after they had looked at the pictures. As I approached Rinor, he said, "No more hospitals." "No more Jobst suit." "No more bandages." The boy was obviously very happy to shed the constant medical reminders that had become an integral part of his life for the last eight years. Then Rinor flashed a big smile and gave me a big hug. We shook hands and I asked him to squeeze my hand as hard as he could. He replied "I don't want to hurt you." His answer brought a smile to my face and I stepped over to Norma to give her a big hug. "I will miss you guys," I said, and she nodded her affirmation that she would miss us as well. Then Gordon and I began to take pictures of the Shriners and Past Potentate as they posed with Rinor and his mother.

The money tree was also a huge success in every sense of the word. Rinor and his mother were shocked and pleasantly surprised by the generosity of their friends. It was only near the end of the reception when Rinor's smile began to fade for the first time. It was as though he suddenly realized this was a final goodbye. He might never see his Shrine friends again. However, Greg and Stella Trejo stayed behind and Rinor's happy mood quickly returned. Rinor posed with Greg and Stella in front of a large wall mural. The mural depicted Ben Hur driving a chariot pulled by a spirited team of horses. Greg was Rinor's favorite hospital van driver. Years earlier Greg had given Rinor his first wrist watch, and strange as it may seem, the watch was made in the Philippines.

On Saturday evening Irma, Gordon, and Rinor went to the Hillbilly dance at the Ben Hur Shrine Temple. Norma wanted to stay home to finish crocheting a goodbye present for Irma. The Hillbilly Club is a Shrine-related social club, open to husbands and wives. Social activities are usually family oriented. Along with social activities the Hillbilly Club sponsors fund-raising activities to help raise money for Shrine charities.

Rinor had a great time at the dance. He enjoyed having the chance to see many ladies of the Shrine and having a chance to say goodbye to them. While at the dance Rinor danced with his favorite Shrine dance partner, LaDell Freudenberg. Unfortunately he had to dance in one spot because LaDell had recently had surgery on one foot. During the intermission Rinor was asked to say something to the group. He hadn't known that he would be asked to address the crowd, but his short talk was sincere and thoughtful. Rinor thanked everyone for what they had done for him and he made Gordon very proud of him as he finished with "God bless you!"

During the evening another generous donation was collected for the Marcial family. Gordon was also approached on both Friday and Saturday nights by other Shriner's who said they would help put Rinor through school with direct contributions or by putting on a fund-raiser or both. Several days later Rinor asked Gordon if he would help him finish school. Gordon told Rinor that he could not promise him anything. Gordon told Rinor that he would have to write to him and let him know how much money he needed for school. Then Gordon could work on raising the necessary money. Norma told Gordon that college had cost one of her daughters $280 a semester plus books. At the current rate Rinor's educational costs would be $560 a year plus books.

In the weeks after the removal of Rinor's elbow apparatus Gordon and Rinor played both tennis and golf. Rinor played golf with Gordon, Bob Oakes, and two of Bob's friends at the Jimmie Clay public golf course in Austin. Gordon paid Rinor's greens fee so that no one could criticize Rinor for being there free. Rinor did well, and the other men let Rinor tee off first and pick up his ball when they had to go in front of him. Then Rinor would putt out. Rinor could hit the ball 150 yards but not very accurately. Rinor's accuracy did not bother him because everyone was having a great time and that was all that mattered.

Rinor also loved to hit a tennis ball. He had a good forehand but could not toss the ball high enough yet to learn to serve. John Fulton, the coach of Gordon's tennis league team and an Austin Community College instructor, worked with Rinor a couple of times on his tennis serve. Rinor still had the United States Tennis Association racquet that was given to him in 1993. When Rinor left Austin, he took the racquet and several tennis balls back home with him.

Before Rinor left for the Philippines, Gordon gave him a book titled *"The Power of Positive Thinking"* by Dr. Norman Vincent Peale. Gordon told Rinor he had read the book several times and recommended that Rinor do the same. *"The Power of Positive Thinking"* is one of a series of small inspirational books by the late Norman Vincent Peale. His short, easy to-read moral lessons are timeless because they are based on God's eternal truth. These books also give numerous examples of how the love and power of God have favorably influenced the lives of ordinary people.

Before Rinor returned home, Gordon thought he should have one last "father and son" talk with the boy. Gordon thought Rinor had been away from home, his father, and his brothers for some of those critical, young, adolescent years. Gordon was curious about what the boy knew and did not know. Gordon asked Rinor if he studied sex education in the Utah school and he replied "no." Then Gordon asked him if he knew anything about sex and Rinor grinned and said, "Yes." "Where did you learn it?" asked Gordon. "Just listening and watching," the boy replied. "Did you ever wake up with your penis hard?" Gordon asked. "Yes," Rinor replied. Gordon was relieved, because in the back of his mind he had feared that the boy's severe burns might have affected his sex life. At this point it appeared that Rinor's sex life would be normal in every way.

"Do you know how babies are made?" Gordon asked. "Yes," Rinor replied. "How do you know?" Gordon asked. The boy related how he had unintentionally seen a young couple "making out" while he was home in the Philippines. "Do you know how to keep a girl from getting pregnant?" Gordon asked. "Yes, by using condoms," Rinor replied. Gordon was satisfied with Rinor's answers and continued to give the boy some fatherly advice. Gordon advised Rinor to be careful and finish his schooling before considering marriage. He also advised Rinor not to marry the first girl he dated. Rinor agreed that Gordon's advice was good advice.

At another time Gordon discussed happiness with Rinor. Gordon told Rinor he should be happy to give and not worry about receiving gifts, money, or job opportunities. A cheerful giver will receive more of the bounty of life than he can possibly imagine. Gordon advised Rinor to put God first, others second, and himself last.

How did Rinor feel about going home to the Philippines? He was happy to be going home to be reunited with his family. He was also sad because he feared he might never see Tito Gordon, Tita Irma, and the people who helped him again. Rinor would miss his friends in Austin, the Shiners, and his new friends in Orem. He is very appreciative of all the people who were so kind to him, unselfishly giving him gifts and presents.

What did Rinor want for the future? In the near future he wanted to learn more about computer programming. His sisters Sidney and Cindy were graduates of a college computer program in computer programming. His brother Norman, who was seventeen years old paints hotels and other commercial buildings, and wants to become a computer engineer.

In the intermediate future Rinor also wanted to graduate from school in the Philippines, get a job, save some money, and buy a house. Rinor has said he would like to become a Shriner. Gordon reminded the boy that he would have to become a Master Mason first and that there was a Masonic Lodge in Manila. Gordon let Rinor read some information about the DeMolay in Manila. The Order of DeMolay is a Masonic-affiliated fraternal organization for young men ages twelve to twenty-one. Rinor also talked about going into missionary work. Perhaps he will be able to accomplish many of these goals. In the distant future Rinor wanted to return to American with some or all of his family.

When Gordon and Irma took Rinor and his mother to the airport, Gordon got the impression from Norma's actions that she was very happy to be returning home. At the airport Norma hugged Gordon and Irma. On her way through the gate she kept telling the Irwins she loved them. Rinor gave Tito Gordon and Tita Irma a big fare well hug. The Irwins felt the same about Rinor and his mother; they were happy they would soon be reunited with the rest of their family. The Irwins were also happy to have their home back. Now they didn't have to worry about their Filipino friends anymore. When Rinor and his mother were home alone, Gordon and Irma tended to worry about many everyday things. Would they be all right being left alone? Would they take the time to fix themselves a good meal? What would they do if some sort of emergency occurred?

As they prepared to leave, Gordon was concerned about Norma and Rinor's luggage. They had eight pieces of luggage and were supposed to take only four pieces of luggage plus their carry-on bags. Gordon was concerned because the American Airlines ticket agent told him that the Philippine Airlines charged $160 extra for each piece of luggage over the limit. Hurriedly they combined one bag into another so that Rinor and his mother ended up with four pieces of luggage and three carry-on bags. The Irwins hoped that Norma and Rinor would not have to pay extra when they transferred to Philippines Airlines. The flight attendant also arranged for Norma and Rinor to catch an earlier direct flight to Los Angeles instead of flying to Dallas-Fort Worth, where they would have to change planes. Gordon hoped they would also be able to get an earlier flight out of Los Angeles for Manila, but he doubted it.

This time Norma and Rinor's flight home was fine until they started their final descent into Manila. A storm had set in, and the plane was violently tossed and bounced around. Finally the plane miraculously broke through the turbulence just before landing. Fear turned to happiness, and passengers clapped their hands and cheered with joy. It was a movie ending to a potential airline disaster.

Gordon had asked Norma to take a picture of the whole family after they got home, and she did. Only the oldest son, Marcial, was not able to be in the pictures because he was working in China. When Marcial came home, it was the first time in 15-years that the family was together again.

Rinor's physical health is now restored to the greatest extent possible. His faith and mental health were never in question. He married to a beautiful Filipino girl on April 2, 2010. As our paths cross, we become a little bit more like everyone we've met, and they become a little bit more like us. The phrase "So mote it be" is used to close Masonic prayers.

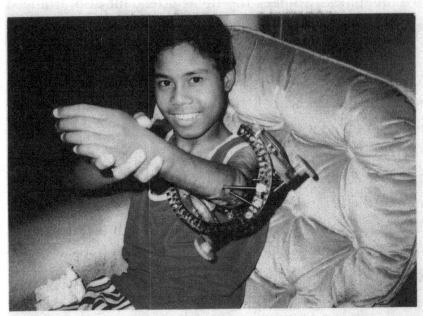

Rinor's second trip to the USA to impove his mobility.

**Rinor's elbow apparatus will eventually allow him to
to move his left elbow through the normal range.**

Left to Right - Rinor, David, Danny holding Ammon, Christopher and Michael Gaffney.

Christmas 1996 with Gaffney family.

Gordon and Paul - Rinor's Farewall

Trip Garza and Potentate Steve Rye @ BHSC

Rinor's Wedding - April 2, 2010.

Chapter 28 – World's Greatest Philanthropy or Justified Target of Criticism?

Every Shriner is a Mason, but not every Mason is a Shriner. So let's talk a little bit about Masons. Freemasonry is the oldest, largest, and best-known fraternity in the world. Freemasonry dates back hundreds of years to a time when workers banded together according to their craft. Years later Masonic Lodges were formed, with fraternal interest replacing the original crafts interests.

The Blue Lodge of Masonry is the basic unit of Masonry. Members earn their first three degrees in Masonry in the Blue Lodge. The first degree is the Entered Apprentice, the second degree is the Fellowcraft, and the third degree is the Master Mason. Masons learn the basic tenants of Freemasonry as they pass from one degree to the next. The third degree of a Master Mason is the highest degree in Masonry.

In order of importance Masons are individuals who put love of God first, love of family second, and love of country third.

Masons are members of a benevolent fraternal brotherhood. Masons do not solicit potential members. No one is asked to join the Masonic fraternity. A man must be drawn to and seek admission to Freemasonry on his own.

Masons are men of good repute who believe in one God, supporting wives, widows, and orphans (Masonic Homes), the church of their choice, the government of the United States, the party of their choice, and the public school systems. Masonry is not a religion and not a secret organization but could be defined as a way of life. The membership of a Masonic Lodge is not secret, but secret words, signs, and oaths are incorporated into the work of the lodge. The authors believe the secret aspects of Masonry were initially instituted to prevent pretenders and eavesdroppers from infiltrating its membership ranks. However, the membership ranks were successfully infiltrated years ago, and there probably are no Masonic secrets today.

Pick up any large book publisher's catalog and you will find numerous books on Masonry, the Knight Templars, Scottish Rite Masons, and the Shriner's, some supporting these organizations and some not supporting them. Anti-Masonic books typically provide the reader with a negative, one-sided, and often untrue view of the goals and work of Masonry. Some books would incorrectly have you believe that Masonry is a religion, but it is not. Some would still have you believe the Knight Templars are a militant group of Masons, but they are not. The Crusades in France ended in the thirteenth century, so nothing could be further from the truth.

Masons may follow one of two paths to become Shriners or members of the Ancient Arabic Order of the Nobles of the Mystic Shrine of North America. By taking one path Christian Masons may seek more light to become Knight Templars. By taking the other path, any Mason having a belief in one God can progress to the 32nd degree of a Scottish Rite Mason. Some Masons become both York Rite and Scottish Rite Masons. These symbolic, historic, and educational journeys through both the York Rite and the Scottish Rite are logical extensions of Masonry. One charity supported by the York Rite is the Knight Templar's Eye Foundation. One charity supported by the Scottish Rite is the Scottish Rite Hospitals for Children. Master Masons, Knight Templars, and 32nd degree Masons may apply for membership in the Shrine.

The Shrine is an international fraternity of about 600,000 members who belong to 191 Shrine Temples throughout the United States, Canada, and Mexico. The first Shrine Temple was the Mecca Shrine founded in New York City in 1872. The Shrine is known for its colorful parades, distinctive red fezzes, and its philanthropy, the Shriner's Burns and Orthopedic Hospitals for Children. Its official philanthropy is known as "the heart and soul of the Shrine." The operating budget for all Shriner's Hospitals is about $425 million a year. Approximately 96 percent of the budget is used for patient care and research; the balance is reserved for capital expenditures. However, the Shrine fraternity and Shrine philanthropy are financially and legally separate entities. The Shrine fraternity is incorporated in the state of Iowa and the Shrine philanthropy is incorporated in the state of Colorado.

The funds for these two entities are kept entirely separate and are audited independently on an individual basis.

Shriner's wear a red fez originally made in the holy city of Fez in Morocco. The fez is a symbol of the Near East theme used by the Shrine and emblematic of the color and pageantry of Shrine ceremonies. The Shrine was tied to a Near East theme by its founders Walter Fleming, a physician, and Billy Florence, an actor. Fleming and Florence needed an exciting, colorful backdrop for their new fledgling fraternity. A tour of Europe provided the inspiration for Florence. According to legend Florence attended a party hosted by an Arabian diplomat in Marseilles, France. At the end of the party the guests became members of a secret society. Florence realized this might provide the ideal vehicle for his new fraternity. He made numerous notes and drawings describing the ceremony he had witnessed.

After returning to the United States Florence shared his experiences with Fleming, and together they created the elaborate rituals and pageantry. The two men also designed the costumes, emblems, and formulated the salutation or greeting. Although the Shrine is not a secret society, it has maintained most of the mysticism and secrecy of its origin. The rest is history.

The motto for the Shriner's Hospitals for Children is, "No one should have to walk alone." There are nineteen orthopedic hospitals for children. These hospitals provide excellent no-cost medical care for children under eighteen having problems with scoliosis and spinal deformities, clubfoot and related deformities, orthogenesis imperfect, spina bifida and myelodyspasia, neuromuscular disorders, hand problems, hip disorders, and orthopedic problems resulting from cerebral palsy, missing limbs, limb deficiencies, leg-length discrepancies', metabolic bone disease, skeletal growth abnormalities, spinal cord injuries, and burn injuries.

Shriner's Hospitals for Children

1. **Boston Hospital, 51 Blossom St., Boston, MA 02114.
2. Canadian Hospital, 1529 Cedar Ave., Montreal, Quebec, Canada H3G 1A6.
3. *Chicago Hospital, 2211 N. Oak Park Ave., Chicago, IL 60707.
4. **Cincinnati Hospital, 3229 Burnet Ave., Cincinnati, OH 45229.
5. Erie Hospital, 1645 W. 8 th St. Erie, PA 16505.
6. **Galveston Hospital, 815 Market St., Galveston, TX 77550.
7. Greenville Hospital, 950 W. Faris Rd., Greenville, SC 29605.
8. Honolulu Hospital, 1310 Punahou St., Honolulu, HI 96826.
9. Houston Hospital, 6977 Main St., Houston, TX 77030-3701.
10. Inter mountain Hospital, Fairfax Rd. at Virginia St., Salt Lake City, UT 84103.
11. Lexington Hospital, 1900 Richmond Rd. , Lexington, KY 40502.
12. Los Angeles Hospital, 3160 Geneva St., Los Angeles, CA 90020.

13. Mexico City Hospital, Suchil No. 152, Col. El Rosario Delg. Coyoacan 04380
14. Mexico, D. F., Mexico.
15. **+Northern California Hospital, 2425 Stockton Blvd., Sacramento, CA 95817.
16. +Philadelphia Hospital, 8400 Roosevelt Blvd., Philadelphia, PA 19152.
17. Portland Hospital, 3101 S.W. Sam Jackson Park Rd., Portland, OR 97201.
18. St. Louis Hospital, 201 S. Lindberg Blvd., St. Louis, MO 63131.
19. Shreveport Hospital, 3100 Samford Ave., Shreveport, LA 71103.
20. Spokane Hospital, 911 W. Fifth Ave., Spokane, WA 99204.
21. Springfield Hospital, 516 Carew St., Springfield, MA 01104.
22. Tampa Hospital, 12502 North Pine Dr., Tampa, FL 33612.
23. Twin Cities Hospital, 2021 E. River Rd. Minneapolis, MN 55414.

**Burn Care Center
+Spinal Cord Injury Rehabilitation Center

For additional information call toll-free 1-(800) 237-5055 in the United States, and 1-(800) 361-7256 in Canada.

The Shriner's Hospitals for Children have been helping children free of charge since the first one was opened in

Shreveport, Louisiana, in 1922. There is never a charge for the care or service provided. No state, local government, or federal funds, are sought or accepted. Shriner's Hospitals for Children are maintained by life memberships, endowments, wills, and gifts. Shriner's also help support Shrine Hospitals financially through their annual $5 hospital assessment fee and the 100 Million Dollar Club. The objective of the 100 Million Dollar Club is for one million Shiners, family members, and friends to join the club by donating $100 each to the Shrine Hospitals. Local Shrine temples and clubs also sponsor fund-raisers to benefit the Shrine Hospitals for Children. To date more than $3.4 billion has been spent operating the Shrine Hospitals and about $770 million has been spent on construction and renovation costs.

The Shriner's orthopedic hospitals were some of the first hospitals in the United States to treat children for orthopedic problems caused by polio. Except in poor third world countries, polio has been virtually eliminated. Today the hospitals are treating other, more specialized orthopedic problems, such as ontogenesis imperfect or brittle bone disease, spina bifida with paralysis of the limbs, and orthopedic problems caused by cerebral palsy. In the early 1960's the Shrine of North America established a first by building three burns hospitals dedicated to treating severely burned children. Research at these hospitals has advanced burn-care treatment worldwide.

Admission to a Shriner's Hospital for Children is based on medical and financial needs. Children from infancy to their eighteenth birthday are eligible for admission if treatment would benefit a child and treatment at another hospital facility would be a financial burden to the child's family. The Los Angeles and Springfield, Massachusetts, hospitals are regional prosthetics and orthotics centers specializing in research and manufacture of braces and artificial limbs.

Application forms for admission to the Shriner's Hospitals for Children can be obtained from Shrine Temple offices, local Shrine clubs, and any Shrine Hospital. Parents or guardians may also write to Shriner's Hospitals for Children, 2900 Rocky Point Drive, Tampa, FL 33607. Completed forms should be returned to the nearest Shriner's Hospital, where they will be evaluated for medical and financial eligibility.

Shrine Hospitals are actively engaged in various research projects looking for cures, more effective treatment for crippling childhood diseases, and improved treatment of burn injuries. The orthopedic hospitals provide expert medical care for children with orthopedic deformities, disease, or injuries such as club-foot, scoliosis, and problems resulting from cerebral palsy. Orthopedic hospitals also treat children with orthopedic problems caused by neuromuscular disorders, Legg-Calve-Perthes (hip) disease. Some units also treat burned children whose wounds have healed but who still need reconstructive surgery, plastic surgery, or rehabilitation. The Shriner's Hospitals are major teaching centers affiliated with some of the top medical colleges and universities in the United States.

Treatment at a Shriner's Hospital for Children unit focuses on a "family-centered care" environment. Shriner's believe medicine can heal the child's body but that it is equally important in the healing process to tend to the child's mind and spirit. Therefore the hospital's staff focuses on the individual patient. Support from family and friends as well as the hospital staff helps each child deal with his or her physical problems.

In the early 1960s Shrine doctors and Shriners became aware that severe burns were another major enemy of children. Each year thousands of children are crippled, disfigured, or killed, by one of the greatest hazards of childhood-fire. Shriner's were quick to recognize that there was a severe lack of burn care expertise at the time. The three Shrine Burns Institutes were opened to help children, conduct burns research, and train medical personnel in the treatment of burns injuries. Since their opening some forty years ago the Burns Institutes have more than doubled a child's chance of survival.

Today the Burns Institutes are still pioneers in burn treatment. They are developing artificial skin and promoting the rapid growth of normal skin. Burns research also includes studies on how to prevent scar formation, the effect of pain drugs on treatment, and the effect of nutrition on healing. Lung functioning and burn infections are other areas of burn's research.

The Shriner's Burns Institutes are prepared to treat children with acute flesh burns, and children in need of plastic surgery, reconstructive surgery, and restorative surgery as a result of healed burns. Healed burns often result in scarring, related contractures, impaired mobility of limbs, and facial deformities. Great advances have already been made in these areas, allowing severely burned children to regain their confidence and self-esteem, and return to normal family life.

If you know of a severely burned child who needs immediate emergency care, your referring physician should telephone the chief of staff at the nearest Shriner's Burns Institute. The referring physician should say that he or she has a patient requiring emergency admission. Such patients are accepted promptly if space is available. The cost of transportation is the responsibility of the family, but the local Shrine Temples can often offer transportation assistance. Every child at a Shrine Hospital is sponsored by a Shriner who acts as liaison between the family and the hospital. Shrine Temples and Shrine clubs often help arrange and pay for transportation for children and parents to the hospitals. Shriner's donate many hours of their time driving family members to and from the hospitals.

For children needing reconstructive surgery and rehabilitation as the result of burn injuries, an application form must be completed and sent to the nearest Shrine Burns Hospital for consideration. Applications may be obtained from locations previously listed.

For spinal cord Injuries (SCI) the Shrine Hospitals in Chicago, Philadelphia, and San Francisco provide the only units in the nation designed to treat children and adolescents. The SCI unit provides long-term rehabilitative care and intensive physical, occupational, and recreational therapy. The goal of SCI units is to help children with spinal cord injuries re-learn the basic skills of everyday life. Counseling helps the children learn to cope with their injury and rediscover that a fulfilling life is still within their reach.

SCI patients learn independent living skills such as cooking meals and ironing clothes. Children and their parents are taught self-care skills because the patient's life changes dramatically after a spinal cord injury. Spinal cord injuries affect not only affect the patient's ability to walk and move their limbs, but the patient's muscles and nerves. Muscle and nerve damage can cause bowel, bladder, and skin problems. Children and their parents are taught the best ways to deal with these problems. The Shriner's Hospitals SCI units are not trauma centers, but they do accept children for treatment until their eighteenth birthday regardless of race, religion, creed, or relationship to a Shriner.

Another major research project is called functional neuromuscular stimulation (FNS). This technique can be used to enable paralyzed people to stand, walk, and grasp objects with their hands. It is hoped that FNS will someday provide enough mobility for paralyzed children to enjoy everyday activity and life in general. Other orthopedic research projects include studies on genetics and its relationship to bone and joint diseases. They are also searching for a cure for juvenile arthritis and investigating the relationship between heredity and disorders of connective tissue.

To date more than 550,000 children have been treated at the Shriner's Hospitals for Children. In 1996 there were 19,928 admissions to orthopedic hospitals and 2,412 admissions to burns hospitals.

The slogan for one famous camera manufacturer was "Image is Everything." For many years the Shrine image was of men wearing strange hats and riding little cars in parades. Perhaps some people remember the Shrine Circus from their childhood days. Few people knew or understood the philanthropy of the Shrine. For many people living in the country the Shrine probably had little to no image at all. In the 1990s the Shrine set about to change their public image. From time to time there would be press releases in local newspapers or perhaps short stories about children who have been helped by the Shrine. However, there was no overt attempt to inform and educate the public about what the Shriner's Hospitals for Children had to offer.

It has only been in recent times that an image of a Shriner carrying a child with a disability has appeared on the back of 18-wheel tractor trailers. The year 2007 marked the eighty fifth Anniversary of the Shrine. Ten years ago Shriner's began publishing a new magazine for family and friends called, *"Your Shrine Hospital"* which featured stories about patients they have helped, hospital news, employee stories, and detailed information about the present day hospitals.

What has caused this desire for a change of image? Shriner's realized that a nearly full hospital is more efficient than a half-empty hospital. You cannot help children if you cannot get them into a hospital for treatment of their problems. Secondly, even the world's greatest philanthropy needs a little favorable publicity and advertising occasionally. In today's competitive world with a host of activities and distractions, sometimes it pays to toot your own horn and let the people know you are alive and well. Recently the Shrine has challenged churches in the United States to seek out and find just one child who needs the services of the Shriner's Hospitals. The Shriner's Hospitals are in better shape today to help children than they have ever been. What a great service for children, their families, and communities!

Part of the title of this chapter is called "Justified Target of Criticism?" Criticism is neither good nor bad, but it is either true or false. If the criticism is true, lessons can be learned from it. If the criticism is false, entities can be destroyed by it. In earlier chapters the author's have been somewhat critical of the Shriner's Burns Hospital-Galveston. This criticism stems from the Galveston Hospital's failure to communicate with local hospitals about Rinor in particular, and his required rehabilitation.

It is annoying to say the least when telephone calls are not returned. It is discouraging to say the least when a hospital creates the impression that the burns care doctor does not communicate properly with an orthopedic doctor or the patient's physical therapists. This criticism comes from a surrogate father and his love for his son. Are there lessons to be learned here? I think there are. Yet despite this criticism the final goal was achieved. The boy who was the subject of our story can walk, run, and play like other boys again! He can also go to school, learn a trade, and become a contributing member of society.

Former Shriners Hospital patients are the greatest word-of-mouth advertising the world has ever seen. For the most part former patients love Shriner's and Shriners Hospitals. Many of these former patients enter child care fields themselves and return as employees of the Shriners Hospitals. These former patients can relate well with current patients because "they have been there." They too have suffered greatly and survived. What better testimony is there?

Chapter 29 – Yellow Journalism

Then there is what I call "yellow journalism criticism. "What is yellow journalism?" One good example is when an investigative reporter and his TV crew show up at the front door of the Shrine Circus demanding to see the local Shrine potentate. When the potentate agrees to see the reporter, the first question he asks is – "Is it true that only one cent out of every dollar taken in by the Shrine Circus goes to the Shriner's Hospital's" If the reporter had done his homework properly, he would have known the answers to these questions before he asked them. He would have known that the profits from the local Ben Hur Shrine Circus go to the operation of the local Shrine Temple and not the Shriner's Hospitals. He would have known the local Shrine Temple has a great deal of flexibility concerning which fund-raisers support the operation of the local Shrine Temple and which fund-raisers support the Shriner's Hospitals for Children. He would have also known that the brotherhood and the philanthropies are separate entities with separate budgets. Apparently this reporter's only purpose is to publicly embarrass a good man and destroy a worthwhile charity.

Perhaps some people think that profits for corporations and operating funds for charities are evil. Well, there would be no corporate employers without corporate profits, and there would be no worthwhile charities without operating funds. The reporter in this real life example had no interest in reporting that about 96 percent of the money donated to Shrine Charities goes directly to child care. Good work and good deeds do not make sensational headlines. Lies, hints of scandals, and false accusations are the fabric of yellow journalism.

In many ways the Shriners of today must feel like the last of the Jedi Knights of *Star Wars* fiction. They are older than many other popular groups and relatively few in numbers. For this reason the Shrine and other Masonic bodies need to attract new young members, men of good character, so that the fraternity can prosper and grow. These modern day Jedi Knights are surrounded by a godless earthy empire that would crush them in a minute if it could. Yet somehow "The Force is with them" and they prevail against overwhelming odds. They must be doing something right, or perhaps God just loves the little children and the youth of the world!

We would challenge the youth of the world to volunteer their help at local hospitals, nursing homes, and Mental Health-Mental Rehabilitation institutes. Be sure to check with your local hospital or volunteer organization to determine if special training is required and available. By helping others you will truly be blessed.

Gordon Irwin and I, the authors of Rinor's story, have tried to be thoroughly honest with the reader. We have not tried to eliminate the negative and accentuate the positive. We hope we have presented both sides of the story to the same degree. Above all we must be true to ourselves. We hope we have accomplished our mission!

Renoir Marcial is the real hero of our story. He suffered much through no fault of his own. He seldom cried around his family and friends. His determination and faith in God inspired everyone he met. Children who are patients at the Shriner's Hospitals seem to have a way of inspiring people, including hospital workers and staff.

Chapter 30 – The Day I Died

While walking Austin's Highland Mall on October 19, 2008, I stopped to take a nitro pill after walking the first lap- about half a mile-and fainted before I could get to a nearby bench. My wife, who was walking another short loop, saw me on the floor and came running. A young lady named Amanda saw me fall, called 911, and stayed on the phone until help arrived, relaying information from my wife to the dispatcher. I was taken to the Heart Hospital of Austin where they thought I might have a heart valve problem, but they couldn't find anything, so I was released the next morning.

Then while walking Highland Mall on November 3, I walked less than half a lap and said, "I don't feel good." Dixie looked at me and saw that I was very pale. There was no place to sit down, so she held me against the railing and got the attention of an employee, Fidel, who was cleaning the escalator. He ran up the down escalator quickly and was soon at Dixie's side, helping her put me gently on the floor. A man walked up behind us and asked if he could help, and Dixie said, "Yes, please call 911."

Another employee, Carlos, saw what was happening and called the guards. A lady guard named Chris had patrolled the outside of the mall in her vehicle for seven years and had never brought in her AED in from her vehicle. However, on this day she had picked up her AED device and was halfway down that wing of the mall when she got the emergency call. She rushed to our aid as did a male guard, Jamael, at about the same time. Rob, head of mall operations, arrived a short time later and asked if anyone was on the phone with 911. Dixie looked to her left where a man who offered to call 911 had been standing, but he was no longer there, so she asked Rob to please call 911, which he did. He also provided the dispatcher with the information he needed.

My wife had already unbuttoned my shirt, and Chris put the AED pads in the locations shown on the device and turned it on. The AED said, "Scanning, needs shock, hands off" so everyone took their hands off me and Chris pushed the shock button, nothing happened. The second time the AED said, "Scanning needs shock, hands off" and Chris pushed the button and my left shoulder twitched, but that was all. The next time the AED said, "Scanning needs chest compressions and mouth-to-mouth." Jamael did the chest compressions while Chris did mouth-to-mouth breathing through her mouthpiece. About thirteen minutes later I woke up and said, "I got to vomit." A young lady from the Aeropostle Store brought out a stack of folded T-shirts to put them under my head. Dixie and the guards rolled me over on my side, and a short time later the EMS crew arrived and took me to the Heart Hospital.

At the Heart Hospital Dr. Roger Gammon, my cardiologist since 1993, did an angiogram, found no blocked arteries, and diagnosed the problem as electric. Dr. Joanne Tsai, the electro-physiologist, was brought in, and the next morning she implanted a pace maker/defibrillator. I went home Thursday and returned to our usual walking at Highland Mall Monday through Friday.

About five weeks later while walking the mall, I rushed to a bench in front of the Edge Store and passed out as soon as I sat down. A lady coming out of the Edge store and asked my wife if I would be all right and she said, "I think so, but would you stay here a moment?" When I regained consciousness, she was praying for my healing, and I thanked her and gave her a hug.

We went to Corpus Christi to celebrate Christmas with our daughter, Linda, and her girls Cheree and Jenifer. We went to see Tom Cruise in the movie Valkyrie. We walked up a short flight of steps and found four seats close to each other. I sat in a seat near the isle. A short time later, I told Dixie, "I don't feel good." My defibrillator kicked me twice in a couple of seconds, and I yelped in pain. Several people near us got up to leave, but Dixie said, "Please don't leave. He will be all right."

We continued our regular morning walks at Highland Mall. I passed out a couple of times, and the last time Jamael took me out to our car in a wheelchair. Dixie emailed Dr. Tsai each time I passed out, and the doctor told us to stop walking the mall.

One Monday while Dixie was doing the laundry, I was mailing out Shrine Circus Advertisement information to potential Shrine Circus program advertisers. I mentioned several times that my head felt hot and my chest hurt. At about 2 p.m., I got up from my computer and went to the dining room. A short time later, I felt really bad and called, "Dixie!" By the time Dixie got to me I had passed out and the defibrillator shocked me. Our dining room chairs have wheels on them, so Dixie kept me in the chair, rolled me over to my recliner next to the phone, and called 911. The ambulance arrived in less than fifteen minutes and took me to the Heart Hospital. That was the sixth time in six months. I asked my doctor, "What do I have to do to get one of the new and improved pacemakers, die?" "Just about," she replied.

On April 7, 2009, I was back in the Heart Hospital. This time my defibrillator was replaced with a new and improved cardiac resynchronization therapy defibrillator that has three wires, one wire in the top chamber and two wires in the bottom chambers to help synchronize the heart. This device also helps strengthen the heart, and I passed out one more time and was shocked again. This time the doctor's changed my medications. I continue to walk the mall and I hope that I won't need another heart cauterization.

On August 3, 2019, while walking the mall, my heart stopped. My defibrillator shocked me once and brought me back to life. They changed my medication and put on Amiodrone with 48 hour I.V. When I came home, I continued to take Amiodrone in the pill form.

On August 25, 2010 while walking my heart stopped again. I was taken to the Heart Hospital again in an ambulance, and spent several hours in the Emergency room being evaluated. The decision was to increase my dose of Amiodrone and Mexiletine, the best medications for A-fibrillation.

**Cris did Mouth to Mouth as Jamael did Chest Compressions
to save my life at Highland Mall on 11/3/08.**

Chapter 31 – Memories

Dixie and I were married August 29, 1958, by the Reverend John Wrenn, who was also a high school teacher. My brother Keith was in one of his classes. He wanted to take care of all our wedding arrangements for a modest cost, at the Tourist Inn where he lived.

At our wedding, the Reverend Wrenn inadvertently pronounced Keith and Dixie man and wife, but the wedding certificate was made out correctly and Keith didn't get to go on the honeymoon. What I didn't know was that my friends from the Savannah River Plant had added some new features to my 1957 Chevy convertible. To begin with the rear axle was sitting on a five-gallon can just off the ground and the front windshield was covered with shaving cream, totally blocking our vision. Condoms filled with toothpaste and other things were hidden in my suitcase because my mother had given them a key to my car without my knowledge. Ward Bond, Harry Hart, and Ronald Frontroth were three of the guilty parties. The car's windshield washers took care of the shaving cream and eventually, my buddies pushed the car off the can, and we finally got started on our honeymoon and spent our first night at the Saluda Motel.

When we started out the next morning, it soon became obvious that the car wasn't hitting on all the cylinders. What we didn't know was that a small smoke bomb had been wired to one of the spark plugs When I found the smoke bomb I removed it but one unnoticed wire kept shorting out one of the sparkplugs. When we got to the next little town, we pulled into the gas station, asked the attendant to check out and wash the car. Then Dixie and I had breakfast at a small restaurant.

There was also Limburger cheese on the manifold, and a fish was in one of the hub caps. When the attendant removed the ground up fish in the hubcap, he said he nearly lost it.

While we lived in South Carolina and our children were young, Mom and Dad, and our family joined the National Camper's and Hiker's Association of America. Between 1966 and 1968 we went on many camping trips together, including one in Pennsylvania where we met some Canadian campers who really liked Dixie's name and gave her a mid-sized Canadian flag.

On one of the campouts our son Tom locked himself inside Mom and Dad's camper. He fell asleep and no one could wake him up, including a marching band that tried to by going around the camper. Mom and Dad didn't have a key with them. Tom finally woke up but, it seemed to take forever.

We let my parents keep each of the children at different times, so that they could get to know their grandparents, and vice versa. Donna's favorite trip with her grandparents was to North Pole, New York, where she saw the real North Pole, the real Santa Clause, and the nativity characters with real beards and long hair, which really impressed her and Dad.

Shortly after we moved to Delaware in June 1968, I was working for the DuPont Chambers Works Plant at Deep Water, New Jersey. DuPont gun powder was stored at Carney's Pont, N.J. just across the Delaware River. Smokeless gunpowder was stored in large underground magazines —they were considered safe. A supervisor left a rail car full of gun powder with a few workers, while he checked in with a company doctor at DuPont Medical. It is believed that one of the workers lit a cigarette that ignited the rail car, which in turn detonated two gun powder magazines in a chain reaction. As a result of these explosions, severe damages were done to the little town Deep Water, as well as to some of the high-rise buildings in Wilmington, Delaware. Al Buhler and I shared an office at DuPont's Cambers Works in Delaware. When the ceiling tiles stated falling, we decided it was time to get out.

One of my co-workers, Doug West, and I liked to go duck hunting during the hunting season when the weather was cold. We took my pickup camper and signed-in for a designated camping spot hoping to get a little sleep that night, and a good blind to hunt from before daybreak. We locked the camper door and went to bed. In the middle of the night someone started banging on the camper door. Doug drew his Colt .45 pistol and I drew mine. When Doug opened the door, we both had a Delaware game warden in our sights, which shook him up quite a bit. We asked him why he woke us up in the middle of the night when we had properly signed in for a camping spot. He didn't have any answer, but he apologized and left. We got out to the blind just before daybreak and shot a few ducks but not many. It wasn't what I'd call a great day.

All of the children wanted me to take them to *Willy Wonka and the Chocolate Factory* (1971). This was a great Gene Wilder movie featuring one nice boy and a bunch of spoiled brats. Be careful what you wish for. A really scary movie the kids wanted to see was *"The Omega Man"* (1971). Dr. Robert Neville (Charlton Heston) is the only survivor of an apocalyptic war with the exception of a few hundred deformed homicidal maniacs determined to kill him. Mathias was the white-haired leader of the killer mutants. One night after the kids went to bed, I put a white mop on my head, opened their bedroom doors and said, "Mathias wants you!" and did my famous mutant walk. It scared the daylights out of them.

On January 14, 1973, we moved our four children, who were between the ages of ten and thirteen, from Wilmington, Delaware, to Corpus Christi, Texas. It was at this time that I started spending a little quality time with each of them.

Tom wanted me to take him to see eight hours of the *Planet of the Apes* movie marathon one Saturday. "Apes don't kill apes" was the theme, and humans were the bad guys. Linda wanted me to take her to see the *Jaws II* a movie in 1978, which scared the life out of her. Apparently the killer shark had developed a taste for teenagers in this movie. I wonder how long it took Linda before she wanted to go swimming at Corpus Christi beach again.

I have had a lot of fun since I became an Al Amin Shrine Clown in 1982. Gene Woodward, aka Grits, was my mentor when I became an Al Amin Shriner. I t was fun being a clown for my granddaughters, as they were growing up. Once a year Shriner's have a "Shake-the-Bucket" campaign at busy intersections collecting money for the Shine Hospitals. The buckets are plastic containers with Shrine emblems on them. Some Shriners will be wearing their familiar red fez's, and Shrine clowns will usually be there in costume. Most kids like to donate money to the clowns.

After the donation was counted, the Potentate of the Al Amin Shrine Temple would ask me if I was ready to go to the bank with him to make the deposit. When I said I was, he knew I had my .45 caliber semi-automatic pistol with me. No one ever tried to rob us at the Shrine Temple or on the way to the bank, so this was just an unnecessary precaution.

After I retired from the Corpus Christi DuPont plant, I liked to take our first granddaughter, Cheree, to the Corpus Christi beach with bags of no-salt, no-butter popcorn to feed the seagulls. All you had to do was throw the popcorn in the air to attract them. On the way home, we'd stop at McDonald's and eat "fry fries" under the funny (plastic) tree with a bench. Cheree got very upset with her aunt Donna one day when she stopped at McDonald's just to use the restroom and did not eat any fry fries under the funny tree.

Dr. Carl Ruthstrom, and his wife, Dolores, knew Dixie when we worked on the 1980 census. We began visiting and socializing with each other. After we became good friends, Carl saw a Texas Nuclear ad for an electrical engineer with experience in nuclear radiation and he immediately thought of me since I had worked at the Savannah River Plant, which had a number of large nuclear reactors. I interviewed for the job and was immediately hired by Texas Nuclear Corporation in Austin, Texas. A few years later the company moved to Round Rock, Texas and changed its name to TN Technologies, Inc.

I worked there for a number of years, until the company folded. Luckily I had a 401 Savings Plan. My next job was as an Environmental Engineer for the state of Texas. I worked there for seven years before accepting a small pension and more of less retiring for good, although I still do a little consulting as a one man firm registered as Paul E. Mix, P.E., Electrical Engineering.

Cheree and Funshine the Clown.

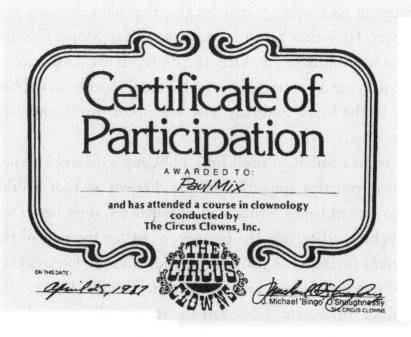

Certificate of Participation

AWARDED TO:

Paul Mix

and has attended a course in clownology
conducted by
The Circus Clowns, Inc.

ON THIS DATE:

April 25, 1987

J. Michael "Bingo" O'Shaughnessy
THE CIRCUS CLOWNS

Chapter 32 – Corpus Christi, Texas' Most Memorable Cold Case Homicide

Corpus Christi may be the Sparkling City by the Sea, but it also has its share of unsolved Cold Cases. Corpus Christi has a total of 56 active, unsolved murder cases. In early June 2007, Sergeant Richard L. Garcia became the cold case unit's first officer. He is now targeting the case of Kay Moore Cramer, who was murdered on Oct. 16, 1981. An assailant stabbed Cramer, age 33, strangled her with a small water hose, stabbed her in the heart, and may have attempted to rob and rape her.

From April 1976 until June 1979, my wife and I owned and operated a tropical fish store known as Fish World. Two retired ladies owned and operated the store before we bought it. They sold the business to us for the cost of the current inventory of fish and supplies, and the fixtures they had purchased, such as a sign with replaceable letters, cash register, stools, etc. Dixie ran the store until I came home from work. Then she would go home and fix supper for the family. All of our children, and some of their friends, worked at the store after school and sometimes on weekends.

We quickly learned that all customers were not honest. We encountered quick-change artists, hot check writers, and outright thieves. We posted hot checks on the register to warn others, and would not let our children make change for customers who tried to give them large bills. One clever trick was to let a child walk out of the store with a small decoration the parent hadn't purchased.

The best thief or all was a man who wanted us to send his "Silent Giant" air pump in for repair. He asked how long will it take to get it repaired? I told him about two weeks. After two weeks, a woman came in and asked if her husband's "Silent Giant" air pump was repaired and ready to pick up. I said that it was, and she paid for the cost of repair. A couple of days later, the man who asked me to send his pump in, came in and asked for his repaired air pump. When I told him his wife had already picked it up, he said that he wasn't married, and demanded a new "Silent Giant" air pump. I told him he didn't bring in a new "Silent Giant" air pump, and he wasn't going to get a new one. I gave him the oldest "Silent Giant" air pump we had in service, and told him to never come back again. After that customer's had to sign for what they sent in for repair, and they were told they were the only one authorized to pick it up.

Fish World's address was 5151 Everhart Road, a short distance from Padre Island Drive. First we greatly expanded the business by adding salt water fish, parakeets, a few large

Parrots, bird cages and supplies. We also sold a wide variety of fish tanks, hoods, air pumps, gravel, fish tank decorations, and other supplies. We periodically advertised sales on our large window sign. The message could be changed based on items we wanted to put on sale. We also used it for messages such as, "We will be closed on Christmas Day" or Thanksgiving Day. We also had a string of sleigh bells on the inside of the front door so we could hear customers entering the store if we were in the center room or back room.

All of our children and some of their friends, worked for Fish World on a part-time basis to earn a little spending money. One day I forgot to reset the check writing machine and made a check out to our son John for "0 Dollars and 0 cents." When he attempted to cash his check at the local H.E.B., the cashier told him "nobody can cash this check," and handed it back to him. I'll guarantee John never accepted a check after that without looking at it.

At first we did not open on Sundays, but eventually we did because many of our customers wanted us to open on Sunday afternoons after church. I checked with our minister, and he gave us his approval to open on Sunday afternoons. Sales turned out to be very good on Sunday afternoon. After buying the business, we built it up by making a customer want list. If more than one customer wanted a new item, we added it on our next order. When new customers became repeat customers, we gave them a Fish World business card with "Present this card for a 10 percent discount on your next purchase" printed on the back. This made repeat customer's very happy, and they purchased more items. People asked us about Pet Grooming for cats and dogs.

Later, we advertised for a groomer and a lady applied for the job. As a contract groomer, she was to supply her own equipment and supplies, and we would receive a small percentage of her sales. We installed a used bath tub for washing pets, and a piece of carpet was mounted on the wall above the bathtub. It was funny to watch her wash, and rinse a cat hanging onto the carpet. Once the cat was wet, it would sink its claws into the carpet and hang there until the groomer was done with the shampoo and rinse. She had a number of cages to keep other animals separated.

We owned the business from April 1976 until June 1979, before we sold it to Mrs. Kay Moore Cramer and her husband. They had a daughter in school, her husband was a musician, and her father was a builder. Shortly after the Cramer's bought the business the "Traveling Texan" did a TV spot featuring the business. The free publicity should have been a big help to her and their business.

Our daughter, Donna, was a tropical fish expert. She knew what fish were compatible and what fish weren't. She knew about both tropical fish and salt water fish. One condition of the sale of the store was that Donna was to stay on and help Mrs. Cramer for a few weeks, or until Mrs. Cramer became more familiar with the business. Donna was abruptly dismissed after a few short weeks, and she was very happy to leave. Today she owns and operates an aquarium maintenance company known as "Tanks-A-Lot" in Anchorage, Alaska.

At about the same time, the dog and cat groomer was asked to leave. Mrs. Cramer tried to keep the groomers cages and tools. I had to show the new owner a copy of the groomer's contract that clearly stated that the groomer was to supply her own tools and cages, everything but the bath tub and carpet mat above the tub. Shortly after we sold the business, a good customer of ours came in, picked up several items, put them on to the counter next to the cash register, and presented his 10% discount card. Mrs. Cramer said, "That card isn't any good" and tore it up. Then she gave him one of her cards. He tore it up and said, "If their card isn't any good, neither is yours". Because Kay was so unfriendly he left his items on the counter and walked out the door. Later, he called us at home to tell us what had happened.

They say there is safety in numbers, and I believe that was very true in this case. For example, if the dog groomer or another adult was there, the murderer may not have had the opportunity. Murder depends on motive, opportunity, and time. In this case, motive and time were probably the most important factors.

On October 16, 1981, Mrs. Cramer was murdered between the hours of 3:00 pm and 5:30 p.m. Police reported that the woman's assailant attempted to rape her and strangled her with a small water hose that was used to refill fish tanks in the center room to make up for water evaporation.

According to Dr. Joseph Rupp, the County Coroner, Mrs. Cramer was stabbed in the heart with a 1-inch wide blade, and left in the back room of the store, that was originally used for pet grooming and storage. The front door was locked.

Robbery did not appear to be the motive although some money was missing. I had a World War II bayonet at home, and the width of the blade was only three-fourths of an inch. Maybe the killer used a hunting knife. The knife wasn't found.

I have always wondered, what was the real motive for this murder? It definitely wasn't money. If you really want money, rob a bank, credit union, Walmart, or Fort Knox. To my way of thinking, the motive for her murder must have been a deep-seated hatred for Kay, or some member of her family. It certainly wasn't money. Only a limited amount of money would have been on her person and in the cash register. If Kay was the only person in the store at the time, then the murderer definitely had the opportunity.

One other thing bothers me about this case. Your rib cage protects your heart at least to some degree. Kay was stabbed once in the heart. Was the killer familiar with Military Special Operations? Was the killer an expert in the Medical field? Did the killer strangle her first and then stab her? Perhaps that could explain why he only had to stab her once. He had time to locate her ribs, and he knew the location of the heart.

According to cold case detectives on television, the murderer always leaves D.N.A. at the scene of a murder. D.N.A. comes from hair and saliva. With the traffic in and out of Fish Word, including the owners, salesmen, delivery men, customers and visitors, there may have been too much D.N.A.

There were trash dumpsters out back and an access road. Someone mentioned seeing an unfamiliar blue sedan on the access road, but no one could provide a good description of the car or its occupant. Looking at the front of the store, there was a veterinarian's office on the right side of Fish World and an auto parts store on the left side. Even though the walls were thin, and we could talk to the vet through the walls, no one heard or saw anything suspicious.

Crime Stoppers

The Corpus Christi Police Cold Case Unit is now targeting the case of Kay Moore Cramer. An assailant stabbed Cramer, age 33, in the heart, and strangled her with a small water hose. There may have been an attempt to rape her. The homicide occurred at Fish World, 5151 Everhart on October 16, 1981, between the hours of 3:00 p.m. and 5:30 p.m. She was the co-owner of Fish World. If you have any information about this homicide, please call Crime Stoppers at 888-TIPS or visit the Crime Stoppers Website at www.888TIPS.com. The information you provide could earn you up to $1,000 in cash. Even though some money was taken from the store, robbery was determined not to be the sole motive. The scary part of this story for me is that under other circumstances my wife, Dixie, or my oldest daughter, Donna, might have been the victim of this tragic and senseless murder. Thank God they weren't!